Cooperative
Task-Oriented Computing

Algorithms and Complexity

Synthesis Lectures on Distributed Computing Theory

Editor
Nancy Lynch, *Massachusetts Institute of Technology*

Synthesis Lectures on Distributed Computing Theory is edited by Nancy Lynch of the Massachusetts Institute of Technology. The series will publish 50- to 150 page publications on topics pertaining to distributed computing theory. The scope will largely follow the purview of premier information and computer science conferences, such as ACM PODC, DISC, SPAA, OPODIS, CONCUR, DialM-POMC, ICDCS, SODA, Sirocco, SSS, and related conferences. Potential topics include, but not are limited to: distributed algorithms and lower bounds, algorithm design methods, formal modeling and verification of distributed algorithms, and concurrent data structures.

Communication and Agreement Abstractions for Fault-Tolerant Asynchronous Distributed Systems
Michel Raynal
2010

The Mobile Agent Rendezvous Problem in the Ring
Evangelos Kranakis, Danny Krizanc, and Euripides Markou
2010

Cooperative Task-Oriented Computing: Algorithms and Complexity

Chryssis Georgiou and Alexander A. Shvartsman

ISBN: 978-3-031-00877-1   paperback
ISBN: 978-3-031-02005-6   ebook

DOI 10.1007/978-3-031-02005-6

A Publication in the Springer series
SYNTHESIS LECTURES ON DISTRIBUTED COMPUTING THEORY

Lecture #7
Series Editor: Nancy Lynch, *Massachusetts Institute of Technology*
Series ISSN
Synthesis Lectures on Distributed Computing Theory
Print 2155-1626   Electronic 2155-1634

Cooperative
Task-Oriented Computing

Algorithms and Complexity

Chryssis Georgiou
University of Cyprus

Alexander A. Shvartsman
University of Connecticut

SYNTHESIS LECTURES ON DISTRIBUTED COMPUTING THEORY #7

ABSTRACT

Cooperative network supercomputing is becoming increasingly popular for harnessing the power of the global Internet computing platform. A typical Internet supercomputer consists of a master computer or server and a large number of computers called workers, performing computation on behalf of the master. Despite the simplicity and benefits of a single master approach, as the scale of such computing environments grows, it becomes unrealistic to assume the existence of the infallible master that is able to coordinate the activities of multitudes of workers. Large-scale distributed systems are inherently dynamic and are subject to perturbations, such as failures of computers and network links, thus it is also necessary to consider fully distributed peer-to-peer solutions.

We present a study of cooperative computing with the focus on modeling distributed computing settings, algorithmic techniques enabling one to combine efficiency and fault-tolerance in distributed systems, and the exposition of trade-offs between efficiency and fault-tolerance for robust cooperative computing. The focus of the exposition is on the abstract problem, called *Do-All*, and formulated in terms of a system of cooperating processors that together need to perform a collection of tasks in the presence of adversity. Our presentation deals with models, algorithmic techniques, and analysis. Our goal is to present the most interesting approaches to algorithm design and analysis leading to many fundamental results in cooperative distributed computing. The algorithms selected for inclusion are among the most efficient that additionally serve as good pedagogical examples. Each chapter concludes with exercises and bibliographic notes that include a wealth of references to related work and relevant advanced results.

KEYWORDS

distributed computing, algorithmics, cooperative computing, fault-tolerance, complexity and lower bounds

Contents

Acknowledgments

The work on robust distributed cooperation presented in this monograph includes results obtained by the authors in collaboration with several colleagues and results obtained by other researchers. The bibliographic notes throughout the monograph provide full details on prior work along with detailed citations.

The authors thank Nancy Lynch, the Series Editor, for inviting them to undertake this project and for her continued encouragement. The authors thank the reviewers of this monograph, Antonio Fernández Anta, Bogdan Chlebus, and Roberto De Prisco, whose meaningful and insightful feedback helped improve the quality of this presentation. Special thanks are due to Diane Cerra, Editor at Morgan & Claypool Publishers, for her encouragement, patience, and perseverance. Without her active participation, liveness of our work could not be guaranteed.

This work was in part supported by National Science Foundation (NSF) Grants 0311368 and 1017232. The work of the first author was partially supported by research funds from the University of Cyprus and from the Cyprus Research Promotion Foundation Grant ΤΠΕ/ΠΛΗΡΟ/0609(ΒΕ)/05.

We will be remiss if we did not mention General and Mrs. Kanellakis, the parents of the late Paris C. Kanellakis (1953-1995) for their continued encouragement and support of research in fault-tolerance that Paris was involved in during the last years of his life. General Eleftherios Kanellakis passed away in 2010 at the age of 97. He is survived by his wife, Mrs. Roula Kanellakis, and the authors are humbly sending the very first copy of this book to her with their respect and appreciation.

Finally, we would like to thank our families.
CG: It is very hard to find the right words for appropriately thanking my wife Agni ($A\gamma\nu\acute{\eta}$), my son Yiorgo ($\Gamma\iota\acute{\omega}\rho\gamma o$), and the newest member of our family, my daughter Despoina ($\Delta\acute{\varepsilon}\sigma\pi o\iota\nu\alpha$). Whatever I write, it will not be enough. So I simply say to all three of you: *Thank you for everything!*
AAS: I thank my wife Sana for her love, joy, care, and, of course, for her encouragement and steadfast support. Thank you, my love! This Dad continues to be proud of his children; congratulations to my son Ted on his CPA, my daughter Ginger on her MD, and to my step-son Arnold on his BS.

Chryssis Georgiou and Alexander A. Shvartsman
July 2011

CHAPTER 1

Introduction

1.1 MOTIVATION AND LANDSCAPE

In 1965, Gordon Moore published an article [76] predicting exponential growth in the density of transistors in integrated circuits. This prediction, now known as the "Moore's Law", has witnessed half a century of doubling of transistor density every two years, as well as other related manifestations that include steady exponential growth in memory storage capacity, hard disk storage, network capacity, uniprocessor throughput, and clock rates. The result is the exponential explosion of the available computing power, high-bandwidth communication networks, and storage capacity in recent decades. Yet the inherent limitations imposed by the laws of physics dictate an inevitable demise of Moore's Law, and its namesake now predicts that in about a decade the existing technology will reach a fundamental barrier [27]. The development of multicore technologies, where increases in throughput are achieved not by designing faster uniprocessors but by packaging multiple uniprocessor cores into a parallel subsystem is a telltale sign. One can no longer rely on improvements in uniprocessor performance to solve computational problems with ever-growing throughput requirements. In fact, driven by the constraints of heat dissipation due to high power consumption by very fast uniprocessors, new processor design is increasingly focusing on multicore, parallel architectures in both shared-memory and message-passing integration approaches. At the same time, we continue to observe substantial growth in the number of networked computers, availability of high communication bandwidths, and volumes of stored data. Thus, the pessimistic outlook for Moore's Law forces the high-speed computing community to seek solutions in large scale distributed computing systems, considering both message-passing and shared-memory system architectures.

Network supercomputing is becoming an increasingly popular mean for harnessing the power of the global Internet computing platform with its high-bandwidth connections and a vast number of interconnected computers. Internet supercomputing comes at a cost substantially lower than acquiring a supercomputer, or building a cluster of powerful machines. Several Internet supercomputing platforms exist today, e.g., [1, 2, 3, 4]. For instance, Internet PrimeNet Server, a project comprised of about 30,000 servers, PCs, and laptop computers, supported by Entropia.com, Inc., is a distributed, massively parallel mathematics research Internet supercomputer. PrimeNet Server has sustained throughput of over 1 Teraflop [3]. Another popular Internet supercomputer, the SETI@home project, also reported its speed to be in Teraflops [61]. In 2009, FightAIDS@home, the biomedical distributed computing project, reported over 100,000 participating processors [2]. A typical Internet supercomputer consist of a *master* computer or server and a large number of computers called *workers*, performing computation on behalf of the master. Here the computational tasks are submitted to the master computer; the worker computers subsequently download and perform the tasks. After completing a downloaded task the worker returns the result to the master, and then proceeds to download another task. The tasks distributed by the master are typically independent and similar in size, and they admit at-least-once execution semantics.

Distributed search and distributed simulation are classical applications that can be naturally abstracted in terms of a system of processors performing a collection of tasks. We now overview several areas that also give rise to similar computational situations.

- In image processing [91] and computer graphics [32], a significant amount of data processing (e.g., operations on large data structures, computing partial and ordinary differential equations) is required, especially in visualization (achieving graphical visual realism) [75, 84]. When the data to be computed can be decomposed into smaller independent "chunks", the usual approach is to load-balance the chunks among the processing units of a parallel machine or the nodes of a cluster [46, 84].

- In databases [29], when querying a large (unsorted) data space, it is often desirable to use multiple machines to search distinct records or sets of records in the database in order to decrease the search time [5].

- In fluid dynamics [43, 52], researchers study the behavior of fluids in different settings by running simulations that involve solving differential equations over very large data spaces. Again, when the data can be decomposed into independent chunks, the chunks are assigned to multiple processing units to achieve fast and reliable computation.

- Airborne radar systems [77] are used to detect and track objects in the presence of a natural and hostile interference. Such radars employ multi-element antenna arrays and require that large amount of data from each antenna element is processed in a short time. Several processing stages in such settings involve large independent data sets that are to be processed concurrently by multiple processors.

- Another example can be found in cryptography [88], specifically in breaking cryptographic schemes. The goal is to search and find a user's private key. A key may be a string of 128 bits, meaning that there are 2^{128} different possibilities to choose a key. Among the various techniques available, the most frequently used is the exhaustive search where multiple processing units search simultaneously for the key, each unit searching different sets of bit permutations.

In this book, we present a study of cooperative computing with the focus on modeling distributed computing settings, algorithmic techniques enabling one to combine efficiency and fault tolerance in distributed systems, and the exposition of trade-offs between efficiency and fault tolerance for robust cooperative computing. The focus of the exposition is on the abstract problem, called *Do-All*, formulated in terms of a system of p cooperating processors that together need to perform a collection of n tasks in the presence of adversity.

When considering computational settings where very large quantities of tasks need to be performed in a distributed setting, a key problem is to ensure the efficiency and progress of the cooperative computation when the distributed computing medium is subject to perturbations. Large-scale distributed systems are inherently dynamic for many reasons, such as failures of computers and network links, planned replacement or removal of obsolete components, integration of new or repaired components, mobility, and varying timing characteristics of cooperating computers. All of these perturbations in the computing medium manifest themselves, and can be modeled, as failures of different types. In a perfect universe, it is sufficient to assign each task to a single worker to ensure its correct and timely execution, thus the total work performed by the system is proportional to the number of tasks. However, in practice, each task may have to be issued to workers multiple times to ensure its execution. Practical observations and theoretical lower bounds strongly support this. Given that the only way to guarantee fault tolerance is through redundancy, there exists an inherent conflict between *efficiency* and *fault tolerance*: efficiency implies elimination of redundancy, while fault tolerance implies introduction of redundancy.

As mentioned already, the model commonly used in the Internet supercomputing includes a master process that supervises the execution of many independent tasks on a large set of worker processes. Despite the simplicity and benefits of a single master approach, as the scale of such computing environments grows, it becomes unrealistic to assume the existence of the infallible master that is able to coordinate the activities of multitudes of workers. A single master creates a performance bottleneck that is also a single point of failure in the system. Additionally, the tasks to be collectively performed by the distributed system may be originating at multiple sources. Thus, it is also necessary to consider peer-to-peer solutions where any worker may generate tasks and where a fully distributed algorithm is employed to perform the tasks dependably and efficiently. From the architectural modeling standpoint, one needs to consider both the message-passing systems, given the popularity of the distributed networks, and the shared-memory systems, in light of the advent of multicore architectures and the observation that it is often easier to develop a distributed algorithm for an abstract shared-memory system and then convert it to the message-passing paradigm.

1.2   BOOK ROADMAP AND CONVENTIONS

1.2.1   ROADMAP

In this book, we focus on models, algorithmic techniques, and analysis. Our goal is to present the most interesting approaches to algorithm design and analysis leading to many fundamental results in cooperative distributed computing. The algorithms selected for inclusion in this work are among the most efficient that additionally serve as good pedagogical examples. Of course, it is impossible to include all such algorithms, and some algorithms that are marginally more efficient are not included if they are too complex or if their analysis is too involved to serve our pedagogical aims. Each chapter concludes with bibliographic notes that include a wealth of references to related work and relevant advanced results.

In Chapter 2, we discuss distributed cooperative computing, fault tolerance, and measures of efficiency. We define the *Do-All* problem of performing a collection of tasks by a set of processors in the presence of adversity. We then present a broad landscape of models of adversity and some of the lower bounds that characterize the inherent costs of providing fault-tolerant solutions for *Do-All*.

In Chapter 3, we present main algorithmic paradigms used in designing solutions for the *Do-All* problem. Each paradigm focuses on a specific style in which processors are allocated to the tasks based on the knowledge about the computation and its progress. We describe three such paradigms: (1) global allocation paradigm, where processors aim to acquire a global view of the computation, (2) local allocation paradigm, where processors use only the local view of the computation, and (3) hashed allocation paradigm, where processors pursue a pseudo-randomized approach. In the second part of the chapter, we describe techniques for implementing the allocation paradigms in shared-memory and message-passing models.

In Chapter 4, we present key algorithms for *Do-All* in the shared-memory model of computation. Among many available algorithms we focus on select few that illustrate the most important techniques and that contain most interesting insights into solving the problem. The efficiency analysis of these algorithms also illustrates the most interesting techniques that reveal noteworthy aspects regarding the behavior of the algorithms in the presence of adversity.

In Chapter 5, we present the most interesting approaches to solving the *Do-All* problem in the message-passing model under different modeling assumptions. As before, we select algorithms that represent interesting techniques for solving the problem, and whose analyses illustrate the behavior of the algorithms and contain noteworthy techniques.

In Chapter 6, we review the most important related work dealing with additional modeling assumption and types of adversity. This includes Byzantine processor failures, solving *Do-All* problem in the model with broadcast channels, solving the problem in the settings where network partitions impose the additional requirement that the results of task execution must be known to all processors, and the model where prolonged periods of network disconnection force processors to schedule their activities in isolation, attempting to reduce redundant work.

At the end of each chapter (except for the final survey chapter) we provide Bibliographic Notes that overview related topics and results. The complete bibliography follows the last chapter. Here we give additional pointers to conference proceedings and archival journals that covering a spectrum of areas related to distributed cooperative computing. Most results in this monograph and related topics on fault-tolerant distributed computation appear as articles in these venues. A reader interested in learning more will be well served by consulting proceedings of at least the following conferences: ACM Symposium on Principles of Distributed Computing (PODC), ACM Symposium on Parallel Algorithms and Architectures (SPAA), ACM Symposium on Theory of Computing (STOC), ACM-SIAM Symposium on Discrete Algorithms (SODA), IEEE Symposium on Foundations of Computer Science (FOCS), IEEE-sponsored Conference on Distributed Computing Systems (ICDCS), EATCS-sponsored Symposium on Distributed Computing (DISC), the Conference on the Principles on Distributed Systems (OPODIS), and the Colloquium on Structural Information and Communication Complexity (SIROCCO). The most relevant journals include the following: Distributed Computing (Springer), SIAM Journal on Computing, Theoretical Computer Science (Elsevier), Information and Computation, Information Processing Letters, Parallel Processing Letters, Journal of the ACM, ACM Journal of Algorithms, Journal of Discrete Algorithms, and Journal of Parallel and Distributed Computing (Elsevier).

1.2.2   CONVENTIONS

In this book, we make the following conventions.

The algorithms are presented using intuitive high level procedural pseudocode. Generally, we present the pseudocode of algorithms with no line-numbering. We number lines only in the pseudocode of algorithms when the text refers to specific lines of the code.

The basis of logarithms is elided in pseudocode when the basis is 2 and in the asymptotic expressions when the basis is a constant and immaterial. In the cases when the basis is significant in asymptotics, we explicitly specify it.

CHAPTER 2

Distributed Cooperation and Adversity

In this chapter, we discuss the efficiency considerations of parallel and distributed cooperative computation, define the main *Do-All* problem central to our study, survey the models of failures, and state the most important lower bounds.

2.1 DISTRIBUTED COMPUTING AND EFFICIENCY

Speeding up computation is one of the central reasons for using distributed (parallel) computing. If a certain task can be done in sequential time T_1 using a uniprocessor, then ideally we would like to perform the same task using p processors (without failures or delays) in parallel time T_p, such that

$$T_p = T_1/p .$$

Obtaining such improvement in time is one of the most important goals of parallel algorithm design.

It is important to measure time improvements relative to the time of the most efficient sequential algorithm—achieving parallel improvements over the time of a poor sequential algorithm is not that meaningful. Now we consider the notion of speed-up in more detail. Let $T_1^\star(n)$ be the time of the best possible uniprocessor algorithm (with respect to a lower bound on time for the problem being solved) for a certain problem with inputs of size n. If a p-processor parallel algorithm solves this problem in time $T_p(n)$, then the achieved speed-up $\mathfrak{s}$ is defined:

$$\mathfrak{s} = T_1^\star(n)/T_p(n) .$$

The speed-up is *linear* when $\mathfrak{s} = \Theta(p)$.

In the setting where multiple processors cooperate on a collection of common tasks, in order to hope to achieve a speed-up close to linear in p, we need to assume that the processors are operating either in synchrony, or at least at comparable speeds. This assumption is in fact implemented in highly parallel computing devices such as systolic arrays and SIMD (single-instruction, multiple-data) devices such as vector processors.

Let us consider the equality signifying linear speed-up, $T_1^\star(n)/T_p(n) = \Theta(p)$, and rewrite it as follows.

$$T_1^\star(n) = \Theta(p \cdot T_p(n)) .$$

The left-hand side represents, asymptotically, the number of basic instructions performed by a uniprocessor in solving the problem. The right-hand side *processor-time product* represents, also asymptotically, the number of basic instructions performed by *all* processors together in solving the problem in the multiprocessor setting. This processor-time product is called *work* and is notated as S. Work is used to assess efficiency of synchronous multiprocessor algorithms in terms of the total number of machine instructions executed by the processors during the computation.

The notion of work for parallel/distributed algorithms naturally generalizes the notion of time for sequential algorithms, thus measuring work is meaningful for uniprocessors as well. Let $T_1(n)$ be the time complexity of a sequential algorithm solving a certain problem on inputs of size n. Since $p = 1$, we observe that $S = p \cdot T_p(n) = 1 \cdot T_1(n) = T_1(n)$, thus the notions of *work* and *time* are equivalent for sequential algorithms.

A parallel/distributed algorithm achieves linear speed-up exactly when its work is the same as the time complexity of the best sequential algorithm. This is of course only meaningful for synchronous computation with infallible processors. Enter failures and delays. Once processor failures and delays (asynchrony) are introduced, measuring work as the processor-time product loses meaning. This is because the computational resource is no longer under the control of the computation—it varies due to failures and delays, and only limited resources may be available to the computation at any given time. Furthermore, local processor clocks may no longer be in synchrony with each other. The efficiency of fault-tolerant parallel computation is more appropriately measured in terms of the processor work-steps that are *available* to the computation.

Example 2.1   *Work and crash failures.* Consider a synchronous p-processor algorithm that terminates in time τ_0 in the absence of failures. The fault-free work $S = \tau_0 \cdot p$ is the area of the dashed rectangle in Figure 2.1. Due to failures, the algorithm begins with $p_{t_0} < p_0$ processors, and then the number of active processors is reduced to p_{t_1}, p_{t_2}, and p_{t_3} at times t_1, t_2 and t_3, respectively. The computation finally terminates at time τ_1. The work performed by the processors in this computation is given by the area bounded by the "staircase" formed by the heavy solid lines and the two axes.

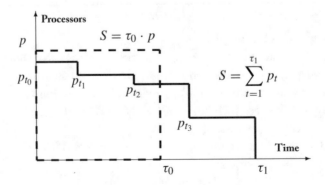

Figure 2.1: Work in the presence of processor crash failures.

In the example, the shape of the "staircase" is determined by an *adversarial pattern* established by an *adversary* that determines when and what processors crash during the computation.

In Example 2.1, we assumed synchronous parallel processors subject to crashes. In this case, the internal clock-ticks of processors are exactly the ticks of some external global clock. Now let us generalize this to the setting where processor failures and restarts, and processor delays are possible. In the most general case, the shape of the "staircase" of Figure 2.1 will instead appear as a "comb" with an irregular pattern of short and missing "teeth", corresponding to the number of processors completing instructions at times determined by some external clock (unknown to the processors), given a pattern of failures, restarts, and delays such as depicted in Figure 2.2.

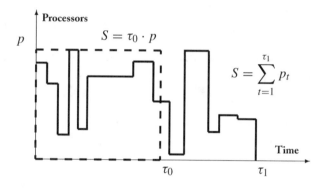

Figure 2.2: Work in the presence of failures, restarts, and delays.

If one considers an extreme case with an interleaved execution and without any true concurrency, the comb may lose all its teeth and the diagram will instead appear as a rectangle of height 1, since at any global clock-tick only one processor can perform a local computation step. Here the work of the algorithm is exactly its time as measured by the external clock (in Figure 2.2, time τ_1 becomes equal to work S).

The time of a computation in the presence of failures, restarts, and delays—unlike the time of a fault-free synchronous algorithm—does not depend exclusively on the number of initial processors and the size of the input. When failures and delays occur, the time depends also on the variations in the size of the available computing resources.

It is conceptually straightforward to provide fault-tolerance by taking advantage of space redundancy: one can use p initial crash-prone processors to solve the computational task, and let each processor run the best sequential algorithm with time complexity $T(n)$, where n is the size of the input. Such solution is as fast as any sequential computation using a single processor. It tolerates up to $p - 1$ failures (assuming no restarts), but its work in the worst case is $S = T(n) \cdot p$, which is achieved in the case without a single failure. This is not an efficient use of the computing resources: for a fault-tolerant p-processor algorithm to be efficient, it must have (multiplicative) work overhead that is substantially lower than p. We will normally consider parallel algorithms on inputs of size n where the number of processors p does not exceed the size of the input, that is, $1 \leq p \leq n$. Therefore, for a fault-tolerant parallel algorithm to be considered efficient, its work overhead must be asymptotically inferior to n. We next define the work complexity measure more formally.

Work complexity. Work accounts for all computation steps performed by the processors available to the computation; this is also called the *available processor steps* measure.

Let A be an algorithm that solves a problem of size n with p processors under an adversarial model $\mathcal{A}$ that defines the types and magnitude of failures and delays caused in each execution of the algorithm. Let $\mathcal{E}(A, \mathcal{A})$ be the set of all executions ξ of algorithm A under adversary $\mathcal{A}$. We denote by $p_i(\xi)$ the number of processors completing a local computation step (e.g., a machine instruction) at time i of the execution, according to some external global clock (not available to the processors).

Definition 2.2   Let A be an algorithm that solves a problem of size n with p processors under adversary $\mathcal{A}$. For any execution $\xi \in \mathcal{E}(A, \mathcal{A})$, let $\tau(\xi)$ be the time (according to the external clock) by which A solves the problem. Then *work complexity* S of algorithm A is:

$$S = S_{\mathcal{A}}(n, p) = \max_{\xi \in \mathcal{E}(A, \mathcal{A})} \left\{ \sum_{i=1}^{\tau(\xi)} p_i(\xi) \right\} .$$

This definition is used to evaluate the efficiency of algorithms and to establish lower bounds. We now define three different notions of efficiency that depend on the multiplicative work overhead relative to the time (or work) of the best sequential algorithm.

For a specific problem, a p-processor parallel algorithm is considered *optimal* when its work on problems of size n is related by a multiplicative constant to the best achievable (or best known) sequential time $T_1^{\star}(n)$ for the same problem. That is, for optimal parallel computation, we require that

$$S = O(T_1^{\star}(n)) .$$

(Note that in the failure-free, synchronous case, this yields a speed-up linear in p.)

We say that the parallel algorithm is *polylogarithmically efficient* (or simply *efficient*) when its work has polylogarithmic overhead relative to the best time of the corresponding sequential algorithm:

$$S = O(T_1^{\star}(n) \cdot \log^{O(1)} n) .$$

We say that a parallel algorithm is *polynomially efficient* when its work has a small polynomial overhead relative to the corresponding best sequential algorithm:

$$S = O(T_1^{\star}(n) \cdot n^{\varepsilon}) ,$$

where ε is a constant, such that $0 < \varepsilon < 1$.

For polynomial efficiency, we require that $\varepsilon < 1$ because if we allow $\varepsilon \geq 1$, then a trivial "parallel" algorithm for $p = n$ processors where each processor simply executes the best sequential algorithm can be considered efficient, since its work is $S = n \cdot T_1^\star(n) = O(T_1^\star(n) \cdot n^1) = O(T_1^\star(n) \cdot n^\varepsilon)$.

Of course for the computation to be practical, in all cases the constants hidden in the asymptotic notation must be small.

In the case of randomized algorithms, we assess *expected work* $ES_A(n, p)$ computed as the expectation of the sum $\sum_{i=1}^{\tau(\xi)} p_i(\xi)$ in Definition 2.2.

Definitions of work complexity do not depend on the specifics of the target model of computation, e.g., whether it is message-passing or shared-memory.

Message complexity. For message-passing algorithms, the efficiency of a fault-tolerant computation is additionally characterized in terms of their *message complexity*. Let A be an algorithm that solves a problem of size n with p processors under adversary $\mathcal{A}$. For any execution $\xi \in \mathcal{E}(A, A)$, let $m_i(\xi)$ be the number of point-to-point messages sent at time i of the execution, according to some external global clock.

Definition 2.3   Let A be an algorithm that solves a problem of size n with p processors under adversary $\mathcal{A}$. For execution $\xi \in \mathcal{E}(A, A)$, let time $\tau(\xi)$ be the time (according to the external clock) by which A solves the problem. Then *message complexity* M of algorithm A is:

$$M = M_{\mathcal{A}}(n, p) = \max_{\xi \in \mathcal{E}(A, A)} \left\{ \sum_{i=1}^{\tau(\xi)} m_i(\xi) \right\} .$$

When processors communicate using broadcasts or multicasts, each broadcast and multicast is counted as the number of point-to-point messages from the sender to each receiver. In the cases where we deal with randomized algorithms, we assess *expected message complexity* $EM_A(n, p)$ computed as the expectation of the sum $\sum_{i=1}^{\tau(\xi)} m_i(\xi)$ from Definition 2.3.

Measuring time. In the analysis of parallel/distributed algorithms in the presence of adversity, the time complexity does not play a central role as compared to the role it plays in the analysis of sequential algorithms. Recall (from the discussion following Figure 2.2) that in the extreme case of interleaving with concurrency, time can be equal to work S. Here the adversity results in at most one processor executing a local computation step for each global time step.

We use the conventional notion of *time* (local or global) to measure the number of steps (e.g., machine instructions) executed locally by a processor in performing activities of interest, or for synchronous models, to measure the time in the conventional sense, for example, in establishing the number of synchronous algorithm iterations.

```
for each processor PID = 1..p begin
    Task[1..n]                                      % Globally known n tasks
    for i = 1 to ⌈n/p⌉ do
        perform Task[PID + p · (i − 1)]
    od
end.
```

Figure 2.3: Solving the *Do-All* problem in the absence of failures and delays.

2.2 COOPERATION PROBLEM: DO-ALL COMPUTING

In this study of the efficiency of distributed cooperative computing in the presence of adversity and the trade-offs between efficiency and fault-tolerance, we focus on the abstract problem of performing a set of tasks in a decentralized setting, called the *Do-All* problem.

Do-All: p processors must cooperatively perform n tasks
in the presence of adversity.

Here we deal with abstract *tasks* as primitive units of work performed by the processors. The tasks are assumed to be *similar*, *independent*, and *idempotent*, which means the following in our context.

Similarity: Any task execution on any processor consumes equal or comparable local resources. In particular, we assume that each task can be performed in constant time (not dependent on n or p).

Independence: The completion of any task does not affect any other task, and any task can be executed concurrently with any other task.

Idempotence: Each task can be executed one or more times to produce the same final result; in other words, tasks admit at-least-once execution semantics.

In the absence of adversity, the problem can be easily solved without any coordination by load-balancing the n tasks among the p processors (here $p \leq n$ is the normal setting where there are at least as many tasks as processors). If the processors and the tasks have known unique identities, each processor simply performs $\lceil n/p \rceil$ tasks, distributed among the processors on the basis of processor identifiers PID, with padding used to include "dummy" tasks when p does not divide n. The pseudocode for such an algorithm is given in Figure 2.3, where each processor is assigned no more than $\lceil n/p \rceil$ and no less than $\lfloor n/p \rfloor$ real tasks. (Alternatively, each processor can be assigned a contiguous "chunk" of $\lceil n/p \rceil$ tasks, but the allocation of real tasks to processors is less intuitive in this case as some processors may get just the dummy tasks.)

In any such algorithm, the total number of tasks performed is $p\lceil n/p \rceil = \Theta(n)$. Given our assumption that each task can be computed by any processor in constant time, the work of such computation is $S = \Theta(n)$. In the absence of adversity, the distributed algorithm performs each task exactly once. This is clearly an optimal solution in terms of tasks, since n tasks must be performed. In particular, the best sequential algorithm to perform n tasks has time complexity $T_1^\star(n) = \Theta(n)$. Furthermore, assuming that each of the p processors progresses at about the same pace through the tasks, the problem is solved in parallel time $T_p(n) = \Theta(n/p)$; this is the number of iterations in the inner loop above. Thus, the algorithm achieves linear speedup: $\mathfrak{s} = T_1^\star(n)/T_p(n) = \Theta(p)$.

In the message-passing settings, we generally assume that each process is able to access the information necessary to perform each task. An algorithm where processors have access to all tasks can be extended with minimal communication and coordination to work in the setting where the tasks are not initially known to all processors. If the subsets of tasks are initially known only to some processors and if a single task can be communicated to a processor in a fixed-size message, then the total number of messages is $M(n, p) = n + p\lceil n/p \rceil = \Theta(n)$. This can be done by communicating all tasks to a chosen master process (e.g., based on the processor ids), which takes n messages. Then the master delivers "chunks" of tasks of size $\lceil n/p \rceil$ to individual processors in a load-balanced fashion, which takes $p\lceil n/p \rceil$ messages.

When adversity is introduced, e.g., failures and delays, developing solutions for the *Do-All* problem that are both efficient and fault-tolerant becomes challenging.

While our main complexity measure is work, it is also important to obtain reasonable message complexity in message-passing systems. In message-passing systems the efficiency of algorithms is sometimes compared using *lexicographic* complexity. Here the complexity functions are pairs $\langle S, M \rangle$, i.e., work and communication, where such pairs are compared lexicographically, first work, then communication. We also note that, intuitively, an efficient messaging algorithm should not require more than n message exchanges for each task. Hence, it is desirable to have algorithms whose message complexity is no worse than quadratic in n.

2.3   COMPUTATION AND ADVERSARIAL SETTINGS

We now describe the basic models of computation, then discuss in detail the different adversarial settings for which fault-tolerant algorithms are to be developed.

Shared-memory model. In this model, the p cooperating processors have access to shared memory. To access memory processors perform read and write operations that take one local processor step (e.g., a machine instruction).

If the processors are synchronous, we assume that processors always compute by executing triples of instructions: a *read* instruction that obtains a value from shared memory, a *compute* instruction that performs a constant time local computation, and a *write* instruction that stores a value in a shared memory location. The memory is atomic, which in our context means that a read operation obtains a value from a memory location that corresponds to the most recent complete write operation (according to some global clock), or the initial value of the location if there is no such write. A read can never return a partially written value. When multiple processors concurrently perform a write to the same memory location, we assume that the values are written in some arbitrary order.

(Although in the algorithms for this model, the processors always write the same value when writing concurrently; this is essentially the COMMON CRCW PRAM model.)

If the processors are asynchronous, then we use the conventional interleaving semantics. Here we also assume that accessing shared memory takes one atomic processor step.

Message-passing model. In this model, the p processors coordinate their activities by means of message passing. Here processors communicate via point-to-point messages. In some models, processors can use broadcast and multicast primitives. From the standpoint of communication efficiency, broadcast or multicast has the same communication cost as the number of messages delivered (see earlier discussion). In synchronous systems, we assume that there is a constant delay between the event of sending a message and the event where the message is received. In asynchronous systems, this delay may be unbounded.

Modeling adversity. Given the scale and complexity of realistic distributed platforms, any algorithm solving *Do-All* must be able to deal with adverse conditions inherent in such platforms that are caused by failures of processors, processor asynchrony, network disconnections, unpredictable message delays, etc. Adversity may impact the system in various ways, and we now discuss failure types that abstract realistic situations occurring in distributed systems where the *Do-All* problem needs to be solved. We first present failure modeling and then discuss corresponding adversarial behaviors.

Processor failures and delays. Adversity manifests itself in terms of processor failures and unpredictable timing associated with asynchronous systems.

- *Processor crashes (or stop-failures).* A processor *crashes* during a computation if it stops (after completing some machine instruction) and does not perform any further actions. In synchronous settings, crash failures can be detected (e.g., by timeouts). Crash failures is the most commonly considered processor failure type.

  When a processor experiences a benign failure, such as a crash, then some tasks assigned to the faulty machine may remain unperformed.

- *Processor crashes and restarts.* Here, following a crash, a processor may *restart* at some point in the computation. If a previously crashed processor restarts in a special well-defined state, the processor can be made aware of the restart. If a processor restarts in the same state it crashed in, such restart is undetectable. This situation is analogous to asynchrony, since arbitrary time may pass between the processor's crash and subsequent restart; however, in a synchronous system correct processors proceed at the same clock rate.

  If a processor is able to restart following a failure, it may come back to life unaware of the overall computation progress.

- *Asynchrony.* Although we take the view that synchrony is instrumental in obtaining parallel speed-up, realistic systems deviate from synchrony even if they are composed of identical processors. For example, a benign page-fault may cause a processor to idle for milliseconds, while its peers execute millions of instructions. When a system is not completely synchronous, then sometimes we are able to make assumptions about the time it takes for a processor to perform a unit of work; such systems are called *timed-asynchronous*. When processors are fully asynchronous, algorithms must be designed to remain correct regardless of the processor speed fluctuations.

  If processors are asynchronous, and their relative processing speeds differ arbitrarily, the tasks assigned to slow processors remain undone for a long time, while the faster processors may idle. In such cases, the negative impact on the efficiency of computation can be substantial.

- *Byzantine processor failures.* Following a Byzantine failure a processor can exhibit arbitrary behavior, e.g., it can do nothing, do something contrary to the algorithm specification, send arbitrary messages, or even behave normally. About the only thing that such a faulty processor cannot do is to impersonate other processors or their messages. Although Byzantine failures are largely outside of our scope, this is an important failure class and we discuss some algorithms that tolerate such failures in the final survey chapter.

  When a processor fails in a malicious way, it may mislead the system into thinking that its tasks have been performed, or it may return incorrect results.

In all such adversarial settings, processors must not only perform their assigned tasks, but also coordinate their activity with other processors in an attempt to detect processor failures and to identify remaining tasks that they can perform should they become idle. In shared-memory settings processors can coordinate their activities by reading and writing shared variables. However, in message-passing settings, where communication is used to coordinate processor activities, the underlying network can also experience adverse conditions.

Communication failures and delays. Adversity affects message-passing systems through of message delays and network failures.

- *Synchrony vs. Asynchrony.* In synchronous settings, all messages sent by correct processors are delivered in constant time. For asynchronous settings, there is no known upper bound on time for message delay. In some cases, and only for the purpose of analysis, we assume that there is an upper bound on delay, but it is not known to the processors, and algorithms in this setting must be correct for completely asynchronous messaging. Message loss is modeled as an unbounded delay on message delivery.

  Unpredictable message delays may cause processors to idle awaiting a needed message. This typically results in inefficient computation.

- *Broadcast failures.* Broadcast or multicast capability is a powerful technique in designing message-passing algorithms. In some models, we assume reliable multicast semantics, meaning that if the sending processor fails, then the multicast message is either delivered to all recipients or to none at all. Unfortunately, it is difficult to implement reliable broadcast in some practical settings, and it is often necessary to model broadcast as point-to-point messages without any semantical benefit.

  When reliable multicast is used to coordinate processor activities, it enables the cooperating processors to quickly build a consistent global view. This is much harder to achieve using point-to-point messages in the presence of failures, resulting in less efficient computation.

- *Intermittent connectivity.* Processors may experience intermittent connectivity, making coordination difficult or impossible. In addition to outright communication failures, in realistic settings, the processors may not initially be aware of the network configuration, which would require expenditure of computation resources to establish communication, for example, in radio networks. During the initial configuration of a network, each processor may start working in isolation pending the completion of system configuration. Regardless of the reasons, it is important to direct any available computation resources to performing the required tasks as soon as possible.

  In all such scenarios, the tasks have to be scheduled for execution by all processors. The goal of such scheduling must be to control redundant task executions in the absence of communication and during the period of time when the communication channels are being (re)established. We survey these issues in Chapter 6.

- *Network fragmentation.* Network may fragment due to communication failures, in which case communication between processors in different partitions is impossible. In Chapter 6, we discuss performing work in networks that are subject to *partitions*. Partitionable networks may undergo dynamic changes in the network topology that partition the processors into non-overlapping *groups*, where communication is only possible for processors within the same group.

In order to model an adversarial setting where failure of a particular type occur, we define the concept of the *adversary* that allows us to abstract and formalize the interference with a computation that is not under the control of the computation. An event caused by the adversary, such as a processor crash or a network fragmentation, interferes with the computation and typically degrades the efficiency of the computation. The concept of the adversary is used in the analysis of algorithms and for obtaining lower bound results for specific problems.

Once an adversary is endowed with the ability to cause specific kinds of failures, it makes decisions when to cause specific failures based on the knowledge it has about the computation. In this regard we distinguish between two main types of adversaries that differ in their knowledge.

(*i*) *Omniscient or on-line*: the adversary has complete knowledge of the computation that it is affecting, and it makes instantaneous dynamic decisions on how to interfere with the computation.

(*ii*) *Oblivious or off-line*: the adversary determines the sequence of failure events it will cause before the start of the computation.

Clearly, the on-line adversary is at least as powerful as an off-line one. However, the distinction between the two types of adversaries vanishes for deterministic algorithms. This is because both types of adversaries can know, before the beginning of the computation, exactly what actions will be taken by the deterministic algorithm and how the algorithm is affected by the events caused by the adversary, e.g., by failures and delays. For randomized algorithms, the distinction between the two adversarial types is significant because the off-line adversaries do not have the knowledge of the random choices, e.g., the outcomes of random "coin tosses", prior to the start of the computation (as opposed to the on-line adversaries that have knowledge of the random tosses, up to the current instant of the computation). Thus, a randomized algorithm may be substantially more efficient in the presence of only off-line adversity.

When presenting algorithms for the *Do-All* problems, we always state explicitly what kind of adversity the algorithm is designed to tolerate. Additionally, for randomized algorithms we always assume off-line adversaries.

2.4 FAULT TOLERANCE, EFFICIENCY, AND LOWER BOUNDS

Appearance of adversity may cause substantial degradation in the efficiency of the computation. The goal of algorithm design for the *Do-All* problem—or any other problem that needs to be solved in the presence of adversity—is combining fault-tolerance (the ability to compute correctly despite the occurrences of failures) and efficiency.

Solving *Do-All* in distributed settings is a source of both challenge and opportunity. On one hand, it is challenging to develop algorithms that achieve high efficiency in solving *Do-All*, while tolerating adversarial conditions. On the other, the fact that we are solving *Do-All* using multiple processors provides us with both the source of parallelism needed to achieve good performance and the source of redundancy that is necessary for fault-tolerance. We elaborate on this below.

Consider a fault-tolerant system with p-fold redundancy in processors designed to tolerate up to $p - 1$ processor failures. A worthwhile objective for such system is to achieve p-fold increase in performance in the absence of adversity, for example, achieve linear in p speed-up. When there are indeed $p - 1$ failures, then the system's performance should approximate the performance of an efficient computation on a uniprocessor.

Similarly, consider a decentralized system consisting of p processors designed to achieve up to p-fold speed-up. Such a system is inherently redundant, and there is no reason why we should not have the goal for the system to tolerate up to $p - 1$ processor failures with graceful degradation in performance as the number of faulty processors increases.

Recall that our primary measure of efficiency is *work*, thus the ultimate goal is to have algorithms that achieve optimal or efficient work. A trivial fault-tolerant solution, where all processors perform all tasks, has work $S(n, p) = \Theta(n \cdot p)$, which is quadratic in n when n and p are comparable. Therefore, efficient algorithms must have work that is *subquadratic* (in n and p), and we will consider interesting only the algorithms that have work $S = n \cdot o(n)$ in the presence of the type of adversity they are designed to tolerate.

In assessing the efficiency of fault-tolerant algorithms, it is also important to consider the relevant lower bounds on work. Clearly, any correct algorithm must perform all tasks, thus there is an immediate work lower bound of $S = \Omega(n)$. Showing substantially stronger lower bounds proved to be very difficult. We now briefly describe the most important lower bounds for *Do-All*.

Lower bound with perfect load balancing. In order to understand the inherent overhead associated with performing a collection of tasks in the presence of adversity, it is interesting to consider the situation where an algorithm is assisted by an *oracle* that has the knowledge of the global state and the history of the computation. In particular, the oracle may be used to assist the processors to load-balance and terminate the computation when all tasks are done. The oracle assumption is used as a *tool* for studying the work complexity patterns of *any* fault-tolerant algorithm since any lower bound developed for this strong model applies equally well to weaker specialized message-passing or shared-memory models.

The strongest possible oracle-based lower bound on work for any synchronous systems with processors prone to crashes is $S = \Omega(n + p \log p / \log \log p)$. This means that work optimality is not achievable in any model of computation for the full range of processors, $1 \le p \le n$. However, if p can be substantially smaller than n, there is hope of designing work-optimal algorithms. Of course, for algorithms to be interesting, p has to be non-trivial, for example, $p = n^{\varepsilon}$, where $0 < \varepsilon < 1$.

Lower bound for synchronous shared-memory. When the processors are synchronous and subject to crash failures, the lower bound on time is $\Omega(\log p)$. This means that the corresponding work lower bound is $S = \Omega(n + p \log p)$. This bound holds even in algorithm executions where no processor crashes. This lower bound is within a less-than-logarithmic factor away from the work of the best known algorithm (we present it in Chapter 4). Thus, no substantial improvements to this lower bound are to be anticipated.

Lower bounds in asynchrony. It is surprising that the best known lower bound for asynchronous systems is also $S = \Omega(n + p \log p)$, as one would expect a high lower bound as compared to synchronous systems. What is interesting in this bound is that it is developed simply by delaying processors, and it holds even if the system is failure-free, that is, even if the processors know that there will be no crashes. This bound applies to both shared-memory and message-passing models. It is very challenging to develop a stronger lower bound, but given that the existing bound is substantially below the upper bounds achieved by known algorithms, it is plausible that a stronger lower bound exists.

The impact of delays in message passing systems. In asynchronous systems the delay on message delivery can be unbounded, thus preventing the processors from effective coordination of their activities. This may yield very inefficient work, and in particular, when the message delivery delay d is $\Omega(n)$, each processor is faced with a decision: either wait for the next expected message or perform tasks in isolation. In either case, work complexity is $S = \Omega(n \cdot p)$. Thus, a sensible goal is to develop asynchronous algorithms that are correct for any delay d, but that achieve reasonable work when d is bounded. The efficiency of these algorithms is evaluated in light of the relevant lower bounds.

In Section 5.4.1, we show that any deterministic algorithm solving *Do-All* performs work $S = \Omega(n + p \min\{d, n\} \log_{d+1}(d + n))$. Here note that when d is small, e.g., a constant, then the lower bound becomes $S = \Omega(n + p \log n)$, and this is exactly what is anticipated by the lower bounds discussed earlier. When d is comparable to n the lower bound becomes multiplicative in p and n, that is, $S = \Omega(n + p\,n)$, and this is unavoidable as we just discussed.

2.5   BIBLIOGRAPHIC NOTES

The *Do-All* problem has been studied in a variety of settings, e.g., in *shared-memory* models [10, 47, 55, 74], in *message-passing* models [21, 28, 33, 83], and in *partitionable networks* [26, 71]. Dwork, Halpern, and Waarts [28] were the first to define and study the *Do-All* problem for message-passing models. De Prisco, Mayer, and Yung were first to study the *Do-All* problem under the work complexity measure we use here. The distributed cooperation problem was first called "*Do-All*" by Chlebus, De Prisco, and Shvartsman [17], who studied it for the model with processor crashes and restarts. Dolev, Segala, and Shvartsman [26] studied the problem of distributed cooperation in the setting of processor groups in partitionable networks. This problem was subsequently called "*Omni-Do*" by Georgiou and Shvartsman in [42], who studied it in the settings with network fragmentation and merges.

In shared-memory models, the *Do-All* problem is known as the *Write-All* problem: *given a zero-valued array of n elements and p processors, write value* 1 *into each array location.* This problem was introduced by Kanellakis and Shvartsman [54], who also defined the work measure (available processor steps).

Do-All algorithms have been used in developing simulations of failure-free algorithms on failure-prone processors, e.g., as in the works of Kedem, Palem, and Spirakis [58], Martel, Park, and Subramonian [73], and Kanellakis and Shvartsman [55, 86]. This is done by iteratively using a *Do-All* algorithm to simulate the steps of failure-free processors on failure-prone processors. Motivated by such algorithm simulations, Georgiou, Russell and Shvartsman [38] formulated the *iterative Do-All* problem and studied it in message-passing and shared-memory models.

Examples of cooperation problems that can be abstracted in terms of *Do-All* computing include distributed search, e.g., SETI@home [61], distributed simulation, e.g., [25], multi-agent collaboration, e.g., [7, 89], image processing [91], computer graphics [32], visualization [46, 75, 84], databases querying [5, 29], fluid dynamics simulations [43, 52], airborne radar applications [77], and cryptography [88].

The definition of the fail-stop model (with or without restarts) is taken from the work of Schlichting and Schneider [85]. Byzantine processor failures were introduced by Lamport, Shostak, and Pease in [67]. The adversarial classifications oblivious/off-line and omniscient/on-line are taken from [14].

The oracle-based lower bound is due to Georgiou, Russell, and Shvartsman [38]. The logarithmic lower bound on time of any execution for deterministic *Do-All* was derived by Kedem, Palem, Raghunathan, and Spirakis in [57]. Martel and Subramonian [74] have extended this logarithmic lower bound to randomized algorithms against oblivious adversaries. The lower bound for asynchronous *Do-All* was derived by Kowalski, Momenzadeh, and Shvartsman [62] using the strategy from the work of Buss, Kanellakis, Ragde, and Shvartsman [16]. The delay-sensitive lower bound is due to Kowalski and Shvartsman [65].

CHAPTER 3

Paradigms and Techniques

The key to obtaining work-efficient solutions for the *Do-All* problem is in load balancing. If an algorithm always manages, in constant time, to allocate each processor to a task that had not been performed, and with no more than one processor allocated to any task, then the work of such an algorithm must be optimal. Indeed, for any n tasks and p processors ($p \leq n$) under this assumption, all tasks are performed with constant computational overhead per task, and since only one processor ever completes an assigned task, the work is $S(n, p) = \Theta(n) + O(p) = \Theta(n)$.

Therefore, *Do-All* algorithms need to perform an effective allocation of tasks to processes: redundant allocation must be avoided when possible. In particular, at a given step, each available processor must decide what task to do next. Ideally, this decision should lead to a *globally optimal* load-balancing allocation, meaning that the available r processors (where $r \leq p$) are only allocated to incomplete tasks, and if the number of incomplete tasks is u, then no more than $\lceil u/r \rceil$ processors are allocated to each incomplete task. In particular, if $u \leq r$, then at most one processor is allocated to each incomplete task.

Assume for the moment that there is an external observer of the distributed system, call it *oracle*, that has a complete global view of the computation. Specifically, the oracle knows what tasks have been performed so far and which processors are available to the computation (e.g., non-faulty). Obviously, with such *perfect knowledge* about the state of the computation, the oracle can implement an optimal task allocation by providing suitable information to each processor. Therefore, the goal of any algorithmic solution developed for the *Do-All* problem is to approximate the oracle-based task allocation in a distributed fashion, where each processor decides by itself what task to do next. In synchronous settings and in the absence of failures, obtaining an optimal allocation is trivial: each processor performs $\lceil n/p \rceil$ distinct tasks, one task at each step (recall the simple algorithm from Section 2.2). However, obtaining a good allocation becomes very challenging in the presence of failures and/or in asynchronous settings.

We consider three broad *algorithmic paradigms* for allocating tasks to processors in constructing robust solutions for the *Do-All* problem in the presence of faults, for synchronous and asynchronous settings, and for the shared-memory and message-passing communication models (Section 3.1). We present algorithmic techniques for implementing these paradigms, with some techniques being hybrid in the sense that they borrow ideas from more than one paradigm (Sections 3.2 and 3.3).

3.1   ALGORITHMIC PARADIGMS

The *Do-All* algorithms can be classified in terms of the algorithmic paradigms for load balancing and processor-task allocation. The paradigms differ in the type and the extent of knowledge used by the processors in allocating themselves to unfinished tasks in a balanced fashion.

3.1.1   GLOBAL ALLOCATION PARADIGM

In the *global allocation paradigm*, processors are allocated using knowledge about the *global* state of the computation. The processors compute and reduce the information that is, in turn, used to synchronize and allocate processors. The global allocation paradigm is most effective in algorithms that can assume a high degree of processor synchrony, since to take advantage of the global view of the computation, a processor needs to know that the view is not going to be changed drastically through the actions of faster processors. Furthermore, processors need to have a way of detecting faulty processors, in order to maintain a consistent view of the set of non-faulty processors; in synchrony, this can be achieved with timeouts.

The goal in the global allocation paradigm is to achieve processor allocation that is as close as possible to the ideal oracle-based allocation discussed above. As we show, it is possible to approximate the oracle-based allocation in logarithmic time, both in the synchronous shared-memory and message-passing models. The algorithmic techniques used to implement the global allocation paradigm differ, however, depending on the communication model assumed (as discussed in Section 3.3).

We now present a simple example that illustrates the global allocation paradigm where each processor makes allocation decisions based on information about the state of *all* processors (be it only 2 processors in the example).

Example 3.1   Consider a 2-processor instance of the *Do-All* problem in the shared-memory model, assuming synchrony, and under the assumption that at most one of the processors may fail by crashing. In the shared-memory model, the processors can synchronize their activities by reading and writing to shared variables. The information about the tasks is stored in shared memory as an array of tasks: $task[1], task[2], \ldots, task[n]$.

The two processors, p_1 and p_2, perform tasks as follows. Processor p_1 performs tasks in sequence from $task[1]$ to $task[n]$, while processor p_2 performs tasks in sequence from $task[n]$ to $task[1]$. We use two shared integer variables *left* and *right* to record the progress of processors p_1 and p_2, respectively. Initially, $left = 0$ and $right = n + 1$, recording the fact that no tasks were performed. We consider the time needed for reading and writing an integer variable to be negligible, compared to the time it takes to perform a task. When p_1 completes a task, it increments *left*, and when p_2 completes a task, it decrements *right*.

The processor uses the global allocation paradigm by comparing the values of *left* and *right*, thus obtaining a consistent global view of the progress of the computation. Specifically, if $left + 1 \leq right - 1$, then $task[left + 1]$ and $task[right - 1]$ have not been recorded as performed yet, and processors proceed to perform these tasks. (However, if $left + 1 = right - 1$, then $task[left + 1]$ and $task[right - 1]$ are one and the same, yet still this task has not been performed.) The two processors learn that the problem is solved when they detect that the next task in their corresponding sequence has already been done, i.e., when $left + 1 > right - 1$.

It is not difficult to see that optimal allocation is achieved in each step of the computation: both processors have a consistent view of the unfinished tasks at each step of the computation. One exception is in failure-free executions for $task[\lceil n/2 \rceil]$ with odd values of n. Both processors see that $left + 1 = right - 1$, and both perform the remaining task.

Since the computation is synchronous and performing a task takes constant time, we measure time and work using units that are sufficiently large to perform a task in one time unit (and read and write an integer variable, but recall that this time is negligible). In the absence of failures by the end of step $i = \lceil n/2 \rceil$, all tasks must be marked as done. The reader can easily check that this solution has work $n \leq S \leq n + 1$.

Now consider a scenario where one processor crashes. If, for example, processor $\mathfrak{p}_1$ crashes during the k-th step of the computation ($k < n/2$), the value of $left$ remains $k - 1$ for the rest of the computation. Processor $\mathfrak{p}_2$ will continue performing tasks until it reaches $task[k - 1]$, at which point, it terminates (note that $task[k]$ may have actually been performed twice: once by $\mathfrak{p}_1$ before it crashed without incrementing $left$, and once by $\mathfrak{p}_2$). Again, the reader can easily check that the work of this solution remains $n \leq S \leq n + 1$. (Also note that the worst case time is bounded from above by $n + 1$; this is achieved when one processor crashes without completing a single task.)   ∎

In the above illustration of a simple global allocation paradigm implementation, the processors perform optimal allocation by computing a consistent global view of the state of the computation, at each step of the computation. It is not difficult to implement the global allocation paradigm in a similar fashion for the analogous synchronous 2-processor *Do-All* problem in the message-passing model (where processors need to maintain a consistent global view by exchanging messages at each step of the computation). This is left as an exercise (see Exercise 3.1).

3.1.2   LOCAL ALLOCATION PARADIGM

In the *local allocation paradigm*, processors make allocation decisions using information about the computation that is *local* to the processors, and without obtaining information about the global progress of the computation. In the shared-memory model, this includes information that the processors can obtain from shared variables in a constant number of shared memory accesses. In the message-passing model, this local information includes information that the processors may obtain by messages received in a constant number of point-to-point message exchanges.

Because no global synchronization of processors is assumed, local allocation algorithms are good candidates for use in *asynchronous* settings. Algorithms using the local allocation paradigm attempt to compensate for the lack of global knowledge available to the processors in the global allocation paradigm algorithms through the use of appropriate data structures in the shared-memory model or logical data structures exchanged via messages in the message-passing model. In other words, algorithmic techniques that need to be employed attempt to turn the local knowledge of processors into some approximation of consistent global knowledge. However, due to asynchrony (and failures), processors might make load-balancing decisions with partial knowledge about the set of unfinished tasks and about the set of non-faulty processors. Here two processors might have very different views of the state of the system. Such an approach is essentially necessary in asynchronous failure-prone systems since it may be difficult or impossible to distinguish a very "slow" processor from a crashed one.

As the result, the algorithmic techniques here will be typically different from the techniques used in the global allocation algorithms that normally assume synchronous processors (we discuss this further in Sections 3.2 and 3.3). The following simple example illustrates the local allocation paradigm using a 2-processor algorithm, where processors do not seek to obtain a consistent global view, but instead are content with making allocation decisions based on locally-available knowledge.

Example 3.2   Consider a 2-processor instance of the *Do-All* problem in the shared-memory model with asynchrony, and under the assumption that at most one of the processors may fail by crashing. The processors will perform allocation to tasks by reading and writing to shared variables. The information about the tasks is stored in shared memory as an array of tasks: $task[1], task[2], \ldots, task[n]$.

The two processors, p_1 and p_2 perform tasks as follows. Processor p_1 performs tasks in sequence from $task[1]$ to $task[n]$, while processor p_2 performs tasks in sequence from $task[n]$ to $task[1]$. We use a shared bit array $done[1..n]$ to record the fact that tasks have been performed. We consider the time needed for reading or writing a single bit to be negligible, compared to the time it takes to perform a task. Initially, $done[]$ contains zeros. Before a processor performs some task $task[i]$, it first checks that $done[i] = 0$; after the processor performs the task, it marks the task as done by setting $done[i]$ to 1. For example, if processor p_1 finds $done[3] = 0$, then it performs $task[3]$ and sets $done[3] = 1$. A processor will never perform $task[i]$, if $done[i] = 1$. Note that either processor does not attempt to determine how many tasks were performed by the other. The two processors learn that the problem is solved when they detect that the next task in their corresponding sequence has already been done.

Since performing a task takes constant local time, we measure work using units that are sufficiently large to perform a task in one (local) time unit (and read and write a single bit, but recall that this time is negligible). In the absence of failures and delays, by the end of step $i = \lceil n/2 \rceil$, all tasks must be marked as done. The reader can easily check that, in this case, the solution has work $n \leq S \leq n + 1$.

Now consider asynchronous scenarios; these include executions with single processor crashes, since a crash can be modeled as an infinite delay. If, for example, processor p_1 completes the first k tasks, reaches $task[k + 1]$ and determines that it was already performed, i.e., $done[k] = 1$, it knows that the problem has been solved. This means that processor p_2 performed tasks in the range from

$task[n]$ to $task[k + 1]$, and also possibly $task[k]$ (if both perform that task simultaneously). Again, the reader can easily check that the work of this solution remains $n \leq S \leq n + 1$.   ∎

The above example is a simple illustration of the local allocation paradigm. Although the processors do not use global knowledge about the progress of the computation, they use shared data structures (an array in the above case) to determine locally whether or not to perform a certain task. Note that a similar solution can be developed for 2 processors in message-passing models under the assumption that messages are not lost. However, some assumptions on the message delay need to be made to analyze the complexity of the algorithm (see Exercise 3.2).

3.1.3   HASHED ALLOCATION PARADIGM

In the *hashed allocation paradigm*, processors are allocated in a hashed fashion, either according to a randomized scheme (e.g., processors are randomly allocated to tasks) or using a deterministic scheme that approximates a particular randomized scheme. Algorithms in the hashed allocation paradigm can be suitable for both synchronous and asynchronous models, but they are particularly well suited for asynchrony.

The most common hashed approach in *Do-All* algorithms uses permutations of tasks. For example, for n tasks, random permutations over $\{1, \ldots, n\}$ are given as schedules for each processor; each permutation determines in what order the processor performs the tasks. Without any additional algorithmic sophistication such an algorithm is bound to have work $\Theta(n \cdot p)$ since each task is redundantly done by each of the p processors. Recall that this work, i.e., with linear overhead in p, makes the algorithm inefficient according to our notions of efficient work. Therefore, the use of permutations is often combined with other algorithmic techniques, including the global allocation paradigm or the local allocation paradigm, to obtain efficient algorithms for *Do-All*.

Note that Examples 3.1 and 3.2 can be viewed as hashed allocation paradigm algorithms. They both use, in essence, permutations that provide task execution orders to the processors: either the sequence $task[1]$ to $task[n]$ or the sequence $task[n]$ to $task[1]$. So, one can view the algorithms in the two examples as variations on the hashed allocation paradigm idea, where some additional technique is used to decide when to terminate the computation.

The applications of the hashed allocation paradigm are discussed in Chapters 4 and 5, where algorithms use processor allocation based on permutations that satisfy certain combinatorial properties.

In the next two sections, we illustrate the main algorithmic techniques used in solving the *Do-All* problem, first in the shared-memory model and then in the message-passing model. We consider two types of techniques: (a) techniques for implementing the paradigms (global, local, and hashed allocation) and (b) techniques for improving the efficiency of *Do-All* algorithms.

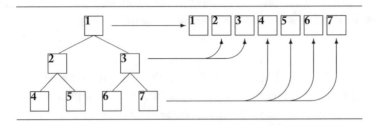

Figure 3.1: Storing a maintenance-free binary tree in an array.

3.2 ALGORITHMIC TECHNIQUES IN THE SHARED-MEMORY MODEL

We begin by presenting the techniques used for implementing the paradigms leading ultimately to efficient solutions for *Do-All*, and then we discuss techniques that can further improve the performance of *Do-All* solutions.

3.2.1 BASIC TECHNIQUES FOR IMPLEMENTING ALLOCATION PARADIGMS

Tree traversals   The tree traversal techniques deal with several issues encountered in solving the *Do-All* problem. They are used for failure detection that in turn allows for the remaining processors to be enumerated so that they can be consistently allocated to remaining tasks. Tree traversal techniques are also used to assess the progress in performing tasks and to implement load balancing. These techniques assume crash-prone processors, our main failure model. The algorithms use full q-ary trees (usually binary trees) for the purposes of accumulation and utilization of the global knowledge about the computation. Hence, such algorithms are well suited for solutions using the global allocation paradigm. Once the utility of such tree traversals in synchronous algorithms becomes clear, their use by algorithms with an asynchronous processor will be also easy to understand.

The tree structures must be resilient to processor failures, and if possible, not require any maintenance of the tree topology. Fortunately, this is easily accomplished by storing a full binary tree in a linear array with implicit tree structure as follows (Figure 3.1). A complete binary tree with n leaves is represented as the linear array $tree[1..2n - 1]$. The root of the tree is the first element of the array, $tree[1]$. Any non-leaf element $tree[i]$ has the element $tree[2i]$ as its left child and the element $tree[2i + 1]$ as its right child. When n is not a power of two, conventional padding techniques can be used.

The algorithms use either the bottom-up or top-down traversal of such full binary trees. The number of leaves is normally equal to, or proportional to the number of *Do-All* tasks n, and the height of the tree is logarithmic in n. In synchronous settings, the bottom-up traversals implement paral-

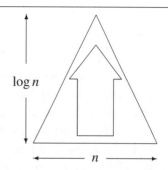

Bottom-up parallel traversal of full binary trees:

- Computes or updates sums of values stored at the leaves
- $\Theta(\log n)$ time
- $O(p \log n)$ work
- Used for error detection and progress estimation

Top-down parallel traversal of full binary trees:

- Divide-and-conquer according to the hierarchy specified by the tree
- $\Theta(\log n)$ time
- $O(p \log n)$ work
- Used for error recovery and load balancing

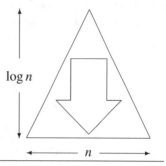

Figure 3.2: Synchronous bottom-up and top-down tree traversals.

lel summation algorithms and the top-down traversals implement a divide-and-conquer processor allocation strategy using a hierarchy, see Figure 3.2.

The tree traversals take logarithmic time, and the computations on the trees are *approximate* in the sense that the values computed are estimates (as we explain in the intuition-building examples that follow).

This tree scheme is readily generalized to trees other than binary, except that for $q > 2$, it is more intuitive to compute the indices of children when the root is placed in $tree[0]$. For example, with the root at $tree[0]$, for ternary trees, a non-leaf element $tree[i]$ has three children: $tree[3i + 1]$, $tree[3i + 2]$, and $tree[3i + 3]$. For q-ary trees with root at $tree[0]$, a non-leaf element $tree[i]$ has q children: $tree[qi + 1], tree[qi + 2], \ldots, tree[qi + q]$.

It is easy to see that the traversals of binary trees can be generalized to logarithmic (base q) traversals of full q-ary trees for some constant q. For most algorithms, the best performance is achieved with binary trees, but in some algorithms, the trees can be parameterized so that the desired performance bounds are achieved when the trees are not binary.

We now illustrate the use of top-down traversal to estimate the number of active processors (that is, processors that have not crashed). As we will see, the value computed is actually an overestimate, since some processors may have crashed during or at the conclusion of the traversal.

Example 3.3   *Processor enumeration:* Consider a processor counting binary tree with $n = 4$ leaves. The tree is stored in the shared array $c[1..7]$, initialized to zeros. There are four processors with PIDs 1, 2, 3, and 4 that start at the leaves and traverse the tree towards its root. At each step, a processor writes into the node corresponding to its location in the tree, the sum of the two child locations; if a processor is at a leaf, it writes 1 into the leaf to account for its presence. Now, if processor 1 crashes prior to the start of the traversal, processor 3 crashes immediately after writing 1 into its leaf $c[6]$, and processor 4 crashes after calculating $c[3] = 2$ as the sum of the contributions recorded in $c[6]$ and $c[7]$, then the tree will look like this after the completion of the traversal.

$$
\begin{array}{rccccc}
c[1]: & & & \boxed{3} & & \\
c[2,3]: & & \boxed{1}\,\boxed{2} & & & \\
c[4,5,6,7]: & \boxed{0}\,\boxed{1}\,\boxed{1}\,\boxed{1} & & & & \\
\mathrm{PID}: & 1 \quad 2 \quad 3 \quad 4 & & & &
\end{array}
$$

Observe that the root $c[1]$ has the value 3, yet the actual number of active processors is 1. The traversal computed an overestimate of the number of active processors. In fact, this will always be so. The root value is exact only when there are no failures during the traversal.   ■

The next example illustrates the construction of the progress tree used to record the progress of the computation and, subsequently, to implement the divide-and-conquer processor allocation. Here we estimate the number of completed tasks based on the information brought to the root of the tree by surviving processors:

Example 3.4   *Progress estimation:* Consider the binary progress tree with four leaves ($n = 4$) stored in the shared array $d[1..7]$. There are 4 processors with PIDs 1, 2, 3, and 4 that begin at the leaves and traverse the tree towards the root. Each processor begins by recording into its leaf the indication that it finished its task; that is, it sets the leaf value to 1. Then each parent gets the sum of its children as processors move up. If, during the bottom-up traversal of the progress tree d, processor 4 crashes prior to the start of the traversal, and processor 3 crashes after the first step of the traversal having written 1 into the leaf $d[6]$, then the tree d will look like this after the completion of the phase.

$$
\begin{array}{rccccc}
d[1]: & & & \boxed{2} & & \\
d[2,3]: & & \boxed{2}\,\boxed{0} & & & \\
d[4,5,6,7]: & \boxed{1}\,\boxed{1}\,\boxed{1}\,\boxed{0} & & & & \\
\mathrm{PID}: & 1 \quad 2 \quad 3 \quad 4 & & & &
\end{array}
$$

Note that each of the processors may have completed its tasks associated with the leaves of the progress tree prior to the start of the traversal. Yet the value of the root $d[1]$ is 2. This indicates that not all tasks were completed, since $d[1] = 2 < 4 = n$. This illustrates why the value at the root of the tree will normally be an underestimate of the actual number of completed tasks. ∎

In the load balancing top-down traversal example that follows, we assume that the progress tree is an exact summation tree, i.e., the value at each internal node is the sum of the values at its two children. Then the processors are allocated at each non-leaf node of the tree in proportion to the number of remaining tasks in each subtree.

Example 3.5   *Load balancing:* Consider the binary progress tree with four leaves ($n = 4$) stored in the shared array $a[1..7]$. There are two surviving processors with PIDs 1 and 2 that begin at the root and traverse the tree towards the leaves.

PID:		{1, 2}		
$a[1]$:		2		
$a[2, 3]$:		2	0	
$a[4, 5, 6, 7]$:	1	1	0	0

At the root, both processors will be sent to the right subtree. This is because out of the two tasks in the left subtree, both have been completed, and none of the tasks in the right subtree are completed. At the internal node $a[3]$, the two processors will be equally divided between the left ($a[6]$) and the right ($a[7]$) subtrees since equal number of unfinished tasks exists in each of the two subtrees. ∎

Note that the progress-estimation traversal in Example 3.4 is not guaranteed to yield the exact summation tree assumed by the load balancing traversal in Example 3.5 above. Algorithms that assume this property (the summation tree) must be able to deal with such situations.

We used *synchronous* tree traversals in the examples. Some traversals of progress trees are also meaningful when processors do so without synchronizing with each other. Consider an *asynchronous* processor that completes its work on a leaf. If the processor traverses the progress tree bottom-up and updates the tree along its path to the root, the tree will still have the property that each node has an underestimate of the tasks completed within the subtree rooted at the node (provided the updates of the tree nodes are atomic). Such tree traversal is useful to implement the local allocation paradigm by using local computation to aggregate the information about the completed tasks. If subsequently an asynchronous processor traverses the progress tree in a top-down fashion, it will eventually reach a leaf of the tree where work still needs to be done (provided any such leaves remain). This leads to an implementation of the allocation of processors to tasks using the local allocation paradigm and the hashed allocation paradigm (see Example 3.6 and Exercise 3.4).

Finally, note that it makes little sense to attempt to enumerate the remaining processors in asynchrony, as there is no way to distinguish a "slow" processor from a crashed one.

Permutations   When we discussed the hashed allocation paradigm, we noted that it can be implemented using permutations. Needed permutations can be constructed based on processor identifiers or task identifiers, as determined by the algorithm design. Such permutations may be precomputed, constructed on-the-fly, or chosen randomly.

Permutations can be used directly to implement the allocation of processors to tasks, and when using tree traversals in shared-memory algorithms, permutations can also be used to balance the allocation of processors to subtrees in top-down traversals. This combines the tree-based aggregation of knowledge with the hashed allocation paradigm when multiple processors need to coordinate their activities at children of a particular tree node. The following example demonstrates the use of permutations with tree traversals for load balancing.

Example 3.6   *Load-balancing with permutations:* Consider the state of the progress tree in Example 3.5, and, in particular, the value 0 of $a[3]$. Suppose, as in the example, that there are two processors that find themselves at the node $a[3]$ of the tree. If the two processors are synchronous, they can use the common global view of the status of the computation, including the fact that both are at $a[3]$, to load balance themselves when descending to $a[6]$ and $a[7]$ (as it is done in Example 3.5). But what if these processors are asynchronous? In this case, each processor may not know that there are two of them at $a[3]$. In this case, the processors must make a local allocation decision. However, with partial knowledge about the state of the computation, both processors might allocate themselves to, say, the left child of $a[3]$, namely $a[6]$. This will lead to poor load balancing. Here permutations can be used to "hash" the two processors with respect to the children of $a[3]$.

In our example, the processors are going to allocate themselves based on the permutations formed by the binary representation of their identifiers. Specifically, the id of each processor can be used at depth h of the node of the progress tree based on the value of the hth most significant bit of the binary representation of the id:

- bit 0 indicates that the processor's order of choosing the leaves is determined by the permutation (*left, right*), meaning that the processor first chooses the left child, then right;

- bit 1 indicates that the processor's order of choosing the leaves is determined by the permutation (*right, left*), meaning that the processor first chooses the right child, then left.

In the example at hand, processor 1 has binary representation 001 and processor 2 binary representation 010 (the tree has depth 3). Hence, at $a[3]$, processor 1 will move to the left child $a[6]$ and processor 2 to the right child $a[7]$. This yields a balanced allocation regardless of the time of arrival of the processors at $a[3]$. Of course, this does not guarantee that any pair of processors necessarily chooses different permutations (e.g., consider processors with ids 1 and 3), but it does provide a mechanism to avoid the situation where all processors choose, say, the left child to start with.   ∎

When dealing with q-ary trees, for $q > 2$, a more involved processor id based permutations can be used. In particular, we discuss predefined permutations that processors select based on their identifiers in Chapter 4.

Finally, we note that while permutations are better suited for asynchronous processors, they can also be useful in synchronous settings.

3.2.2   TECHNIQUES FOR IMPROVING ALGORITHM EFFICIENCY

So far, we have seen techniques for implementing the allocation paradigms. We will now discuss two more techniques that can lead to more efficient *Do-All* solutions in shared-memory models.

Oversaturation   For the *Do-All* problem, it is sensible to assume that $p \leq n$; that is, the number of processors p is no larger than the number of tasks n, thus there is at least one task for each processor to perform. It is often the case that the efficiency of algorithms improves if the number of processors is asymptotically somewhat smaller than the number tasks, e.g., $p = O(n/\log n)$ or $p = O(\sqrt{n})$. The challenge here is to improve work complexity while still being able to use non-trivial number of processors, thus extracting substantial speedup in the absence of adversity. This general approach is called *oversaturation*; that is, we oversaturate the processors with tasks. (In the literature this is sometimes called "taking advantage of processor slackness", meaning that using "too many" processors leads to the inability of keeping them sensibly busy.)

Oversaturation is used in conjunction with tree-traversing algorithms, where the idea is to use the main tree that has p leaves (instead of n leaves), then attaching a list of tasks of size n/p to each leaf (instead of having just one task at each leaf), thus oversaturating the leaf and the processor(s) associated with the leaf.

Let us consider a parameterization with $p = \Theta(n/\log n)$, making the height of the tree to be $\log p = \Theta(\log n)$, where each leaf has a list of $\log n$ tasks, see Figure 3.3. Note that if a processor starts at the "bottom" task at any leaf of such a tree, then it takes $\Theta(\log n)$ local time steps to reach the root; this is the same asymptotic complexity as for full trees with n leaves (assuming that each task takes $\Theta(1)$ unit of time). If a processor is allocated to a leaf of such tree, it sequentially performs $\log n$ tasks.

Oversaturation, in many cases, leads to improved work efficiency, and in synchronous algorithms, optimal work can be obtained. In Section 4.1, we present an algorithm that achieves optimal work efficiency using this approach.

Composite Tree Traversals   As already mentioned, tree traversals is a powerful technique for implementing algorithms in the global allocation paradigm and the local allocation paradigm. One can also use composite tree structures with multiple levels of trees, where additional trees are attached to

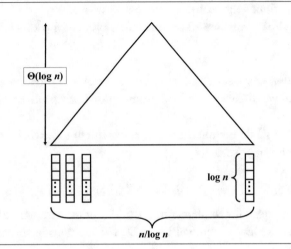

Figure 3.3: An oversaturated progress tree.

the leaves of the top level tree. The use of such composite trees can lead to improved task allocation, yielding more efficient *Do-All* solutions.

In Section 4, we discuss in detail algorithms that use such composite tree traversals. Here we present a simple example to illustrate the idea of the composite trees. Let n be the number of tasks and p the number of processors ($p \leq n$). Consider a q-ary progress tree of n leaves and depth $\log_q n$; call such a structure $Tree(n)$. We split this tree into two levels, see Figure 3.4:

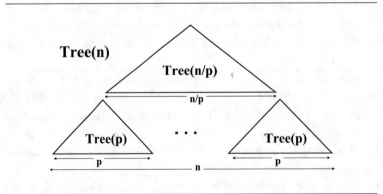

Figure 3.4: Two-level composite tree.

- the top level tree with n/p leaves, call it $Tree(n/p)$, and

- n/p lower level trees, each with p leaves, call each of them $Tree(p)$.

Thus, each $Tree(p)$ is rooted at the internal node of $Tree(n)$ at depth $\log_q(n/p)$.

The idea is to use different traversal methods for the top level subtree $Tree(n/p)$, and each subtree $Tree(p)$. The choice of the traversal method for a subtree is determined on the basis of the state of the computation, as observed by any processor at the the time the processor commences the traversal of the subtree.

For example, if a processor estimates that there are many processors poised to traverse the subtree, it may use an approach that attempts to balance processor loads to avoid congestion. On the other hand, if a processor estimates that there are few processors traversing the subtree, it may choose to traverse the subtree using a simpler algorithm that does not waste resources on load balancing; this latter case is very similar to the oversaturation approach. We present details in Sections 4.3 and 4.5.

3.3 ALGORITHMIC TECHNIQUES IN THE MESSAGE-PASSING MODEL

In the absence of a common shared address space, the processors need to coordinate their activities and perform the task allocation by exchanging messages. The additional care needed to handle coordination via message exchanges renders the development of message-passing algorithms harder than shared-memory algorithms. As a result, the algorithmic techniques used to implement the paradigms in the message-passing model generally differ from the ones used in the shared-memory model, especially for the global allocation paradigm. However, some techniques are similar, such as the use of permutations. Also, as we show in Section 5.1, one can develop specialized techniques that *emulate Do-All* algorithms developed for the shared-memory model in the message-passing model, with the additional overhead due to the cost of the emulation. Such emulations can be quite efficient; however, as one would expect, algorithms developed entirely from scratch for the message-passing model can be more efficient. (We present details in Chapter 5.)

We begin by presenting the techniques used for implementing the allocation paradigms leading to efficient solutions for *Do-All*, then we discuss techniques that can further improve the performance of *Do-All* solutions.

3.3.1 BASIC TECHNIQUES FOR IMPLEMENTING ALLOCATION PARADIGMS

Manipulation of Local Data Structures   To enable efficient solutions, the processors need to maintain information on what tasks are not yet completed during the course of the computation. In synchronous settings, the processors may also maintain information on which processors are still operational (as discussed previously, this is not meaningful in asynchronous settings). For manipulating this kind of information, either sets or lists are used. Also, as we will see in Section 5.2, additional hierarchical structures, e.g., binary trees, may be used for improved efficiency.

In the absence of communication–due to network failures or asynchrony–the processors may continue computing tasks based on their local information. This guarantees that no single processor will perform the same task twice; hence, the processors make local progress in solving *Do-All*, contributing to the overall global progress. Therefore, the manipulation of local data structures implements the local allocation paradigm. When communication is possible and timely, and hence the processors can exchange their local knowledge, more effective global progress can be made. Therefore, when close coordination is possible, as we will see next, local information can help in implementing the global allocation paradigm.

Coordinator-based Coordination   Recall that in message-passing systems, besides work complexity, we are also concerned with message complexity. In synchronous settings, and in the absence of message-loss (i.e., communication is reliable), a standard technique is to use a *coordinator*. The coordinator can be used for failure detection and load balancing while keeping the message complexity low. Processors periodically report their local information to the coordinator, for example, using convergecast communication. The coordinator collects and combines this information and reports, using broadcast, the updated information to the other processors. This technique is used to implement the global allocation paradigm, as each time the processors receive an update from the coordinator their local information on the sets of unfinished tasks and active processors becomes consistent. Once the processors have such consistent global information, effective load balancing is achieved (we show this in Section 5.2). In synchronous settings, failure detection can be implemented with the use of timeouts. If the coordinator does not receive a report from a processor at the predefined time, this processor is considered to have crashed and it is removed from the list of active processors.

Clearly, in asynchronous settings or in the absence of reliable communication, the coordinator-based approach does not work well; it can be the case that no message from the coordinator reaches the processors in a timely manner, or vice versa. This ultimately leads to quadratic worst case work complexity. Even in synchronous settings and in the presence of processor crashes, the coordinator-based technique may not lead to efficient *Do-All* solutions, since the coordinator constitutes a single-point of failure. If the coordinator fails, and when this is detected, a new coordinator must be selected by the other processors. Again, the new coordinator may fail and so on, causing substantial inefficiency in work complexity. It is not difficult to see that any algorithm that uses the single-coordinator approach is bound to have work $S = \Omega(n + (f + 1)p)$, where f is the number of processor crashes. Namely, consider the following adversarial behavior: while there is more than one operational processor, the adversary stops each coordinator immediately after it becomes one and before it sends any messages. This creates pauses of $\Omega(1)$ steps, giving the $\Omega((f + 1)p)$ part. Eventually there remains only one processor that performs all tasks; because it has never received any messages, this gives the remaining $\Omega(n)$ part. Hence, one may conclude that the use of the single coordinator-based technique trades fault-tolerance for message-complexity.

Another approach is to use multiple coordinators. This substantially improves performance of algorithms, provided at least one coordinator succeeds in communicating with other processors. However, there is a challenge of maintaining a consistent view among the coordinators. This can be achieved in synchronous systems by using reliable broadcasts among the coordinators. However, a reliable broadcast primitive itself is difficult to implement, and it is important to have efficient algorithms that use only simple asynchronous point-to-point messaging (or simple broadcast). The multiple coordinator approach can lead to better efficiency, and we discuss this in more detail below in the section on performance improvement. The next technique we present uses simple messaging, and it trades message complexity for fault-tolerance.

Gossip-based Coordination   As we have discussed above, the use of a coordinator-based approach might not be effective in asynchronous settings and because coordinators present vulnerable points of failure. Another technique that can be used both in synchronous and asynchronous settings is to have all the processors to broadcast their local information to all other processors. This *all-to-all* message exchange is also called *gossiping*: every processor has a *rumor* (its local information in our case) and the goal is to periodically (based on processors local clocks) have each processor to learn the rumors of all other processors. Clearly, this approach requires more messages to be sent as compared to the coordinator approach, but on the other hand, it is more resilient to failures: the loss of any single processor does not have the same negative impact as the loss of a coordinator.

Gossip-based coordination is suitable for asynchronous settings, and it does not normally assume reliable communication. Each processor, once it performs a task, can broadcast its local knowledge (set of unfinished tasks) to the other processors and continue to perform the next task. If and when it receives messages from the other processors, it updates its local knowledge. Clearly, the better the communication, the better the global progress that can be achieved. This technique can be viewed as an implementation of a hybrid, local/global allocation paradigm: processors schedule their activities locally in the absence of communication, then try to acquire global knowledge when communicating. As we will see in Chapter 5, the gossip-based technique, when combined with permutations (presented next), can lead to efficient solutions for *Do-All*.

Permutations   In message passing systems, permutations are used for performing load-balancing allocation of tasks to processors similar to the shared-memory model. Permutations implement the hashed allocation paradigm, but for more effective solutions, they are used in conjunction with gossiping (that approximates the global allocation paradigm, depending on the quality of communication). Algorithms using permutations choose the next task to perform based on the permutations of tasks in the absence of communication (due to connectivity failures or asynchrony). If these permutations are wisely chosen, then potential message exchange helps the processors to achieve a more effective global progress.

The following simple example demonstrates the benefit of using permutations with gossiping.

Example 3.7   *Permutations and Gossiping:* Consider the *Do-All* problem in the message-passing model with two asynchronous processors p_1 and p_2. Each processor iteratively performs a task and sends this information to the other processor until it learns that all the tasks have been performed. Say that due to asynchrony, no message is reached from one processor to the other until each of them have performed $n/2$ tasks. Once each processor delivers all messages in transit, no further messages are delivered, e.g., due to complete network collapse. Hence, from this point on, each processor will have to compute all remaining tasks in isolation. The processors cease sending messages when each sends the last message reporting that all tasks are done. Now consider two cases.

(a) The processors do not use specifically-designed permutations on tasks; that is, they perform the tasks in some ad hoc order. In the worst case, the processors may have been performing the tasks in the same order. In this case, no new information is received by the processor when communication is available. This results in total work $S = 2(n/2) + 2(n/2) = 2n$, and of message complexity $M = 2n$.

(b) The processors use permutations where one is the reverse order of the other. That is, p_1 uses permutation $(task_1, task_2, \ldots, task_n)$, and p_2 uses $(task_n, task_{n-1}, \ldots, task_1)$. In this case, during the absence of communication, the processors perform different tasks (until each performs $n/2$ tasks). Hence, when the communication is re-established, both processors learn that all tasks have been performed and no further messages are sent. This solution has work $S = n$ and message complexity $M = n$. The work in this scenario is optimal, and overall, this is a substantially more efficient algorithm. ∎

For more than two processors, more complex permutations with certain properties need to be used, and we address this in Sections 5.3 and 5.4.

3.3.2   TECHNIQUES FOR IMPROVING ALGORITHM EFFICIENCY

We now present two techniques that can be used to develop more efficient *Do-All* solutions in the message-passing model. The first employs multiple coordinators, and the second uses expander graphs.

Multiple, Concurrent Coordinators   As we have discussed, the coordinator-based technique has good message complexity, but requires multiple coordinators to achieve good performance as single-coordinator approaches invariably lead to linear work overhead because a coordinator is a single point of failure. On the other hand, the gossip-based technique can provide better fault-tolerance and improved work with higher message-complexity. One can view gossiping as a technique where all processors are acting as coordinators concurrently. It is only natural to consider dynamic approaches where one or a few coordinators are active when failures are not numerous, and where many or all processors can act as coordinators when a substantial number of failures is encountered.

We now discuss such a technique that is well-suited for synchronous settings, where processors can communicate using *reliable multicast*: if a processor crashes while performing a multicast, then either all targeted processors receive the message or none. (This, in fact, approximates the behavior of broadcast in local area networks.) Instead of having only one coordinator, there could be many coordinators. But to reduce messaging overhead, the number of coordinators is kept as low as possible. A *martingale strategy* is employed for this purpose: begin with a single coordinator; if this coordinator crashes, then use two coordinators; if both coordinators crash, then use four coordinators, etc. In other words, as long as all prior coordinators fail, double the number of coordinators. This substantially increases the resilience to coordinator failures, and assuming that the adversary is not allowed to crash all processors, there will be at least one coordinator that succeeds in its role.

The computation could proceed in an iterative manner as in the single-coordinator case: the processors send their local information to the coordinators, the coordinators collect and combine this information and broadcast the new updated information to the processors. The assumption of reliable multicast assures that the information sent from the different coordinators is consistent.

To save on message complexity, the following optimization can be used: if at a given iteration at least one coordinator does not fail, then in the next iteration, a single coordinator is used and the martingale strategy is followed again. If the system experiences few or no failures, a constant number of coordinators will normally be used. The resulting message complexity can be asymptotically close to that of the single-coordinator approach. If many processor crashes are encountered, then messaging overhead is increased, but it is rarely as high as with the gossiping (all-coordinators) approach. This technique combines the benefits of both worlds: low message complexity and high fault-tolerance. In Section 5.2, we present in detail a *Do-All* algorithm that relies on this technique.

Note, however, that this technique does not work well in the absence of reliable multicast or in asynchronous settings.

Expander Graphs and Multicast   When only point-to-point messaging is available, and when failures are frequent, the gossip-based coordination technique is the most promising. Gossip enables fault-tolerant coordination among processors, but it does so with high message complexity, due to all-to-all broadcast. We now present another gossip-based technique that, instead of using all-to-all broadcast, uses "controlled" multicast; in particular, it uses *expanding communication graphs*.

A communication graph is a data structure that can be used to constrain communication so that communication occurs only along the edges of the graph. The communication graph has the processors as its nodes. A processor can send (or multicast) messages to its non-faulty neighbors in the graph. To maintain low message complexity, initially, the communication graph should have a constant degree. As processors crash, meaning that nodes are "removed" from the graph, the neighborhood of the non-faulty processors changes dynamically – the graph expands its degree – so that the resulting graph guarantees "progress in communication". Informally speaking, progress in communication according to such a graph is achieved if there is at least one "good" connected component that evolves suitably with time and satisfies the following properties: (i) the component contains "sufficiently many" nodes so that collectively "sufficient" new information will be learned, e.g., local information about unfinished tasks, (ii) it has "sufficiently small" diameter so that information can be shared among the nodes of the component without "undue delay", and (iii) the set of nodes of each successive good component is a subset of the set of nodes of the previous good component (to insure that knowledge is not lost). Figure 3.5 depicts an expansion of the neighborhood of a node in such a communication graph.

In cooperating on tasks, the processors use these graphs to exchange information, and as long as there are not many failures, the information is aggregated with a low messaging overhead. When

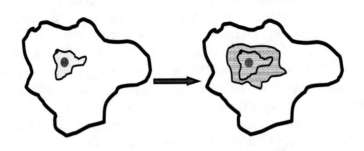

Figure 3.5: The "amoeba" on the left represents a node within its neighborhood in a graph. When a sufficient number of crashes occur, the neighborhood of the node expands as shown on the right graph. This is done for all non-faulty processors to ensure progress in communication.

crashes occur, the graph expands in such a way that information is disseminated in a timely manner while still keeping communication costs relatively low. In Section 5.3, we present an efficient *Do-All* algorithm that combines expanding communication graphs with permutations. There, the notion of a communication graph is formally defined as well as the properties that need to be satisfied for the purpose of the specific algorithm. Generally speaking, expander communication graphs can be constructed efficiently.

3.4   EXERCISES

3.1.   Describe a simple algorithm that implements the global allocation paradigm to solve the 2-processor synchronous *Do-All* problem in the message-passing model, where one of the processors could crash. Assume that messages are not lost. What are the work and message complexities of your solution? *Hint: Use similar reasoning as in Example 3.1.*

3.2.   **(a)** Describe a simple algorithm that implements the local allocation paradigm to solve the 2-processor asynchronous *Do-All* problem in the message-passing model, where one of the processors could crash. *Hint: Use similar reasoning as in Example 3.2.*
(b) Assuming that a message from one processor is received by the other within d time units (measured by an external clock not available to the processors), compute the work and message complexities of your solution. *Hint: Consider various cases depending on the relationship between d and n (the number of tasks).*

3.3.   Describe a non-trivial algorithm that implements the local allocation paradigm to solve the 3-processor asynchronous *Do-All* problem in the shared-memory model, where up to two of the processors could crash. Analyze the work complexity of your algorithm. *Hint:*

Use similar reasoning as in Example 3.2 for the two processors and think how the third processor would "traverse" the linear array.

3.4. Consider the following progress tree with $n = 8$ and assume that only processors with PIDs 1, 3, and 7 are operational. Given that all three processors are currently at $a[1]$, explain how each processor will traverse the tree if the allocation strategy described below is used. A processor at $a[i]$ uses the following allocation strategy:

- If $a[2i] = a[2i + 1] = 1$, then the processor moves to $a[\lfloor i/2 \rfloor]$.

- If $a[2i] = 1$ and $a[2i + 1] = 0$, then the processor moves to $a[2i + 1]$.

- If $a[2i] = 0$ and $a[2i + 1] = 1$, then the processor moves to $a[2i]$.

- If $a[2i] = a[2i + 1] = 0$, then the processor moves according to the binary representation of its id and the depth of $a[i]$ in the tree, as explained in Example 3.6.

PID:				{1, 3, 7}			
$a[1]$:				1			
$a[2, 3]$:			1		0		
$a[4, 5, 6, 7]$:		1	1		0	0	
$a[8, 9, 10, 11, 12, 13, 14, 15]$:	1	1	1	1	0	0	0	0

The processors are asynchronous, but for the sake of discussion, assume that they traverse the tree synchronously (the processors do not know this). Once a processor reaches a leaf node, it stays there.

3.5. Consider the synchronous *Do-All* problem in the message-passing model with n fault-free processors and n tasks. Assume that communication is not reliable, that is, a message from one processor to another may be arbitrarily delayed or be lost. Thus, we consider the *Do-All* problem against an adversary that can "control" the delivery of messages. Show formally that any *Do-All* algorithm that uses the coordinator-based technique in this setting has quadratic (with respect to n) work complexity. In particular, construct an adversarial strategy that would cause any coordinator-based *Do-All* algorithm to exhibit that much work.

3.6. Consider the synchronous *Do-All* problem in the message-passing model with n processors and n tasks under an adversary that can cause processor crashes. Also consider the multiple-coordinator-based technique along with the martingale strategy as explained in the paragraph "Multiple, Concurrent Coordinators" of Section 3.3. Explain how the absence of reliable multicast can lead to inefficient solutions to the *Do-All* problem in this setting.

3.5   BIBLIOGRAPHIC NOTES

The categorization of the algorithmic paradigms into the global allocation paradigm, the local allocation paradigm, and the hashed allocation paradigm follows the one presented by Kanellakis and Shvartsman [55] for the *Do-All* problem in the shared-memory model. We have extended it to also cover the message-passing model.

Binary-tree traversals and how they can be used for processor enumeration, allocation, and progress estimation for the synchronous *Do-All* problem in the shared-memory model was first presented by Kanellakis and Shvartsman [54]. Buss, Kanellakis, Ragde, and Shvartsman [16] were the first to demonstrate how binary-tree traversals can also be used for the asynchronous *Do-All* problem in the shared-memory model.

Anderson and Woll [10] formulated the permutation-based approach to solving the asynchronous shared-memory *Do-All* problem, they developed several algorithms and showed the existence of appropriate permutations that make the work of their algorithms efficient. One of their algorithms uses traversals of q-ary trees, $q > 2$.

Oversaturation is a standard technique used, for example, for parallel summation algorithms [51]. The composite tree traversal has been used by Groote, Hesselink, Mauw and Vermeulen [47] and Kowalski and Shvartsman [64] for efficiently solving the asynchronous *Do-All* problem in the shared-memory model.

De Prisco, Mayer, and Yung [83] were the first to employ the coordinator-based technique to solve the *Do-All* problem in the message-passing setting with synchronous crash-prone processors. In the same work the lower bound $S = \Omega(n + (f + 1)p)$ ($f < p$ being the maximum number of processor crashes) for any *Do-All* algorithm using the single-coordinator technique was shown.

Chlebus, De Prisco, and Shvartsman [17] developed a *Do-All* algorithm that beats the above lower bound by using the multi-coordinator-based technique. However, to do so, reliable multicast was assumed. Georgiou, Kowalski, and Shvartsman [37] developed a *Do-All* algorithm that also beats the above lower bound, but by neither using coordinators nor assuming reliable multicast; instead it uses the gossip-based coordination technique in conjunction with permutations satisfying certain properties and expander graphs. Kowalski, Musial, and Shvartsman [63] explore ways of efficiently constructing such permutations. Expander graphs have been considered in various settings, see, for example, [8, 9, 18, 69, 90].

Kowalski and Shvartsman [65] used permutations in conjunction with gossiping to develop a solution to the *Do-All* problem in the asynchronous message-passing setting.

CHAPTER 4

Shared-Memory Algorithms

In this chapter, we present several algorithms for the *Do-All* problem in the shared-memory model. The algorithms are as follows.

- Algorithm W: This is an algorithm in the global allocation paradigm for synchronous systems with processor crashes. The algorithm obtains polylogarithmic work efficiency for the full range of processors, that is, for $1 \leq p \leq n$. It can be made work-optimal by reducing the number of processors to $p = O(n \log \log n / \log^2 n)$.

- Algorithm X: This is an algorithm in the local allocation paradigm for asynchronous systems, and it obtains polynomial work efficiency for the full range of processors. Namely, the algorithm has $O(np^{\log(3/2)})$ work for $1 \leq p \leq n$.

- Algorithm *Groote*: This is another algorithm in the local allocation paradigm for asynchronous systems. It solves the *Do-All* problem with $n = m^k$ tasks and $p = 2^k$ processors ($p \leq n$) for some parameter m and constant $k > 0$ using work $O(np^c)$, where $0 < c = \log(\frac{m+1}{m}) < 1$.

- Algorithm AW^T: This is another polynomially efficient *Do-All* algorithm for asynchronous systems. The processors are allocated according to a combination of the local allocation paradigm and the hashed allocation paradigm. The work of the algorithm is $O(np^\varepsilon)$ for any $\varepsilon < 1$ and for the range of processors $1 \leq p \leq n$.

- Algorithm *TwoLevelAW*: This algorithm is constructed as a two-level nested algorithm and makes use of a careful parametrization of algorithm AW^T. The work of the algorithm is $O(n + p^{2+\varepsilon})$ for any $\varepsilon > 0$ and for the range of processors $1 \leq p \leq n$. When $p = O(n^{1/(2+\varepsilon)})$ the algorithm is work-optimal as opposed to algorithms X, *Groote*, and AW^T that require superlinear work when $p = \Omega(n^{1/4})$.

4.1   ALGORITHM W

Algorithm W implements the global allocation paradigm by using tree traversals: a bottom-up traversal for processor enumeration, a top-down traversal for processor allocation, and a bottom-up traversal for progress estimation. The algorithm tolerates dynamic processor crashes as long as at least one processor does not fail, and it has work $S = O(n + p \log^2 n / \log \log n)$ for any pattern of up to $p - 1$ crashes. The algorithm is polylogarithmically efficient, and as of this writing, it is the most efficient *Do-All* algorithm for synchronous systems with processor crashes.

4.1.1   DESCRIPTION OF ALGORITHM W

For simplicity of presentation, we assume that the number of processors is the same as the number of tasks in the *Do-All* problem, that is $p = n$. The algorithm works for any $p \leq n$ without any modification; assume that the algorithm starts with n processors, and that $n - p$ processors crash prior to the first step of the algorithm. We describe algorithm W in terms of its inputs, outputs, data structures, and control flow. The algorithm models tasks as a shared array $task[1..n]$, initialized to 0's. Performing a task takes the form of writing the value 1 to the corresponding array element. This does not affect the complexity analysis since it takes constant time to perform any task.

Input: Shared array $task[1..n]$; $task[i] = 0$ for $1 \leq i \leq n$.

Output: Shared array $task[1..n]$; $task[i] = 1$ for $1 \leq i \leq n$.

Data structures: The algorithm uses full binary trees to (1) enumerate processors, (2) allocate processors, (3) perform work ($task[i] := 1$), and (4) estimate progress. There are three full binary trees, each of size $2n - 1$, stored as linear arrays in shared memory (as explained in Section 3.2.1). The trees are: $count[1..2n - 1]$ used for processor counting and allocation, $done[1..2n - 1]$ used for progress counting, and $aux[1..2n - 1]$ used for top-down auxiliary accounting. They are all initially 0.

   The input is in a shared array $task[1..n]$, where the n elements of this array are associated with the leaves of the trees $done$ and aux. Element $task[i]$ is associated with $done[i + n - 1]$ and $aux[i + n - 1]$, where $1 \leq i \leq n$. Similarly, processors are initially associated with the leaves of the tree $count$, such that processor with identifier PID is associated with $count[PID+n - 1]$.

   Each processor uses some constant amount of local memory. For example, this local memory may be used to perform some simple arithmetic computations. An important local variable is $pnum$ which contains a dynamically changing processor number (as a result of processor enumeration). The total shared memory used is $O(n + p)$.

Control flow: Algorithm W consists of the parallel *loop*; the high level code of the algorithm is given in Figure 4.1. This loop consists of four phases, W1, W2, W3, and W4, and the loop is performed synchronously by all processors that have not crashed. At the start, two phases are executed, phases W3 and W4. Note that processors can crash at any time during the algorithm. We next proceed with a high level description of the phases, and then provide additional technical details.

Phase W1, *processor enumeration phase*: The processors traverse bottom-up the processor counting tree, starting with the leaves associated with processor identifiers (PIDs) and finishing at the root. After this traversal, the processors are assigned a processor number. As explained in Section 3.2.1, such a tree traversal takes $O(\log n)$ time.

---

forall processors PID=1..*n* **parbegin**
    Phase W3: Visit leaves based on PID to perform work, i.e., write to the input tasks
    Phase W4: Traverse the *done* tree bottom up to measure progress.
    while the root of the *done* tree is not *n* **do**
        Phase W1: Traverse tree *count* bottom-up to enumerate processors
        Phase W2: Traverse the *done, aux, count* trees top down to allocate processors
        Phase W3: Perform work, i.e., write to the input tasks
        Phase W4: Traverse the *done* tree bottom up to measure progress
    od
parend.

Figure 4.1: A high level view of algorithm *W*.

Phase W2, *processor allocation phase*: The processors are allocated using the processor number obtained in phase W1 in a dynamic top-down traversal of the progress tree (starting with the root and finishing at the leaves associated with unfinished tasks) to assure load balancing. As explained in Section 3.2.1, such a tree traversal takes $O(\log n)$ time.

Phase W3, *work phase*: The processors perform work at the leaves they reached in phase W2. The work takes the form of writing to the array of tasks, specifically, setting the values of array *task*[] to 1. Hence, this phase takes $O(1)$ time. (Note that the algorithm can perform any equally-sized tasks, ranging from a single assignment statement to the execution of a complex program. Of course, the complexity analysis needs to be performed with the knowledge of how long it takes to perform a task.)

Phase W4, *progress measurement phase*: The processors begin at the leaves of the progress tree where they ended in phase W3 and update the progress tree, using a bottom-up traversal, to estimate the progress of the algorithm. Again, such traversal takes $O(\log n)$ time.

From the description of the phases, it is evident that each iteration of the *loop* takes $O(\log n)$ time.

Algorithm *W* technical details   The complete pseudocode of algorithm *W* is given in Figures 4.2 and 4.3. We now describe the operation of the algorithm in more detail.

In **phase W1**, each processor PID traverses tree *count* bottom-up from the location PID $+ n - 1$. The $O(\log n)$-node path of this traversal, is the same (static) for all the loop iterations. As processors perform this traversal, they calculate an overestimate of the surviving processors. This is done using a standard $O(\log n)$ time version of a parallel summation algorithm (recall discussion in Section 3.2.1 and Example 3.3). Tree *count* holds the sums for the current *loop* iteration. During this traversal, surviving processors also calculate new processor numbers *pnum* for themselves, based on the same sums, in a prefix-sum pattern. Detailed code for this procedure is given in Figure 4.2.
    Each processor PID starts by writing a 1 in the leaf *count*[PID $+ n - 1$] of the tree *count*. If a processor fails *before* it writes 1, then its action will not contribute to the overall count. If a

```
                                          procedure W1(integer pnum)
                                            shared integer array
                                               count[1..2n − 1];
                                            private integer
                                               i, i₁, i₂,-- parent, left/right child indices
                                               subt;-- running subtree total

                                            i₁ :=PID +(n − 1);-- start at a leaf
Algorithm W :                               pnum := 1;-- assume this PID is number 1
forall processors PID = 1..p parbegin       subt := 1;-- count PID once
  shared integer array
     task[1..n], count[1..2n − 1],        -- traverse the tree from leaf to root
     done[1..2n − 1], aux[1..2n − 1];       for 1..log n do
  private integer pnum, k;                     i := i₁ div2;-- parent of i₁ and i₂
                                                if 2 ∗ i = i₁ -- i₁ came from ...
  k := PID;-- initial work item for PID         then i₂ = i₁ + 1 --...left
  W3(k);-- do work at the leaf                   else i₂ = i₁ − 1 --...right
  W4(k);-- measure progress                      fi
                                                count[i₂] := 0;-- assume no active sibling(s)
  while done[1] ≠ n do -- Main loop             count[i₁] := subt;-- self is active
                                                subt := count[i₁] + count[i₂];-- update total
     W1(pnum);-- enumerate processors           if i₁ > i₂ -- came from right
     W2(pnum, k);-- processor allocation         then pnum := pnum + count[i₂] fi
     W3(k);-- do work at the leaf               i₁ := i;-- advance to parent
     W4(k);-- measure progress                od
                                              count[1] := subt;-- record the total
  od                                        end.
parend.
```

Figure 4.2: Detailed code of algorithm W: Main loop and phase W1.

processor fails *after* it writes 1, then this number can still contribute to the overall sum if one or more processors were active at a sibling tree node and remained active as they moved to the ancestor tree node. The same observation applies to counts written subsequently at internal nodes, which are the sums of the counts of the children nodes in tree *count*.

It is easy to show that phase W1 will always compute in *count*[1] an *overestimate* of the number of processors, which are surviving at the time of its completion (see Example 3.3 for intuition and see Lemma 4.1 for formal argument). In addition, we need to enumerate the surviving processors. This is accomplished by each processor assuming that it is the only one, and then adding the number of the surviving processors it estimates to its left. This enumeration creates the dynamic processor number *pnum*.

Finally, in phase W1, we must be able to reuse our tree during several iterations of the main loop. This presents a problem. For example, if a processor had written 1 into its tree leaf and then failed, then the value 1 will remain there for the duration of the computation, thus preventing us from computing monotonically tighter estimates of the number of surviving processors. This is corrected by processors always clearing (writing zero to) the sibling's value in the tree before writing their own

```
procedure W2(integer pnum, integer k)
    shared integer array
        count[1..2n − 1], done[1..2n − 1],
        aux[1..2n − 1];
    private integer
        i, i₁, i₂,-- current/left/right indices
        size,-- number of leaves at current node
    i := 1;-- start at the root
    size := n;-- the whole tree is visible
    aux[1] := done[1];
    -- traverse the tree from to root to leaf
    while size ≠ 1 do
        i₁ := 2 * i;  i₂ := i₁ + 1;-- left/right
        -- compute accounted node values
        if done[i₁] + done[i₂] = 0 then aux[i₁] := 0
        else aux[i₁] := aux[i] * done[i₁]
                    div (done[i₁] + done[i₂]) fi
        aux[i₂] := aux[i] − aux[i₁];
        -- processor allocation to left/right sub-trees
        count[i₁] := count[i] * (size/2 − aux[i₁])
                    div (size − aux[i]);
        count[i₂] := count[i] − count[i₁];
        -- go left/right based on processor number
        if pn ≤ count[i₁] then i := i₁
        else i := i₂; pn := pn − c[i₁] fi
        size := size div 2;-- half of leaves
    od
    k := i − (n − 1);-- assign based on i
end.
```

```
procedure W3(integer k)
    task[k] := 1;-- perform a task
end.


procedure W4(integer k)
    shared integer array
        done[1..2n − 1];
    private integer
        i, i₁, i₂;-- parent and left/right child indices
    -- mark the leaf done
    i₁ := k + (n − 1);-- leaf index
    done[i₁] := 1;-- done!
    -- traverse the tree from leaf to root
    for 1.. log n do
        i := i₁ div2;
        if 2 * i = i₁ -- j₁ came from . . .
        then i₂ := i₁ + 1 -- . . . left
        else i₂ := i₁ − 1;-- . . . right
        fi
        -- update progress tree and advance
        done[i] := done[i₁] + done[i₂];-- update
        i₁ := i;-- advance to parent
    od
end.
```

Figure 4.3: Detailed code of algorithm W: phases W2, W3, and W4.

total value. If there are no active siblings, then the value 0 correctly represented the number of such siblings. If there are active siblings, they will overwrite the zero with their own total.

In **phase W2**, all surviving processors start at the root of the progress tree *done*. In $done[i]$, there is an underestimate of the work already performed in the subtree defined by i. Now the processors traverse *done* top-down and get allocated according to the work remaining to be done in the subtrees of i; see Figure 4.3.

It is essential to balance the work loads of the surviving processors. In the next section, we argue that the algorithm meets the goal of balancing (Lemma 4.2). Although the divide-and-conquer idea based on *done* is sound, some care has to be put into its implementation.

In the remaining discussion of phase W2, we explain this implementation, which is based on the *auxiliary progress tree aux*. The values in *aux* are *defined* from the values in *done*. All values in *aux* are defined given *done*, although only part of *aux* is actually *computed*. The important points are that (1) *aux* represents the progress made *and* fully recorded from leaves to the root, and (2) the value of each $aux[i]$ is defined based only on the values of *done* seen along the unique path from the root to the node i.

At each internal node i, the processors are divided between the left and right subtrees in proportion to the leaves that either have not been visited *or* whose visitation was not fully recorded in *done*. This is accomplished by computing $aux[2i], aux[2i+1]$ and using these values instead of $done[2i], done[2i+1]$ in order to discard partially recorded progress (occurring when crashes cause processors to record progress in *done* only part way to the root).

A partially recorded progress is detected in *done* when a value of an internal node in *done* is less than the sum of the values of its two descendants. Thus, at i, after computing the values $aux[2i], aux[2i+1]$, the allocation of work is done using divide-and-conquer in proportion to the values $n_i - aux[2i]$ and $n_i - aux[2i+1]$, where n_i is the number of leaves at each of the two children of node i (n_i is computed in the pseudocode as $size/2$, where the variable $size$ records the number of leaves in the subtree of node i).

Formally, the nonnegative integer values in *aux* are constrained top down as follows: The root value is $aux[1] = done[1]$. For the children of an interior node i ($1 \le i \le n-1$), we have $aux[2i] \le done[2i], aux[2i+1] \le done[2i+1]$, and $aux[2i] + aux[2i+1] = aux[i]$.

These constraints do not uniquely define $aux[]$. However, one can realize a unique definition by making $aux[2i]$ and $aux[2i+1]$ proportional (up to round-off) to the values $done[2i]$ and $done[2i+1]$. Thus, the dynamic top-down traversal given in Figure 4.2 implements one way of uniquely defining the values of *aux* satisfying these constraints.

The constraints on the values of $aux[]$ assure that (1) there are exactly $done[1] = aux[1]$ number of leaves whose *done* and *aux* values are 1—such leaves are called *accounted*, and no processor will reach these leaves, and (2) the processors reach leaves with the *aux* values of 0—such leaves are called *unaccounted*.

In **phase W3** all processors are at the leaves reached in phase W2; see Figure 4.3. Phase W3 is where the work gets done. Each processor writes 1 in the *task* array element associated with the leaf it is allocated to. Prior to the start of the first iteration of the *loop*, each processor PID writes 1 to *task*[PID]. (Here we model performing a task that takes constant time as writing 1 to the task array. When using the algorithm to perform real tasks, this is where the code for the task is placed.)

In **phase W4**, the processors record the progress made by traversing tree *done* bottom up and using the standard summation method (recall discussion in Section 3.2.1 and Example 3.4). The $O(\log n)$ paths traversed by processors can differ in each *loop* iteration, since processors start from the leaves where they were in phase W3. What is computed each time is an underestimate of the progress made (it is an underestimate because crashes can prevent the complete recording of the progress). The details of this bottom up traversal are in Figure 4.3.

As we argue in the next section, the progress recorded in *done*[1] in phase W4 grows *monotonically*, and it *underestimates* the actual progress (see Lemma 4.3). This guarantees that the algorithm terminates after at most n iterations, since $done[1] \ne n$ is the guard that controls the main *loop*.

4.1.2 ANALYSIS OF ALGORITHM *W*

We begin with an outline of the complexity analysis. Lemma 4.1 shows that in each loop iteration, the algorithm computes (over)estimates of the remaining processors. Lemma 4.2 argues that processors are only allocated to the unaccounted leaves, and that all such leaves are allocated a balanced number of processors. Lemma 4.3 assures monotonic progress of the computation, and thus its termination. In Lemma 4.4, we develop an upper bound on the work performed by the processors in terms of logarithmic block-steps. These lemmas are used to show the main Theorem 4.5.

The following notation is used in the remainder of the section. Consider the j-th iteration of the *loop*, where $1 \leq j \leq n$. Note that the first iteration consists only of phases W3 and W4. Let U_j be the estimated remaining work, i.e., the value of $N - done[1]$ right before the iteration starts, right after phase W4 of the previous iteration; we let U_1 be n. Let P_j be the real number of surviving processors, right before the iteration starts, i.e., right after phase W4 of the previous iteration; P_1 is p. Finally, let R_j be the estimated number of surviving processors, that is the value of $count[1]$ right after phase W1 of the j-th iteration; R_1 is p.

The following is shown by a simple induction on tree *count* (and it is left as an exercise).

Lemma 4.1 *In algorithm W, for all loop-iterations j, we have: $P_j \geq R_j \geq P_{j+1}$, as long as at least one processor survives.*

The next lemma argues that the processor allocation to the unaccounted leaves is balanced, and it can be shown by using an invariant for the algorithm of phase W2 (and is left as an exercise).

Lemma 4.2 *In phase W2 of each loop-iteration j of algorithm W: (1) processors are only allocated to unaccounted leaves, and (2) no leaf is allocated more than $\lceil P_i / U_i \rceil$ processors.*

The following lemma shows that for each loop-iteration, the number of unvisited leaves is decreasing monotonically, thus assuring termination of the main loop after at most n iterations. (The worst case of exactly n iterations corresponds to a single processor surviving at the outset of the algorithm.) The lemma is proved using simple inductions on the structure of the trees used by the algorithm (and is left as an exercise).

Lemma 4.3 *In algorithm W, for all loop-iterations j, we have: $U_j > U_{j+1}$, as long as at least one processor survives.*

We now come to the main lemma. We treat the three $\log n$ time tree traversals, plus the constant time work phase, performed by a single processor during each iteration of the algorithm as a single ***block-step*** of cost $O(\log n)$. We charge each processor for each such block step, regardless of whether the processor actually completes the traversals or whether it crashes somewhere in-between. This coarseness does not distort our results.

Lemma 4.4   *The number of block-steps of algorithm W using p processors, on input of size n using progress tree with n leaves, is $B_{n,p} \leq n + p \log n / \log \log n$, for $p \leq n$.*

Proof. Consider the jth iteration of the main *loop* of algorithm W.

At the beginning of the iteration, P_j is the overestimate of active processors, and U_j is the estimated remaining unvisited leaves. At the end of the jth iteration (i.e., at the beginning of the $j + 1^{st}$ iteration), the corresponding values are P_{j+1} and U_{j+1}. From Lemmas 4.1 and 4.3, we know that $P_j \geq P_{j+1}$ and $U_j > U_{j+1}$. Recall that $P_1 = p$ and $U_1 = n$.

Let τ be the final iteration of the algorithm, i.e., $U_\tau \geq 0$ and the number of unvisited elements after the iteration τ is $U_{\tau+1} = 0$. We examine the following two major cases:

Case 1: Consider *all* block steps in which $P_j < U_j$:

By Lemma 4.2, each leaf will be assigned no more than 1 processor; therefore, the number of block steps $B_{Case\ 1}$ accounted in this case will be no more than

$$B_{Case\ 1} \leq \sum_{j=1}^{\tau}(U_j - U_{j+1}) = U_1 - U_{\tau+1} = n - 0 = n \ .$$

Case 2: We now account for *all* block-steps in which $P_j \geq U_j$ in the following two subcases:

(2.a) Consider all block steps after which $U_{j+1} < \frac{U_j}{\log n / \log \log n}$:

This could occur no more than $O(\frac{\log n}{\log \log n})$ times since $U_{j+1} < U_j = n$. No more than p processors complete such block-steps; therefore, the total number of blocks $B_{Case\ (2.a)}$ accounted for here is

$$B_{Case\ 2.a} = O(p \frac{\log n}{\log \log n}) \ .$$

(2.b) Finally, consider block steps such that $P_j \geq U_j$ and $U_{j+1} \geq \frac{U_j}{\log n / \log \log n}$:

Consider a particular iteration j. By Lemma 4.2, at most $\lceil \frac{P_j}{U_j} \rceil$ but no less than $\lfloor \frac{P_j}{U_j} \rfloor$ processors were assigned to each of the U_j unvisited leaves. Therefore, the number of failed processors is at least

$$U_{j+1} \left\lfloor \frac{P_j}{U_j} \right\rfloor \geq \frac{U_j}{\log n / \log \log n} \cdot \frac{P_j}{2U_j} \geq \frac{P_j}{2 \log n / \log \log n} \ .$$

This can happen no more than τ times. The number of processors completing step j is no more than $P_j(1 - \frac{1}{2\frac{\log n}{\log \log n}})$. In general, for p initial processors, the number of processors completing ℓ^{th} occurrence of case (2.b) will be no more than $p(1 - \frac{1}{2\frac{\log n}{\log \log n}})^\ell$.

Therefore, the number of block-steps $B_{Case\ 2.b}$ accounted for here is bounded by:

$$
\begin{aligned}
B_{Case\ 2.b} &\leq \sum_{\ell=1}^{\tau} p\left(1 - \frac{1}{2^{\frac{\log n}{\log \log n}}}\right)^{\ell} \leq p\sum_{\ell=1}^{\infty}\left(1 - \frac{1}{2^{\frac{\log n}{\log \log n}}}\right)^{\ell} \\
&= p\frac{1}{1 - (1 - \frac{1}{2^{\frac{\log n}{\log \log n}}})} = p\cdot 2^{\frac{\log n}{\log \log n}} = O\left(p\frac{\log n}{\log \log n}\right).
\end{aligned}
$$

The total number of block steps $B_{n,p}$ of all cases considered is then

$$
B_{n,p} = B_{Case\ 1} + B_{Case\ 2.a} + B_{Case\ 2.b} = O(n + p\frac{\log n}{\log \log n}),
$$

as desired. $\square$

The next theorem follows from the above lemma and the definition of a block-step.

Theorem 4.5   Algorithm W solves the *Do-All* problem using $p \leq n$ crash-prone processors with work $S = O\left(n \log n + p \log^2 n / \log \log n\right)$.

This result proves that algorithm W has polylogarithmic efficiency. In the next section, we show how oversaturation can be used to obtain an optimal algorithm.

4.1.3   IMPROVING EFFICIENCY WITH OVERSATURATION

One immediate observation based on the result of Theorem 4.5 is that if $p = n/\log n$ processors are used, then the work of algorithm W is $O(n \log n)$. This observation makes one wonder whether it is possible to construct an optimal algorithm for *Do-All* using a non-trivial number of processors. We now show that this is possible using oversaturation.

Recall from Section 3.2.2 (paragraph "Oversaturation") that this technique involves the traversal of trees that have $n/\log n$ leaves instead of n. The progress tree is now associated with $\log n$ different *Do-All* tasks (recall Figure 3.3).

Let algorithm W_{os} be the version of algorithm W where trees *count*, *done*, and *aux* have $n/\log n$ leaves. Furthermore, each leaf of tree *done* is associated with $\log n$ distinct *Do-All* tasks. Observe that each block-step still has the cost $\Theta(\log n)$: the tree traversals in phases W1, W2, and W4 take $\Theta(\log(n/\log n)) = \Theta(\log n)$ time, and given that each *Do-All* task takes $\Theta(1)$ time, phase W3 also takes $\Theta(\log n)$ time (a processor at the leaf sequentially performs the $\log n$ tasks associated with the leaf).

Furthermore, each processor, instead of using its PID during the computation, uses the PID modulo $\frac{n}{\log n}$. When the number of processors p is such that $p > \frac{n}{\log n}$, it is not difficult to see that this assures that there is a uniform initial assignment of at least $\lfloor p/\frac{n}{\log n}\rfloor$ and no more than $\lceil p/\frac{n}{\log n}\rceil$ processors to the work elements at each leaf of the progress tree.

We now prove the efficiency of algorithm W_{os}.

Theorem 4.6   Algorithm W_{os} solves the *Do-All* problem using $p \leq n$ crash-prone processors with work $S = O(n + p \log^2 n / \log \log n)$.

Proof. We factor out any work that is wasted due to failures by charging this work to the failures. Since the failures are crashes, there can be at most p failures, and each processor that crashes can waste at most $O(\log n)$ steps corresponding to a single iteration of the algorithm. Therefore, the work charged to the failures is $O(p \log n)$, and it will be amortized in the rest of the work.

We next evaluate the work that directly contributes to the progress of the algorithm by distinguishing two cases below. As discussed above, each block-step (and each iteration) of the algorithm takes $O(\log n)$ time.

Case 1: $1 \leq p < \frac{n}{\log n}$. In this case, at most one processor is initially allocated to each leaf of the progress tree. We use Lemma 4.4 to establish an upper bound on the blocks-step of the algorithm, except that instead of n leaves, the progress tree has $n / \log n$ leaves. Each block-step and leaf visit takes $O(\log n)$ time; therefore, the work is:

$$S = B_{\frac{n}{\log n}, p} \cdot O(\log n) = O\left(\left(\frac{n}{\log n} + p \frac{\log n}{\log \log n} \right) \cdot \log n \right) = O(n + p \log^2 n / \log \log n) .$$

Case 2: $\frac{n}{\log n} \leq p \leq n$. In this case, no more than $\lceil p / \frac{n}{\log n} \rceil$ processors are initially allocated to each leaf. Any two processors that are initially allocated to the same leaf, should they both survive, behave identically throughout the computation. Therefore, we can estimate the number of block steps assuming $n / \log n$ processors and then use $\lceil p / \frac{n}{\log n} \rceil$ processor allocation as a multiplicative factor in estimating the work.

By Lemma 4.4, we establish the number of block-steps:

$$B_{\frac{n}{\log n}, \frac{n}{\log n}} = O\left(\frac{n}{\log n} + \frac{n}{\log n} \frac{\log n}{\log \log n} \right) = O\left(\frac{n}{\log \log n} \right) .$$

From this, and the cost of a block-step of $O(\log n)$, the work is:

$$S = \left\lceil p / \frac{n}{\log n} \right\rceil \cdot O\left(\frac{n}{\log \log n} \right) \cdot O(\log n) = O(p \log^2 n / \log \log n).$$

The results of the two cases combine to yield $S = O(n + p \log^2 n / \log \log)$.   □

The following corollary shows the processor range for which the algorithm is optimal.

Corollary 4.7   *The work of algorithm W_{os} using $p \leq n \log \log n / \log^2 n$ crash-prone processors is $S = O(n)$.*

4.2   ALGORITHM X

In this section, we present an asynchronous algorithm for the *Do-All* problem, called algorithm X. The algorithm can also be used in failure models with *detectable restarts* [1]. The important property of this algorithm is that it has bounded sub-quadratic work for any pattern of failures and restarts. In particular, for both models (synchronous processors with crashes and detectable restarts or asynchronous processors), algorithm X has work $S = O(n \cdot p^{\log_2 \frac{3}{2}})$ using $p \le n$ processors.

Like algorithm W, algorithm X utilizes a progress tree of size $2n - 1$, but it is traversed by the processors independently, not in synchronized phases. This reflects the local nature of the processor allocation in algorithm X—it implements the local allocation paradigm—as opposed to the global allocation used in algorithm W. Each processor, acting independently, searches for work in the smallest immediate subtree that has work that needs to be done. It then performs the necessary work, and moves out of that subtree when all work within it is completed.

4.2.1   DESCRIPTION OF ALGORITHM X

We first describe algorithm X and then discuss some technical details.

Input: Shared array $task[1..n]$; $task[i] = 0$ for $1 \le i \le n$.

Output: Shared array $task[1..n]$; $task[i] = 1$ for $1 \le i \le n$.

Data structures: The algorithm uses a full binary tree of size $2n - 1$, stored as a linear array in $done[1 \ldots 2n - 1]$ in shared memory. An internal tree node $done[i]$, $i = 1, \ldots, n - 1$, has the left child $done[2i]$ and the right child $done[2i + 1]$. The tree is used for progress evaluation and processor allocation. The values stored in array $done[]$ are assumed to be initially 0. The n elements of the input array $task[1 \ldots n]$ are associated with the leaves of the tree. Element $task[i]$ is associated with $done[i + n - 1]$, where $1 \le i \le n$.

Each processor uses some constant amount of private memory to perform simple arithmetic computations. The total shared-memory used is $O(n + p)$.

Control flow: The algorithm consists of a single initialization and of the parallel *loop*. A high level view of the algorithm is in Figure 4.4; all line numbers refer to this figure. (The detailed code for the algorithm is given in Figure 4.5 that is discussed later).

The initialization (line 01) assigns the p processors to the leaves of the progress tree so that the processors are assigned to the first p leaves. The *loop* (lines 02-11) consists of a multi-way decision (lines 03-10). If the current node u is marked done (that is, $done[u]$ is 1), then the processor moves up the tree (line 03). If the processor is at a leaf, it performs work (line 04). If the current node is an unmarked interior node and both of its subtrees are done, the interior node is marked by changing

---

[1]In the model with crashes and detectable restarts, a processor that crashes may recover, and it is aware of the crash upon the restart. A restarted processor can join the computation at a predefined step, specifically to ensure the continued synchrony of processors.

```
00    forall processors PID=0..p − 1 parbegin
01         Perform initial processor assignment to the leaves of the progress tree
02         while there is still work left in the tree do
03              if subtree rooted at current node u is done then move one level up
04              elseif u is a leaf then perform the work at the leaf
05              elseif u is an interior tree node then
06                   Let uL and uR be the left and right children of u, respectively,
07                   if the subtrees rooted at uL and uR are done then update u
08                   elseif only one is done then go to the one that is not done
09                   else move to uL or uR according to PID bit values
10                fi fi
11         od
12    parend.
```

Figure 4.4: A high level view of the algorithm X.

its value from 0 to 1 (line 07). If a single subtree is not done, the processor moves down appropriately (line 08).

For the final case (line 09), the processors move down when neither child is done. This last case is where a non-trivial decision is made. The PID of the processor is used at depth h of the tree node based on the value of the hth most significant bit of the binary representation of the PID: bit 0 will send the processor to the left, and bit 1 to the right. (Recall Example 3.6 in Section 3.2.1.)

If each processor was traversing the tree alone, it would traverse it in a post-order fashion using the bits of its PID to re-interpret the meaning of "left" and "right". Bit value 0 leads to the "standard" interpretation of "left" and "right", while value 1 reverses them. This results in each processor "intending" to traverse the leaves of the tree according to a permutation determined by its PID, except that the progress by other processors effectively prunes the progress tree when sub-trees are finished. In effect, each processor traverses a sub-tree with the same root.

Regardless of the decision made by a processor within the *loop* body, each iteration of the body consists of no more than four shared memory reads, a fixed time computation using private memory, and one shared memory write, as one can observe from the detailed code given in Figure 4.5.

In the code, the notation "PID[$\log(k)$]" is used to denote the binary true/false value of the $\lfloor \log(k) \rfloor$-th bit of the $\log_2 n$ bit representation of PID, where the most significant bit is the bit number 0, and the least significant bit is bit number $\log_2 n$. Note that the algorithm can also solve the *Do-All* problem "in place", by using the array $task[1..n]$ as a tree of height $\log_2(n/2)$ with the leaves $task[n/2..n − 1]$, and doubling up the processors at the leaves, and using $task[n]$ as the final element to be initialized and used as the algorithm termination sentinel. With this modification, the array $done[1..2n−1]$ is not needed. The asymptotic efficiency of the algorithm is not affected.

One of the advantages of this algorithm is that it can be used in the settings with detectable failures and restarts such that the recovered processors lose their private memory but restart in specially designated states. However, some extra care needs to be taken for handling recovery events,

```
forall processors PID = 1..p parbegin
    shared integer array task[1..n];          -- the Do-All array, initially all values zero
    shared integer array done[1..2n − 1];     -- the progress tree, initially all values zero
    private integer where, done;              -- current node index and its "done" value
    private integer left, right;              -- left/right child values in progress tree   where := n+PID−1;−
- initial assignment at the leafs
    while done[1] ≠ 1 do-- as long as the root is not marked as done
        done := d[where];-- doneness of this subtree
        if done then where := where div 2;-- move up one level
        elseif not done ∧ where > n − 1 then-- at a leaf
            if task[where − n + 1] = 0 then task[where − n + 1] := 1;-- perform Do-All task
            elseif task[where − n + 1] = 1 then d[where] := 1;-- indicate "done"
            fi
        elseif not done ∧ where ≤ n − 1 then-- interior tree node
            left:= done[2 ∗ where]; right := done[2 ∗ where + 1];-- left/right child values
            if left ∧ right then done[where] := 1;-- both children done
            elseif not left ∧ right then where := 2 ∗ where;-- move left
            elseif left ∧ not right then where := 2 ∗ where + 1;-- move right
            elseif not left ∧ not right then-- both subtrees are not done
                -- move down according to the PID bit
                if not PID[log(where)] then where := 2 ∗ where;-- move left
                elseif PID[log(where)] then where := 2 ∗ where + 1;-- move right
                fi
            fi
        fi
    od
parend.
```

Figure 4.5: Algorithm X detailed pseudocode.

and the processors need to copy their private memory to the shared memory which is non-volatile. Modifying the algorithm to handle detectable failures and restarts is left as an exercise (see Exercise 4.8).

4.2.2   ANALYSIS OF ALGORITHM X

We first show that Algorithm X indeed solves the *Do-All* problem; that is, if a non-faulty processor ceases executing the algorithm, then it is the case that all tasks have been performed. Note that no guarantee on the time the problem is solved by algorithm X can be given in an asynchronous environment.

Lemma 4.8   *Algorithm X with p processors is a correct solution for the asynchronous Do-All problem of size n. All non-faulty processors cease executing the algorithm after $O(p \cdot n)$ collective loop iterations.*

Proof. First observe that the processor loads are localized in the sense that a processor exhausts all work in the vicinity of its original position in the tree before moving to other areas of the tree. If a processor moves up out of a subtree then all the leaves in that subtree were visited. Also observe that it takes exactly one iteration to (i) change the value of a progress tree node from 0 to 1, (ii) to move up from a (non root) node, or (iii) to move down left, or (iv) down right from a (non leaf) node. Therefore, given any node of the progress tree and any processor, the processor will visit and spend exactly one loop iteration at the node no more than four times.

Since there are $2n - 1$ nodes in the progress tree, any processor will be able to execute no more than $O(n)$ loop iterations. If there are p processors, then all processors will be able to complete no more than $O(p \cdot n)$ loop iterations. Furthermore, at any point in time, at least one processor is active. Note that once a processor marks the root of the progress tree as done, all other processors cease executing the algorithm in their next iteration (this can take arbitrary time due to asynchrony). Therefore, from the above and the fact that once a leaf node of the progress tree is marked done, it is not unmarked, it follows that it will take no more than $O(p \cdot n)$ sequential loop iterations of constant size for the algorithm to solve the problem.

Finally, observe that all paths from a leaf to the root are $\log_2 n$ long; therefore, at least $\log_2 n$ loop iterations per processor are required to solve the problem.   □

Now we prove the main work lemma. Note that in this lemma, we assume $p \geq n$. (The processors are initially allocated to the leafs based on their PID modulo n.)

Lemma 4.9   *Algorithm X for the Do–All problem of size n with $p \geq n$ asynchronous processors has work* $S = O(p \cdot n^{\log_2 \frac{3}{2}})$.

Proof. Let $S_{x,y}$ denote the work that algorithm X requires to solve the *Do–All* problem of size x using y processors. We show by induction on the height of the progress tree that there are positive constants c_1, c_2, c_3 such that $S_{n,p} \leq c_1 p \cdot n^{\log_2 \frac{3}{2}} - c_2 p \log n - c_3 p$.

For the base case: we have a tree of height 0 that corresponds to an input array of size 1 and at least as many initial processors p. Since at least one processor, and at most p processors, will be active (in the sense that are not slow), this single leaf will be visited in a constant number of steps. Let the work expended be $c'p$ for some constant c' that depends only on the lexical structure of the algorithm. Therefore, $S_{1,p} = c'p \leq c_1 p \cdot 1^{\log_2 \frac{3}{2}} - c_2 p \cdot 0 - c_3 p$ when c_1 is chosen to be larger than or equal to $c_3 + c'$ (for any constant c_3).

Now consider a tree of height $\log_2 n$ (≥ 1). The root has two subtrees (left and right) of height $\log_2 n - 1$. By the description of algorithm X, no processor will leave a subtree until the subtree is *marked*, i.e., the value of the root of the subtree is changed from 0 to 1. Due to asynchrony, one of the subtrees is marked before the other.

Assume without loss of generality that the left subtree is marked-one first with $S_L = S_{n/2,p/2}$ work being expended in this subtree. Any active processors from the left subtree will start moving via the root to the right subtree. The length of the path traversed by any processor as it moves to the right subtree after the left subtree is finished is bounded by the maximum path length from a leaf to another leaf $c' \log_2 n$ for a predefined constant c'. No more than the original $p/2$ processors of the left subtree will move, and so the work of moving the processors is bounded by $c'(p/2) \log_2 n$.

We observe that the cost of an execution in which p processors begin at the leaves of a tree (with $n/2$ leaves) differs from the cost of an execution where $p/2$ processors start at the leaves, and $p/2$ arrives at a later time via the root, by no more than the cost $c'(p/2) \log_2 n$ accounted for above. This is so because a simulating scenario can be constructed in which the second set of $p/2$ processors, instead of arriving through the root, start their execution with a delay, and then traverse along a path through the marked nodes (if any) in the progress tree, until they reach an unmarked node that is either a leaf or whose descendants are marked.

Having accounted for this difference, we see that work S_R to complete the right subtree using up to p processors is bounded by $S_{n/2,p}$ (by the definition of S, if $p_1 \leq p_2$, then $S_{n,p_1} \leq S_{n,p_2}$). After this, each processor spends a constant number of steps moving to the root and stopping. This work is bounded by $c'' p$ for some small constant c''.

The total work S is the following:

$$S \;\leq\; S_L + c' \frac{p}{2} \log_2 n + S_R + c'' p \leq S_{n/2,p/2} + c' \frac{p}{2} \log_2 n + S_{n/2,p} + c'' p.$$

Hence, we have that

$$
\begin{aligned}
S \;\leq\;& c_1 \frac{p}{2} \left(\frac{n}{2}\right)^{\log_2 \frac{3}{2}} - c_2 \frac{p}{2} \log_2 \frac{n}{2} - c_3 \frac{p}{2} + c' \frac{p}{2} \log_2 n + c_1 p \left(\frac{n}{2}\right)^{\log_2 \frac{3}{2}} - c_2 p \log_2 \frac{n}{2} - c_3 p + c'' p \\
=\;& c_1 p n^{\log_2 \frac{3}{2}} - c_2 p \log n \left(\frac{3}{2} - \frac{c'}{2c_2}\right) - c_3 p \left(\frac{3}{2} - \frac{c''}{c_3} - \frac{3c_2}{2c_3}\right) \\
\leq\;& c_1 p \cdot n^{\log_2 \frac{3}{2}} - c_2 p \log_2 n - c_3 p,
\end{aligned}
$$

for sufficiently large c_2 and c_3, depending on fixed c' and c'', e.g., $c_2 \geq c'$ and $c_3 \geq 3c_2 + 2c''$.

Since the constants c', c'' depend only on the lexical structure of the algorithm, the constants c_1, c_2, c_3 can always be chosen sufficiently large to satisfy the base case and both the cases (1) and (2) of the inductive step. This completes the proof. □

We now derive the work complexity of algorithm X for $p \leq n$ by increasing the work done by the processors at the leaves of the progress tree.

Theorem 4.10   Algorithm X solves the *Do-All* problem of size n using $p \leq n$ asynchronous processors with work $S = O(n \cdot p^{\log_2 \frac{3}{2}})$.

Proof. When $p \leq n$, we use the following parameterization: (*i*) the algorithm uses the progress tree with p leaves, and (*ii*) instead of one task at each leaf, the algorithm associates $\lceil n/p \rceil$ tasks with each leaf (using padding in both cases as necessary). The analysis is exactly the same as for the case $p = n$, except that the processing at each node (any node) of the progress tree takes not $O(1)$ work, but $O(n/p)$ work, since a node (a leaf) may have $\lceil n/p \rceil$ tasks associated with it.

By Lemma 4.9, $S_{p,p} = O(p \cdot p^{\log_2 \frac{3}{2}})$. Thus, the overall work is $S = S_{p,p} \cdot O(n/p) = O(\frac{n}{p} \cdot p \cdot p^{\log_2 \frac{3}{2}}) = O(n \cdot p^{\log_2 \frac{3}{2}})$, as desired. $\qquad\qquad\qquad\square$

4.3   ALGORITHM *GROOTE*

We now present another asynchronous algorithm for the *Do-All* problem which we call *Groote*. We first present in an incremental way the idea behind the algorithm, and then we describe the complete algorithm.

4.3.1   A HIGH-LEVEL VIEW OF THE ALGORITHM.

The algorithm is a generalization of the two-processor algorithm based on processor collisions (recall Example 3.2): a situation where two (or more processors) concurrently and redundantly perform the same task and then detect that they have "collided" on this task. The tasks are represented in a linear array and are numbered from 1 to n. The first processor inspects and then performs tasks sequentially starting at task number 1 and moving up; the second processor inspects and then performs tasks sequentially starting with task number n and moving down. Each processor stops when it inspects a task that has already been performed by the other processor. (We show, in the next section, that the work spent inspecting tasks for completion is subsumed by the work spent on performing tasks.) We denote by C_2 the cost of work performed by two processors. Then, it is easy to see that C_2 is at most $n + 1$: each task but the final one is performed exactly once, while the final task is performed at most twice if both processors collide, finding the task not done and performing it concurrently.

We now consider the *Do-All* problem for 4 processors and n tasks. We assume that n is perfect square, i.e., $n = m^2$ for some m (if n is not a perfect square, we use padding). We arrange the tasks in a 2-dimensional m by m array. The processors work in pairs on each row of the matrix: the first processor pair starts at the top row and moves down, the second pair starts at the bottom row and moves up. When working on a row, each pair of processors follows the two-processor algorithm described above. Prior to starting on a new row, each pair checks whether or not the next row is done, if so, the algorithm terminates: either all rows are now done, or the two pairs have collided on a row also meaning that all rows are done. Figure 4.6 illustrates the algorithm.

Using the analysis for the two-processor algorithm, the cost of the work of each pair on a single row of tasks is no more than $m + 1$. There are m rows, and when the two pairs of processors collide, the final row is done twice. Thus, in the worst case, the number of rows of tasks performed by the 4 processors is $m + 1$. The total cost C_4 of the work is therefore: $C_4 = C_2 \cdot (m + 1) = (m + 1) \cdot (m + 1) = (m + 1)^2$.

This idea is extended to 8 processors as follows. We assume that n is perfect cube, i.e., $n = m^3$ for some m (if n is not a perfect cube, we use padding). We arrange the tasks in a 3-dimensional m by m by m array. The processors work in quadruples on each 2-dimensional "slice" of the cube: the first processor quadruple starts at the front surface of the cube and moves "in", the second quadruple starts at the back surface and moves "out", one slice at a time. When working on a slice, each quadruple of

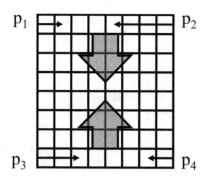

Four-processor algorithm for $n = 64 = 8^2$. Each pair works on one row at a time (i.e., a one-dimensional instance of the problem). The algorithm terminates when the two pairs of processors "meet" (collide).

Figure 4.6: Algorithm *Groote* for 4 processors.

processors follows the 4-processor algorithm described above. Prior to starting on a new slice, each quadruple (i.e., each processor in the quadruple) checks whether or not the next slice is done, and if so, the algorithm terminates: either all 2-dimensional slices of the cube are now done, or the two quadruples have collided on a slice also meaning that all tasks are done. Figure 4.7 illustrates the algorithm.

Using the analysis for the 4-processor algorithm, the cost of the work of each quadruple on a single slice of tasks is no more than $C_4 = (m + 1)^2$. There are m 2-dimensional slices, and when the two quadruples of processors collide, the final slice is done twice (at most). Thus, in the worst case, the number of slices of tasks performed by the 8 processors is $m + 1$. The total cost C_8 of the work is therefore: $C_8 = C_4 \cdot (m + 1) = (m + 1)^2 \cdot (m + 1) = (m + 1)^3$.

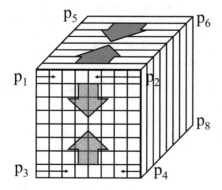

Eight-processor algorithm for $n = 512 = 8^3$. Each quadruple works on one 8 by 8 slice of the cube (i.e., a two-dimensional instance of the problem) at a time. The algorithm terminates when the two quadruples "meet" (collide).

Figure 4.7: Algorithm *Groote* for 8 processors.

As one can see, this algorithm implements the local allocation paradigm using a multi-level approach similar to hierarchical trees as described in Section 3.2.2 (paragraph "Composite Tree Traversals"). We next present the parameterization of this algorithm for many processors.

4.3.2   THE ALGORITHM FOR $p = 2^k$ AND $n = m^k$

This idea is generalized to $p = 2^k$ processors as follows. We assume that $n = m^k$ for some integer $m \geq 2$. We arrange the tasks in a k-dimensional array with coordinates from $[m]$.

The processors work in "opposing" groups of $p/2$ $(= 2^{k-1})$ processors on each $(k-1)$-dimensional "slice" of the k-cube: the first group starts at the "bottom surface" of the cube (i.e., starting with coordinate 1) and moves "up" (by incrementing the coordinate after completing a slice), the second group starts at the "top surface" (i.e., starting with coordinate m) and moves "down" (by decrementing the coordinate after completing a slice), one slice at a time.

Note that each slice is a $(k-1)$-dimensional array. When working on a $(k-1)$-dimensional slice, each group of processors performs the (2^{k-1})-processor algorithm. Prior to starting on a new slice, each group (i.e., each processor in the group) checks whether or not the next slice is done by the opposing group of processors, and if so, the algorithm terminates: either all slices of the k-cube are now done, or the two groups have collided on a slice, likewise meaning that all tasks are done. The algorithm operates recursively at lower dimensions.

The checks for completion of slices are implemented by associating one completion *trit*, a trinary bit, initialized to 0, with each slice in each of the k dimensions. Processors proceeding from slice 1 to slice m set the associated trit to 1 upon completing the slice, and opposing processors proceedings from slice m to slice 1 set the trit to -1 upon completing the slice. Prior to commencing the work on a next slice a processor checks the trit. If the bit value is 0, the processor proceeds to work on the slice and sets the trit accordingly. If the trit is not 0 and is not marked by the opposing group of processors, the processor proceeds to the next slice. Else if the trit is marked by the opposing group of processors, indicating either a collision or the completion of all slices in the current dimension, the processor proceeds to the next higher dimension. When the highest dimension is done, the algorithm terminates. The pseudocode for the algorithm is left as an exercise (see Exercise 4.9).

We now analyze the complexity of algorithm *Groote*. We first prove the cost for performing tasks and then the cost for checking for completion of slices.

Lemma 4.11   *Algorithm Groote solves the Do-All problem with $n = m^k$ tasks and $p = 2^k$ asynchronous processors using task-based cost $C_p = O(np^\gamma)$, where $0 < \gamma = \log_2(\frac{m+1}{m}) < 1$.*

Proof. We first express work C_p in terms of the parameters k, the number of dimensions, and m, the size of each dimension. This work is computed as follows:

$$C_p = C_{p/2} \cdot (m+1) = C_{p/4} \cdot (m+1) \cdot (m+1) = \ldots = C_2 \cdot (m+1)^{k-1} = (m+1)^k.$$

Now, to express work in terms of $p = 2^k$ and $n = m^k$, we perform the following reformulation:

$$C_p = (m+1)^k = n \cdot \left(\frac{m+1}{m}\right)^k = n \cdot \left(\frac{m+1}{m}\right)^{\log_2 p} = n \cdot p^{\log_2\left(\frac{m+1}{m}\right)}.$$

Given that $m \geq 2$, we have that $0 < \log_2((m+1)/m) < 1$ (also note that the basis 2 of the logarithm is significant in the asymptotic expression for work). $\square$

Noteworthy, the work above is always subquadratic in n and p.

Checking for completion of slices involves reading and writing trits. We let R denote the trit-based cost spent for checking for completion of slices.

Lemma 4.12 *Algorithm Groote solves the Do-All problem with $n = m^k$ tasks and $p = 2^k$ asynchronous processors using trit-based cost $R = O(n \log p)$.*

Proof. We need to compute the number of trits that need to be examined. From the description of the algorithm, it follows that with dimension k, there are $m^k + m^{k-1} + \ldots + m^1$ bits to be examined. However, not all of them are examined by the same number of processors.

As mentioned in the description of the algorithm, the processors are divided into groups, and when working on a $(k-1)$-dimensional slice, each group of processors performs the (2^{k-1})-processor algorithm. Given a one-dimensional array, it can be seen that in the worst case, $m+2$ trits must be examined: each of the m trits are examined once, and at most two extra trits are checked by the opposing processors to realize that the whole array has been checked.

At the highest level, there is $1 (= m^0)$ instance of $m + 2$ trits examined by 2^{k-1} processors each. At the next level, there are m instances of $m + 2$ trits examined by 2^{k-2} processors each. At the next level, there are m^2 instances of $m + 2$ trits examined by 2^{k-3} processors each and so on. Hence, at the lowest level, there are m^{k-1} instances of $m + 2$ trits examined by $1 (= 2^0)$ processors each. Summing these gives us the total number of trits examined. Note that each trit examination may incur two work units (one for reading and one for writing) in the worst case. Therefore,

$$ R \leq 2 \sum_{i=0}^{k-1} m^{k-i}(m+2)2^{i-1} = 2(m+2) \sum_{i=0}^{k-1} m^{k-i}2^{i-1}. \tag{4.1} $$

Note that $m \geq 2$, thus $m + 2 \leq 2m$. Replacing 2^{i-1} with m^{i-1} in Equation (4.1), we get $R \leq 4mkm^{k-1} = 4km^k = 4n \log p$. $\square$

We now give the overall complexity result.

Theorem 4.13 Algorithm *Groote* solves the *Do-All* problem with $n = m^k$ tasks and $p = 2^k$ asynchronous processors $(p \leq n)$ using work $S = O(np^\gamma)$, where $0 < \gamma = \log_2(\frac{m+1}{m}) < 1$.

Proof. The work S of the algorithm is the sum of C_p and R. From Lemmas 4.11 and 4.12, we see that R is asymptotically subsumed by C_p. $\square$

Note that if we want $n = p$, we choose $m = 2$. In this case, the work becomes $O(n^{\log_2 3})$. Earlier, we studied a binary tree based algorithm, called algorithm X. As we saw, its work for $n = p$ is also $O(n^{\log_2 3})$. This is not surprising because algorithm X is very similar in its approach to the algorithm we described here for $m = 2$. In algorithm X, the binary progress tree is used to control the execution, where a "collision" occurs when some two subtrees are completed.

4.4   ALGORITHM AW^T

In this section, we present an algorithm for the asynchronous *Do-All* problem that uses *generalized progress trees* for detection of unfinished work in the style of the local allocation paradigm, and that uses permutation schedules to select potential work in the style of the hashed allocation paradigm. We call this algorithm, algorithm AW^T. As we show, the data structures of algorithm AW^T can be parameterized, so that its work is $S = O(n^{1+\varepsilon})$ for $p = n$, and for any $\varepsilon > 0$. Hence, this algorithm has better work complexity than the other asynchronous algorithms we have seen so far.

Recall that in algorithm X, the processors traverse the work elements in the order determined by the processors' PIDs and the structure of the progress tree (which is a binary tree). At each internal node of the tree, a processor chooses between the two children based on whether any of the children are not "done", and based on the bit in that processor's PID corresponding to the depth of the node. This bit can be interpreted as a permutation of the two children. When a processor arrives at a node, it uses one of the two permutations to choose the order of the progress tree traversal. The choice of the permutation is based on the bit in the binary expansion of the processor's PID in position corresponding to the depth of the node.

Algorithm AW^T generalizes this approach using a q-ary progress tree ($q \geq 2$) and permutations for the processors to traverse the tree. Before we describe algorithm AW^T, we define the term *contention* of permutation schedules and explain how this is related with redundant work.

4.4.1   CONTENTION OF PERMUTATIONS

In this section, we present and generalize the notion of *contention* of permutations and give properties of contention (without proofs). Contention properties turn out to be important in the analysis of Algorithm AW^T as well as other algorithms presented in later sections.

We use braces $\langle \ldots \rangle$ to denote an ordered list. For a list L and an element a, we use the expression $a \in L$ to denote the element's membership in the list, and the expression $L - K$ to stand for L with all elements in K removed.

We now provide a motivation for the material in this section. Recall the 2-processor asynchronous *Do-All* problem considered in earlier chapters: Two asynchronous processors, p_1 and p_2, need to perform n independent tasks with known unique identifiers from the set $[n] = \{1, \ldots, n\}$. Assume that before starting a task, a processor can check whether the task is complete (e.g., by checking a data structure stored in shared memory); however, if both processors work on the task concurrently, then the task is done twice because both find it not to be complete. We are interested in the number of tasks done redundantly.

Let $\pi_1 = \langle a_1, \ldots, a_n \rangle$ be the sequence of tasks giving the order in which $\mathfrak{p}_1$ intends to perform the tasks. Similarly, let $\pi_2 = \langle a_{s_1}, \ldots, a_{s_n} \rangle$ be the sequence of tasks of $\mathfrak{p}_2$. We can view π_2 as π_1 permuted according to $\sigma = \langle s_1, \ldots, s_n \rangle$. That is, π_1 and π_2 are permutations. With this, it is possible to construct an asynchronous execution for $\mathfrak{p}_1$ and $\mathfrak{p}_2$, where $\mathfrak{p}_1$ performs all n tasks by itself, and any tasks that $\mathfrak{p}_2$ finds to be unperformed are performed redundantly by both processors.

In the current context, it is important to understand how the structure of π_2 affects the number of redundant tasks. Clearly, $\mathfrak{p}_2$ may have to perform task a_{s_1} redundantly. What about a_{s_2}? If $s_1 > s_2$, then by the time $\mathfrak{p}_2$ gets to task a_{s_2}, it is already done by $\mathfrak{p}_1$ according to π_1. Thus, in order for a_{s_2} to be done redundantly, it must be the case that $s_2 > s_1$. It is easy to see, in general, that for task a_{s_j} to be done redundantly, it must be the case that $s_j > \max\{s_1, \ldots, s_{j-1}\}$. Such s_j is called the *left-to-right maximum* of σ. The total number of tasks done redundantly by $\mathfrak{p}_2$ is thus the number of left-to-right maxima of σ. Not surprisingly, this number is minimized when $\sigma = \langle n, \ldots, 1 \rangle$, i.e., when π_2 is the reverse order of π_1, and it is maximized when $\sigma = \langle 1, \ldots, n \rangle$, i.e., when $\pi_1 = \pi_2$. The notion of *contention* of permutations captures the relevant left-to-right maxima properties of permutations that are to be used as processor schedules. We proceed with a formal presentation of this term.

We refer to a list of task identifiers as a *schedule*. When a schedule for n tasks is a permutation of task identifiers π in $\mathcal{S}_n$, we call it a *n-schedule*. Here $\mathcal{S}_n$ is the symmetric group, the group of all permutations on the set $[n]$; we use the symbol $\circ$ to denote the composition operator, and $\mathbf{e}_n$ to denote the identity permutation. For a n-schedule $\pi = \langle \pi(1), \ldots, \pi(n) \rangle$, a *left-to-right maximum* is an element $\pi(j)$ of π that is larger than all of its predecessors, i.e., $\pi(j) > \max_{i<j}\{\pi(j-i)\}$.

Given a n-schedule π, we define $\mathrm{LRM}(\pi)$, to be the number of left-to-right maxima in the n-schedule π. For a list of permutations $\Psi = \langle \pi_0, \ldots, \pi_{n-1} \rangle$ from $\mathcal{S}_n$ and a permutation δ in $\mathcal{S}_n$, the *contention* of Ψ with respect to δ is defined as $\mathrm{Cont}(\Psi, \delta) = \sum_{u=0}^{n-1} \mathrm{LRM}(\delta^{-1} \circ \pi_u)$. The *contention of the list of schedules* Ψ is defined as $\mathrm{Cont}(\Psi) = \max_{\delta \in \mathcal{S}_n}\{\mathrm{Cont}(\Psi, \delta)\}$. Note that for any Ψ, we have $n \le \mathrm{Cont}(\Psi) \le n^2$. It turns out (see bibliographic notes) that it is possible to construct a family of permutations with the following low contention (H_n is the nth harmonic number, $H_n = \sum_{j=1}^{n} \frac{1}{j}$).

Fact 4.14   For any $n > 0$ there exists a list of permutations $\Psi = \langle \pi_0, \ldots, \pi_{n-1} \rangle$ with $\mathrm{Cont}(\Psi) \le 3n H_n = \Theta(n \log n)$.

For a constant n, a list Ψ with $\mathrm{Cont}(\Psi) \le 3n H_n$ can be found by exhaustive search. This costs only a constant number of operations on integers (however, this cost might be of order $(n!)^n$).

4.4.2   DESCRIPTION OF ALGORITHM AW^T

We now describe algorithm AW^T.

Input: Shared array $task[1..n]$; $task[i] = 0$ for $1 \le i \le n$.

Output: Shared array $task[1..n]$; $task[i] = 1$ for $1 \le i \le n$.

Data structures: For the *Do-All* array of size n, the progress tree is a q-ary ordered tree of height h, thus $n = q^h$. Each interior node of the tree has a data bit, indicating whether the sub-tree rooted at the node is done (value 1) or not (value 0).

The progress tree is stored in a linear array $done[0..(qn-1)/(q-1) - 1]$ using the same technique as used to store a binary tree, with $done[0]$ being the root and the q children of the interior node $done[v]$ being the nodes $done[qv + 1], done[qv + 2], \ldots, done[qv + q]$. We define n_T, the size of the progress tree, to be $(qn-1)/(q-1)$. The space occupied by the tree is $O(n)$. The *Do-All* array elements are attached to the leaves of the progress tree, such that the leaf $done[v]$ is mapped to the *Do-All* array element $task[n - n_T + v + 1]$.

We use $p = n$ processors, and we represent their PIDs in terms of their q-ary expansion. Such expansion requires $h = \log_q n$ of q-ary digits, and for the processor whose PID is $\mathfrak{p}$, we denote such expansion by $\mathfrak{p}_0\mathfrak{p}_1 \ldots \mathfrak{p}_{h-1}$. The q-ary expansions of PID is stored in the array $\mathfrak{p}[0..h-1]$.

The order of traversals within the progress tree is determined by the set $\Psi = \{\pi_0, \pi_1 \ldots, \pi_{q-1}\}$ of permutations over $[q]$, i.e., over $\{1, 2 \ldots, q\}$.

Control flow: Each processor uses, at the node of depth d, the dth q-ary digit of its PID $\mathfrak{p}$ to select the permutation $\pi_{\mathfrak{p}_d}$. The processor traverses the q subtrees in the order determined by $\pi_{\mathfrak{p}_d}$, but it visits a subtree only if the corresponding done bit is not set. The pseudocode for Algorithm AW^T is given in Figure 4.8 in terms of the recursive procedure AWT (lines 10-23) that is executed in parallel by all processors.

4.4.3   ANALYSIS OF ALGORITHM AW^T

It is not difficult to see that this algorithm solves the *Do-All* problem since, as in algorithm X (see Lemma 4.8), a processor leaves a subtree only when there is no work left to be done. In particular, if only a single processor is active, it will traverse the entire tree in search of work. We now give the analysis of work S for Algorithm AW^T.

Let S_p be the work of algorithm AW^T with p processors using the progress tree with p leaves. We calculate S_p using a recurrence, similarly to the analysis of algorithm X. At depth 1 of the progress tree, all processors will traverse the q nodes in search of work. This contributes the quantity $p \cdot q$ to S_p. At depth 1 and below, the processors use only their q-ary digits $\mathfrak{p}[1..d-1]$ (line 20 of Figure 4.8). There are q groups of p/q processors such that their PIDs differ only in the first q-ary digit. The work of such a group of processors in traversing any of the subtrees with roots at depth 1 of the progress tree is at most $S_{p/q}$. Whether or not at least one processor in such a group traverses and completes a subtree and marks it done is determined by the contention of the set of permutations Ψ used by the algorithm.

```
00    forall processors PID=0..p − 1 parbegin
01        shared π₀, . . . , π_{q−1} -- read-only set of permutations Ψ
02        shared integer array task[1..n] -- Do-All array
03        shared integer array done[0..(qn−1)/(q−1) − 1] -- q-ary progress tree of size n_T
04        private v init = 0 -- current node index, begin at the root
05        private d init = 0 -- current depth in the tree
06        AWT(v, d)
07    parend.

10    procedure AWT( -- Recursive progress tree traversal
11                      v, -- current node index
12                      d -- depth of the current node )
13        private p[0..d − 1] const = PID₍q₎ -- d digits of q-ary expansion of PID
14        if done[v] = 0 -- any work to be done here?
15        then -- current node is NOT done – still work left
16          if d = h        -- is v a leaf?
17          then task[n − n_T + v + 1] := 1; done[v] := 1; -- Perform work on the leaf
18          else -- not a leaf – visit subtrees
19            for j = 1 . . q do -- visit subtrees in the order of π_{p[d]}
20                AWT(done[qv + π_{p[d]}(j)], d + 1) -- visit subtree in the j-th position of π_{p[d]}
21            od
22          fi fi
23    end.
```

Figure 4.8: Pseudocode for Algorithm AW^T for fixed q and h.

Thus, we have the following recurrence: $S_p \leq p \cdot q + S_{p/q} \cdot \mathrm{Cont}(\Psi)$. The solution to the recurrence is (the sum is a geometric series):

$$S_p \leq q \cdot p \sum_{k=0}^{\log_q p} \left(\frac{\mathrm{Cont}(\Psi)}{q}\right)^k \leq 2q \cdot p \left(\frac{\mathrm{Cont}(\Psi)}{q}\right)^{\log_q p} = O\left(q \cdot p^{\log_q \mathrm{Cont}(\Psi)}\right).$$

To solve the *Do-All* problem for $n > p$, we use the algorithm $\lceil n/p \rceil$ times and get the following work bound:

Lemma 4.15 *Algorithm AW^T with p processors solves the Do-All problem of size n ($p \leq n$) using a q-ary progress tree and a set Ψ of q permutations on $[q]$ in the asynchronous model with work $S = O(q\, n \cdot p^{\log_q \mathrm{Cont}(\Psi)-1})$.*

We can obtain algorithm X with $p = n$ from Algorithm AW^T by choosing $q = 2$ and $\Psi = \{(1\ 2), (2\ 1)\}$. It is easy to calculate that $\mathrm{Cont}(\Psi) = 3$, and so for algorithm X, we have $S = O(2n \cdot p^{\log_2 3-1}) = O(n \cdot p^{\log \frac{3}{2}})$, as expected.

It turns out that algorithm AW^T can be parameterized so that it is not only polynomially efficient, but it can be made more efficient (asymptotically) than the other polynomial algorithms we have seen so far:

Theorem 4.16   For any $\varepsilon < 1$, there exist q and Ψ such that algorithm AW^T with p processors using q-ary trees and permutations in Ψ is a polynomially efficient algorithm that solves the *Do-All* problem of size n ($p = n$) in the asynchronous model with work $S \leq O(n \cdot p^\varepsilon)$.

Proof. We begin by choosing Ψ such that $\mathrm{Cont}(\Psi) \leq cq \log_2 q$ where c is a small constant. As we have indicated, such Ψ exist and can be constructed (see Fact 4.14). Since q is a parameter that does not depend on p, even a brute force approach that computes contention for all possible Ψ is acceptable (but not practical for larger q). By substituting $cq \log q$ for $\mathrm{Cont}(\Psi)$ in Lemma 4.15, we get the following:

$$\begin{aligned} S &= O(q\, n \cdot p^{\log_q \mathrm{Cont}(\Psi)-1}) & &= O(q\, n \cdot p^{\log_q (cq \log_2 q)-1}) \\ &= O(q\, n \cdot p^{\log_q q-1} \cdot p^{\log_q (\log_2 q^c)}) & &= O(q\, n \cdot p^{\log_q (\log_2 q^c)}). \end{aligned}$$

Since $\lim_{q \to \infty} \log_q (\log_2 q^c) = 0$, one can find q such that $\log_q (\log_2 q^c) < \varepsilon$ for any $\varepsilon > 0$. Note that for large q, the algorithm is not very practical.   □

4.5   ALGORITHM *TWOLEVELAW*

In this section, we present an algorithm for the asynchronous *Do-All* problem that is constructed as a two-level nested algorithm, where the pivotal decision leading to its efficiency is whether and when to allow the processors to work in isolation, and when to enforce cooperation. When cooperating, the processors use a careful parameterization of algorithms AW^T presented in the previous section. For this reason, we call this algorithm, algorithm *TwoLevelAW*.

The work complexity of algorithm *TwoLevelAW* is $O(n + p^{2+\varepsilon})$, for any $\varepsilon > 0$ which is optimal when $p = O(n^{1/(2+\varepsilon)})$, while all other known *Do-All* deterministic algorithms (including algorithms X, *Groote*, and AW^T) require super-linear work when $p = \Omega(n^{1/4})$.

In more detail, Algorithm *TwoLevelAW* is based on a two-level nested application of q-ary progress tree algorithms (such the ones used by algorithm AW^T). At the lowest level, the processor is forced to make a decision on whether to work in isolation using a sequential algorithm and a local schedule, or to cooperate. A processor cooperates when it believes that a certain collection of *Do-All* tasks is *saturated* with processors. By carefully choosing the saturation point, the algorithm can be made optimal for a non-trivial range of processors. The algorithm is additionally parameterized by a set of permutations. It is correct for any set of permutations, but its efficiency depends on selecting a set of permutations with certain combinatorial (contention) properties that are known to exist. These permutations require the same properties as the ones used by algorithm AW^T and were described in Section 4.4.1.

In the remainder, we will be referring to algorithm *TwoLevelAW* with p processors and n *Do-All* tasks parameterized by q and t as algorithm TLAW(q, t). In Section 4.5.2, we show that for any $\varepsilon > 0$ there are parameters q and t such that the work of algorithm TLAW(q, t) is indeed $O(n + p^{2+\varepsilon})$.

4.5.1   DESCRIPTION OF ALGORITHM TLAW(q, t)

We now describe algorithm TLAW(q, t).

Input: Shared array $task[1..n]$; $task[i] = 0$ for $1 \leq i \leq n$.

Output: Shared array $task[1..n]$; $task[i] = 1$ for $1 \leq i \leq n$.

Data structures: The main data structure in the algorithm is a complete q-ary *progress tree* with p leaves. Parameter q, typically a constant, corresponding to the number of children at each interior node, also parameterizes schedules used in the algorithm. The n tasks are partitioned into p *jobs*, where each job consists of t *chunks* of tasks (thus there are $p \cdot t$ chunks, each chunk consists of $n/(p \cdot t)$ tasks). This structuring is illustrated in Figure 4.9.

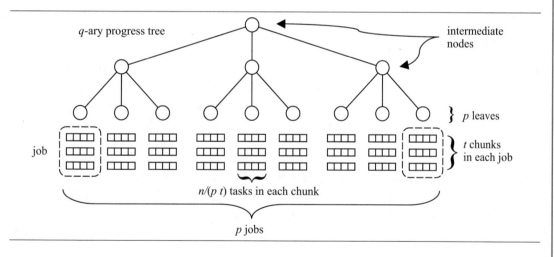

Figure 4.9:   Illustration of the q-ary progress tree, and job and chunk structuring for $n = 108$ tasks, $p = 9$ processors, $q = 3$, and $t = 3$. Each chunk has $n/(pt) = 108/(9 \cdot 3) = 4$ tasks.

The algorithm uses a list Ψ of q schedules (permutations) from S_q, $\Psi = \langle \pi_0, \ldots \pi_{q-1} \rangle$ (recall permutation-related notation from Section 4.4.1). We assume that $\log_q p$ is a positive integer. If it is not, we pad the processors with at most qp "infinitely delayed" processors, so this assumption is satisfied (given that q is a constant, this padding does not affect the asymptotic complexity of the algorithm). Note that we focus our attention to the case of $n \geq p^2$, as for larger p, algorithm AW^T

yields a solution with the sought work $O(np^\varepsilon) = O(p^{2+\varepsilon}) = O(n + p^{2+\varepsilon})$.

Control flow: The complete q-ary *progress tree* with p leaves used in the algorithm is stored in the boolean-valued array T. The n tasks are represented by the n locations of the array $task[1..n]$. Recall that we divide the n tasks into p *jobs*, each of size at most $\lceil n/p \rceil$. Each job is associated with a leaf of the progress tree. The nodes of the progress tree are initially 0. When all jobs corresponding to the leaves of a given subtree are complete, the root of the subtree is set to 1. When the root of the tree is set to 1, all jobs are complete. The processors traverse the progress tree in search of unfinished jobs as with algorithm AW^T (and X). Each processor chooses the order of traversal according to its PID and the permutations from Ψ. When a processor reaches a leaf, it checks whether the job at the leaf is complete. If not, it starts a procedure for performing the job. The key idea of the algorithm that leads to optimality is to augment the tree traversal with a subtle procedure for performing jobs. Each job is divided into t *chunks*, where each chunk consists of at most $\lceil (n/p)/t \rceil$ tasks. When a processor works on a job, it chooses a different algorithm depending on the knowledge of how many processors are performing this job. Within a job, the tasks are processed at the granularity of chunks.

We now present the algorithm in detail. The code is given in Figure 4.10 (state components and progress tree traversal) and in Figure 4.11 (doing jobs). The line numbers in the presentation below refer to these figures.

PROGRESS TREE TRAVERSAL

Recall that the boolean-valued *progress tree* is a complete q-ary tree of height h with p leaves, where $h = \log_q p$. Each of the n *tasks* consists of writing to one shared memory location of the *Do-All* array $task[1 .. n]$. The tasks are partitioned into p *jobs* associated with the leaves of the progress tree, each job consisting of $\lfloor n/p \rfloor$ or $\lceil n/p \rceil$ tasks. Each job is statically divided into t chunks. This division is recorded in the constant array $JobChunks[1..p]$, where each element of the array records the identities of the t chunks comprising the particular job. To perform a job j means setting to 1 all elements of $task[\cdot]$ associated with all chunks of the job, i.e., the chunks in $JobChunks[j]$. (The assignment of tasks to jobs and chunks is also done statically, and we do not discuss this further.)

The progress tree is stored in a boolean array $T[0 .. g - 1]$ (line 5), where $g = \sum_{i=0}^{h-1} q^i = (q^{h+1} - 1)/(q - 1) = (pq - 1)/(q - 1)$. Here $T[0]$ is the root, and the q children of the interior node $T[d]$ are the nodes $T[qd + 1], T[qd + 2], \ldots, T[qd + q]$. The space occupied by the tree is $O(p)$. Initially, all nodes of the progress tree are set to 0 (false) indicating that not all jobs have been performed. The node of tree is set to 1 (true) whenever all jobs in a subtree rooted at that node are complete. Note that such updates of the progress tree T are always monotone: initially, each node contains 0, then once a node changes its value to 1, it remains 1 forever. Thus, no race conditions arise, which in turn allows the algorithm to use read/write memory without any additional synchronization primitives.

The progress tree is traversed using the recursive procedure DOALL (lines 30-43). Each processor independently searches for work in the smallest immediate subtree that has remaining

```
00   const q -- Arity of the progress tree
01   const Ψ = ⟨π_r | 0 ≤ r < q ∧ π_r ∈ S_q⟩ -- Fixed list of q permutations of [q]
02   const h = log_q p -- The height of the progress tree
03   const g = (q^{h+1} − 1)/(q − 1) -- The size of the progress tree
04   shared array task[1 .. n] of {0, 1} initially {0}^n -- The Do-All array
05   shared array T[0 .. g−1] of {0, 1} initially {0}^g -- The progress tree
06   shared array Chunk[1 .. p][1 .. t] of [p] × [p · t] -- Array of pairs (job, chunk) for processors
07   const array JobChunks[1 .. p] of set of [p · t] -- Fixed sets of chunks in jobs
08   private set Local_PID of [p · t] -- Local set of performed chunks in current job
09   private array Pos_PID[0 .. p − 1] of [t] -- Local array of indices of right-most chunks
10   private set Coop_PID of P -- Local set of processors performing same job

20   forall processors PID = 0 to p − 1 parbegin -- Traverse progress tree in search of work
21       const array α[0 .. h − 1] of integer PID_{(base q)} -- h digits of q-ary expansion of PID
22       integer d initially 0 -- Current node index is d, begin at the root T[0]
23       integer l initially 0 -- Current depth in the tree
24       DoAll(d, l)
25   parend.

30   procedure DoAll(d, l) -- Recursive progress tree traversal
31       -- d : current node index; l : depth of the current node
33       if T[d] = 0 then -- Current node is not done – still work left
34           if l = h then -- Node T[d] is a leaf
35               DoJob(d + p − g) -- Do the job at the leaf T[d]
36           else -- Node d is not a leaf
37               for j = 1 to q do -- Visit subtrees in the order of π_{α[l]}
38                   DoAll(q · d + π_{α[l]}(j), l + 1) -- Visit subtree in the j-th position of π_{α[l]}
39               od
40           fi
41           T[d] := 1 -- Record completion of the subtree rooted at node d
42       fi
43   end.
```

Figure 4.10: Algorithm TLAW(q, t): constants, state, and progress tree traversal at processor PID.

work. It then performs any jobs it finds, and moves out of that subtree when all jobs within it are complete. When exploring the subtrees rooted at an interior node at height l, a processor visits the subtrees in the order given by one of the permutations in $\Psi = \langle \pi_0, \pi_1, \ldots, \pi_{q-1} \rangle$. We represent the PID of each of the p processors in terms of its q-ary expansion stored in the local array $\alpha[0 .. h − 1]$. The processor then uses the permutation $\pi_{\alpha(l)} \in \Psi$, where $\alpha(l)$ is the value of the l-th digit in the q-ary expansion of its PID (lines 37-39). The processor performs a traversal within a subtree only if the corresponding bit in the progress tree is not set (line 33). In other words, each processor PID traverses its progress tree in a post-order fashion using its PID and the permutations in Ψ to establish the order of the traversals, except that the traversal can be pruned based on the progress of other processors recorded in the tree. When a processor reaches a leaf corresponding to an unfinished job, it performs the job by calling the procedure DoJob (line 35).

```
50    procedure DoJob(j)
51        Local_PID := ∅ -- No chunks done for the job
52        Coop_PID := {PID} -- No other cooperating processors
53        Pos_PID[1..p] := {0}^p -- Clear all processors' positions
54        Chunk[PID][1..t] := (⊥, ⊥)^t -- No chunks are yet done by processor PID
55        while JobChunks[j] ≠ Local_PID do -- While not all chunks in job j done
56            Check(j) -- Check for done chunks and update the set of cooperating processors
57            if |Coop_PID| > s then -- Has the job been saturated with processors?
58                AllTasks(j) -- The job is saturated, run cooperative algorithm
59            else
60                DoChunk(j) -- The job is not saturated, do another chunk
61            fi
62        od
63    end.
```

```
70    procedure Check(j)
71        forall w ∈ P − {PID} while |Coop_PID| ≤ s do -- Check others, while job is not saturated
72            if Pos_PID[w] < t then -- Is there more chunks to check?
73                (job, chunk) ← Chunk[w][Pos_PID[w] + 1] -- Get next chunk
74                while job = j ∧ Pos_PID[w] + 1 ≤ t do -- While w working on the same job
75                    Coop_PID := Coop_PID ∪ {w} -- Record w's PID
76                    Local_PID := Local_PID ∪ {chunk} -- Add chunk
77                    Pos_PID[PID] := Pos_PID[PID] + 1 -- Advance own position
78                    Chunk[PID][Pos_PID[PID]] ← (job, chunk) -- Record progress for others
79                    Pos_PID[w] := Pos_PID[w] + 1 -- This chunk of w is now recorded
80                    if Pos_PID[w] + 1 ≤ t then -- More chunks to check?
81                        (job, chunk) ← Chunk[w][Pos_PID[w] + 1] -- Get next chunk of w
82                    fi
83                od
84                if w ∈ Coop_PID ∧ job ≠ ⊥ then -- Processor w moved to another job
85                    Local_PID := JobChunks[j] -- This means all chunks are done
86                fi
87            fi
88        od
89    end.
```

```
90    procedure DoChunk(j)
91        c := Balance(PID, j, Coop_PID, Local_PID)
92        perform chunk c -- Do all t tasks in chunk c
93        Local_PID := Local_PID ∪ {c} -- Record the local progress
94        Pos_PID[PID] := Pos_PID[PID] + 1 -- Advance own position
95        Chunk[PID][Pos_PID[PID]] ← (j, c) -- Record own progress for others
96    end.
```

Figure 4.11: Algorithm TLAW(q, t): doing a job at processor PID.

PERFORMING JOBS

In partitioning the jobs into t *chunks*, we have each chunk consisting of $\lfloor \frac{n}{pt} \rfloor$ or $\lceil \frac{n}{pt} \rceil$ tasks, where t is a parameter of the algorithm. (As with jobs, the assignment of tasks to chunks is done statically, and we do not detail this.) Two different procedures are used to perform tasks within a job, depending on how many processors participate in working on the same job. The code is given in Figure 4.11.

Let s be a fixed threshold (that depends on t; the value of s is defined explicitly in Section 4.5.2). We say that a job is *saturated*, if more than s processors are working on the job; otherwise, the job is *unsaturated*. If a processor thinks that a job is unsaturated, it performs the tasks in the job, one chunk at a time. Else, when it learns that a job is saturated, it runs an instance of algorithm AW^T for p processors and n/p tasks corresponding to the job (procedure ALLTASKS, which is discussed later).

The top level procedure DoJOB implements this process (lines 50-63). The threshold s is used to decide whether to perform procedure DoCHUNK(j) or procedure ALLTASKS(j).

Shared array $Chunk[1..p][1..t]$ has size $p \cdot t$ and, for every processor PID, $Chunk[\text{PID}][i]$ is a pair $(job, chunk)$, where job is the number of a job and $chunk$ is the number of a chunk. Note that since $1 \le job \le p$ and $1 \le chunk \le p \cdot t$, each element of $Chunk[\cdot][\cdot]$ stores $\log p + \log(p \cdot t) = O(\log(p+n))$ bits.

Row $Chunk[\text{PID}]$ is written only by processor PID, while it can be read by any processor (this is a property of the algorithm and not a model assumption).

While executing procedure DoJOB(j), the following local structures are used. Each processor PID maintains a local list $Local_{\text{PID}}$ of the chunks performed in its current job j. It also has a local array Pos_{PID} containing integers from 0 to t. The intuition behind $Pos_{\text{PID}}[w]$ is that if processor w performs the same job as processor PID, then PID has already read all chunks stored in $Chunk[w][1 .. Pos_{\text{PID}}[w]].chunk$. Additionally, processor PID stores the subset $Coop_{\text{PID}}$ of processors, about which it has learnt that they perform the same job as PID does.

When a processor PID starts on a new job j, it clears its data structures (lines 51-54), then checks for the progress of other processors on the same job by examining the list of chunks performed by other processors. This is done using the call to procedure CHECK(j) in line 56. If the job is not saturated, then PID does another chunk from the job using the call to procedure DoCHUNK(j) in line 60. If the job is saturated, the processor starts executing the chunks of job j cooperatively with other processors. This is done using a call to procedure ALLTASKS(j) in line 58.

Procedure ALLTASKS(j) is the same as the top-level algorithm of DoALL($\cdot, \cdot$). (In fact, it can be implemented as a parameterized recursive call to DoALL, but the parameterization would unnecessarily obscure the code in Figures 4.10 and 4.11.) ALLTASKS is a procedure specified for p processors and n/p tasks (array locations) that correspond to all tasks in job j. We use the same parameter q as the arity of the progress tree with n/p leaves. The main difference between ALLTASKS and DoALL is that in ALLTASKS a processor performs one task at a leaf of the progress tree, instead of doing one job in DoALL at line 35.

CHECKING PROGRESS OF OTHER PROCESSORS

We now describe the procedure CHECK(j) (lines 70-89). Although the code is detailed, the idea is very simple: while the job j is not saturated, the processor PID executing the procedure checks the array $Chunk[w][\cdot]$ for all other processors w and records any progress of other processors on job j. If w is also working on the same job, then PID adds it to its local variable $Coop_{\text{PID}}$ (lines 74-75).

In more detail, processor PID takes the following actions for every other processor $w \neq$ PID (lines 72-83): it checks which job is being done by w by reading from $Chunk[w][Pos_{\text{PID}}[w] + 1]$ (line 73) and examining the job field (line 74). The loop in lines 74-83 records the progress on the chunks in $Local_{\text{PID}}$ (line 76) and in $Chunk[\text{PID}][Pos_{\text{PID}}[\text{PID}]]$ (line 78), and advances to the next chunk. Finally, if processor w previously worked on job j, but is found to be working on some other job, this means that all chunks in job j are complete (lines 84-86).

DOING ONE CHUNK AND FUNCTION BALANCE

When processor PID decides to perform the next chunk of the unsaturated job j (lines 57 and 60), it calls procedure DOCHUNK (lines 90-96). The process chooses the next chunk c according to the load-balancing implemented by the function BALANCE (line 91); we next describe this function.

Intuitively, this function balances all chunks in job j that processor PID does not know to be finished (those chunks are $JobChunks[j] - Local_{\text{PID}}$) among processors cooperating on the same job j (stored in $Coop_{\text{PID}}$). Although each processor PID uses its local data $Local_{\text{PID}}$ and $Coop_{\text{PID}}$ to perform this balancing, it is shown in the analysis that this balancing is sufficiently good from the global point of view. Formal definitions follows.

Function BALANCE(PID, j, $Coop_{\text{PID}}$, $Local_{\text{PID}}$) returns the chunk number, say c, within the current job j. Recall that the chunks for job j are stored in $JobChunks[j]$. Processor PID chooses chunk c as follows.

- Processor PID lists the sorted chunks in $JobChunks[j] - Local_{\text{PID}}$, yielding an ordered list $c_1, \ldots, c_x$ of chunks, where $x = |JobChunks[j] - Local_{\text{PID}}|$;

- Processor PID lists the sorted processors in $Coop_{\text{PID}}$, yielding an ordered list $w_1, \ldots, w_y$ processors, where $y = |Coop_{\text{PID}}|$;

- Let z be such that PID $= w_z$, then the chosen chunk is $c := c_{\lceil zx/y \rceil}$.

Processors keep local sets $JobChunks[j] - Local_{\text{PID}}$ and $Coop_{\text{PID}}$ sorted, which means that additions to, and deletions from, these sets can take $O(\log t)$ and $O(\log p)$ time, respectively. With this, function BALANCE can be done in (local) time $O(t)$, contributing $O(t)$ to the work complexity.

Having determined the next chunk c, the processor performs it (line 92), i.e., it performs all $O(n/(pt))$ tasks in the chunk. The processor then updates $Local_{\text{PID}}$, advances its position $Pos_{\text{PID}}[\text{PID}]$, and records its progress in the location $Chunk[\text{PID}][Pos_{\text{PID}}[\text{PID}]]$ (lines 93-95).

4.5.2 ANALYSIS OF ALGORITHM TLAW(q, t)

Before we analyze the performance of algorithm TLAW(q, t), we argue that the algorithm correctly solves the *Do-All* problem with asynchronous processors.

Correctness of Algorithm TLAW(q, t). The correctness of the algorithm TLAW(q, t) follows from the following observations.

Lemma 4.17 *In algorithm TLAW(q, t), if any processor returns from procedure call to* DoALL *in line 24, then each leaf of the progress tree $T[\cdot]$ is set to 1.*

Proof. This follows from the correctness of algorithm AW^T (see section 4.4). A processor exits a subtree by returning from a recursive call to DoALL if and only if all roots of the subtrees are set to 1 (at the lowest level of the tree, the leaves are set to 1). When a processor returns from the top-level call to DoALL, all leaves are marked. □

In procedure DoALL, a leaf of $T[\cdot]$ can be set to 1 only at line 41. This is done after a processor determines that it reached a leaf (line 34), and after the processor completes the call to DoJob for that leaf (line 35). Thus, we need to show that upon the return from that DoJob, all tasks in the corresponding job are done and the corresponding leaf is set to 1.

We start with preliminary lemmas describing certain properties of the algorithm.

Lemma 4.18 *In algorithm TLAW(q, t), if a processor* PID *adds a chunk to Local$_{PID}$ then this chunk is done.*

Proof. By induction—the processor either performs the chunk by itself, or it learns about it by reading information in $Chunk[v][\cdot]$ recorded by some other processor v. The first time any processor v writes the pair (j, c) in $Chunk[v][\cdot]$ (line 95) is after it performs chunk c in job j by itself. □

Lemma 4.19 *In algorithm TLAW(q, t), if any processor returns from procedure call to* DoJob(j) *in line 35, then all tasks in job j are done.*

Proof. A processor PID returns from DoJob after it finds that its variable Local$_{PID}$ contains all chunks in the corresponding job (line 55). Consider the first such processor. If the job ever becomes saturated, then the processor calls ALLTASKS. When the processor returns from ALLTASKS, then all tasks are indeed performed (the proof of this is the same as the proof above for DoALL in Lemma 4.17). (Recall that in ALLTASKS writing 1 in the leaf of the progress tree used in that procedure is equivalent to performing a single task associated with this leaf.) Else the job never becomes saturated from the local point of view of the processor. In this case, the processor either does chunks by itself (DoCHUNK), or it learns that the chunks were done from other processors (using CHECK), and it records its progress in Local$_{PID}$. By Lemma 4.18, this means that all tasks in the current job are done. In all cases, all tasks for each chunk of the job are complete. □

Lemma 4.20   *In algorithm TLAW(q, t), if processor PID writes 1 into leaf corresponding to job j then all tasks in job j are complete.*

Proof. Any leaf of $T[\cdot]$ is set to 1 only at line 41. This happens after the return from DoJob corresponding to the leaf. By Lemma 4.19, all tasks in the job are complete.   □

Next, we argue termination, assuming that there is at least one processor that is not delayed forever (otherwise, the *Do-All* problem is not solvable).

Lemma 4.21   *Any execution of algorithm TLAW(q, t) takes finite time for at least one processor.*

Proof. The progress tree used by the algorithm has finite number of nodes. By code inspection, each processor executing the algorithm makes at most one recursive DoAll call per each node of the tree. By the same reasoning, there is a finite number of calls to AllTasks. Procedures Check and DoChunk clearly take finite time. Thus, any call to DoJob takes finite time. It therefore follows that at least one processor completes the algorithm in finite time.   □

Putting all of this together leads to the following.

Theorem 4.22   Algorithm TLAW(q, t) performs all tasks in finite time.

Proof. By Lemma 4.21, at least one processor completes the algorithm in finite time. By Lemma 4.19, each return from DoJob(j) means that all tasks in job j are done. By Lemma 4.17, each leaf of the main progress tree is set to 1. By Lemma 4.20, setting any leaf to 1 means that the job at the leaf is done. Therefore, all tasks are done.   □

Complexity Analysis of Algorithm TLAW(q, t). We now analyze the work complexity of algorithm TLAW(q, t) and its range of optimality.

Recall the notation $S(n, p)$ that denotes the work performed by p processors using (in this case) algorithm TLAW(q, t) to solve the n-size instance of the *Do-All* problem. Fix $\varepsilon > 0$. We need to show that there is a constant integer parameter $q > 0$ and an integer parameter t, such that algorithm TLAW(q, t) has work $S(n, p) = O(n + p^{2+\varepsilon})$. It is sufficient to show this result for $\varepsilon \leq 1/2$; for $\varepsilon > 1/2$ one can use the same algorithm parameterization as for $\varepsilon = 1/2$. Let $\xi = \varepsilon/9$ and let $t = p^{6\xi}$. Parameter q will be set later, once some preliminary results are proved. We fix threshold $s = \sqrt[3]{t} = p^{2\xi}$.

We say that processor v *starts job* j if it makes a call to DoJob(j). We say that a job is completed if 1 is written into the corresponding leaf. Consider the leaf of the progress tree corresponding to job j. For an execution of the algorithm, let p_j denote the total number of processors that ever call

DoJob(j). We start with preliminary lemmas. The first lemma reasons about the order of certain events.

Lemma 4.23 *If processor v adds processor w to set $Coop_v$ during some step of the execution of DoJob(j), then w started job j before that step.*

Proof. Processor v adds another processor w to $Coop_v$ only upon reading a pair (j, c), for some c, from $Chunks[w][\cdot]$. Only processor w can write to $Chunks[w][\cdot]$. This happens when w performs chunk c of job j by itself, and only during the execution of DoJob(j) by processor w. Thus, w started job j earlier. □

Now we focus on complexity. We first state a result that follows from the analysis of algorithm AW^T.

Lemma 4.24 *For every constant $\xi > 0$ there exist constants $p_\infty, q \geq 0$ such that for every integer parameters $t > 0, n > 0$ and $p > p_\infty$:*
(a) the total number of calls to DoJob($\cdot$) in algorithm $TLAW(q, t)$ is less than $p^{1+\xi}$,
(b) if for any job j, AllTasks(j) is executed by all processors, the resulting work is $O(\frac{n}{p} \cdot p^\xi + p^{1+\xi})$.

Proof. The top-level structure of algorithm $TLAW(q, t)$ is the same as that of the q-ary progress tree algorithm of algorithm AW^T. The existence of p_∞ and q such that clause (a) is satisfied follows directly from the work analysis of AW^T (presented in Section 4.4.3) for p processors and the progress tree with p leaves. Here the constant $q > 0$ can be chosen depending on ξ. More precisely, we can choose q such that algorithm $TLAW(q, t)$ makes $O(p^{1+\xi/2})$ calls to procedure DoJob($\cdot$). It follows that there are positive constants p', c such that for every $p > p'$ the number of calls is at most $c \cdot p^{1+\xi/2}$. We choose the constant p_∞ such that $p_\infty^{\xi/2} > \max\{c, p'\}$. Thus, for every $p > p_\infty > p'$, the number of calls is at most $p_\infty^{\xi/2} \cdot p^{1+\xi/2} \leq p^{1+\xi}$.

Clause (b) follows similarly. In procedure AllTasks, we have a q-ary progress tree with n/p leaves and p processors. Note that the above analysis does not depend on parameter t. □

Let q and p_∞ be the constants satisfying Lemma 4.24 for ξ. We partition the leaves of the progress tree into two sets: A and B. Set A contains all leaves corresponding to the unsaturated jobs j such that $p_j \leq s \; (= \sqrt[3]{t} = p^{2\xi})$. Set B contains all remaining leaves; these correspond to the saturated jobs. By Lemma 4.24 (a) and the counting argument, we get that $|B| \leq p^{1-\xi}$.

We now give some helpful intuition. If a job is saturated, then processors switch to procedure AllTasks causing p^ξ work overhead, which is not too high by the property that $|B| \leq p^{1-\xi}$. If a job is unsaturated, then we perform an increased number of reads to gain the knowledge needed for balancing (this is amortized by a polynomial in p since additional structures have small size depending on p only). What we gain is optimal task balancing (up to a constant factor and a small additive summand)—consequently, we get optimal work plus some a small polynomial in p.

The technical difficulty is to guarantee that the above properties hold in any asynchronous execution, e.g., some processors may think that job j is saturated, while others may think that it is unsaturated. Lemma 4.26 argues how to overcome this. Another difficulty is how to balance (nearly optimally) the chunks in an unsaturated job—this is argued in Lemma 4.25.

Lemma 4.25   *For an unsaturated job, $j \in A$, the total number of local steps spent by processors executing* DoJob(j) *is* $O(\frac{n}{p} + pts \log p) = O(\frac{n}{p} + p^{1+9\xi})$.

Lemma 4.26   *For a saturated job, $j \in B$, the total number of local steps spent by processors executing* DoJob(j) *is* $O(\frac{n}{p} \cdot p^{\xi} + p^{1+9\xi} + p_j \cdot p \log p)$.

We are now ready to prove the work complexity of the algorithm.

Theorem 4.27   *For every constant $\varepsilon > 0$, there is a constant q and a parameter t, such that p-processor algorithm* TLAW(q, t) *on inputs of size n performs work* $O(n + p^{2+\varepsilon})$.

Proof. By Lemma 4.25, we get that the work spent on each job in A is $O(\frac{n}{p} + p^{1+9\xi})$, where $|A| \leq p$. By Lemma 4.26, we get that the work spent on each job in B is $O(\frac{n}{p} \cdot p^{\xi} + p^{1+9\xi} + p_j \cdot p \log p)$. Recall that $|B| \leq p^{1-\xi}$ from the conclusion of Lemma 4.24 and the counting argument. Using Lemma 4.24 (a), we also obtain that $\sum_{j \in B} p_j \leq p^{1+\xi}$. Putting all of the above together with $\varepsilon = 9\xi$, we obtain that the total work $S(n, p)$ is bounded from above as follows.

$$
\begin{aligned}
S(n, p) &= O\left(\frac{n}{p} + p^{1+9\xi}\right) \cdot p + O\left(\sum_{j \in B} \left(\frac{n}{p} \cdot p^{\xi} + p^{1+9\xi} + p_j \cdot p \log p\right)\right) \\
&= O\left(n + p^{2+9\xi}\right) + O\left(|B| \cdot \left(\frac{n}{p} \cdot p^{\xi} + p^{1+9\xi}\right)\right) + O\left(\sum_{j \in B}(p_j \cdot p \log p)\right) \\
&= O(n + p^{2+\varepsilon}),
\end{aligned}
$$

as desired. $\square$

As an immediate corollary, we have that the algorithm is optimal when $p^{2+\varepsilon} \leq n$. (This is, by far, the strongest optimality result as of this writing.)

Corollary 4.28   *For every constant $\varepsilon > 0$, there is a constant q and a parameter t, such that p-processor algorithm* TLAW(q, t) *on inputs of size n performs optimal work* $O(n)$ *when* $p^{2+\varepsilon} \leq n$.

We note that the algorithm, for the case when optimal work is achieved, uses $O(n)$ space (so space is not traded for optimality).

4.6   EXERCISES

4.1. Algorithm W assumes that the linear array representing the progress tree is initially zeroed. What would be the problem if this assumption was not in place? What changes need to be made to the algorithm to remove this assumption? What is the resulting work complexity?

4.2. Algorithm W uses phase W1 for processor enumeration. Assume that this phase is not used, and instead in phase W2, processor allocation is done using permanent processor identifiers (in effect assuming that there are no crashes). Does this affect the correctness of the algorithm? Explain. Does this affect the work efficiency of the algorithm? Explain.

4.3. Algorithm W uses in phase W2 an auxiliary progress tree *aux* for processor allocation. Is it necessary to represent this tree as a *shared* structure? Can this structure be replaced, for example, by some constant number of local variables without affecting the correctness or efficiency of algorithm W?

4.4. Prove Lemmas 4.1–4.3.

4.5. Write a detailed pseudocode for Algorithm W_{os}.

4.6. Algorithm X uses a binary progress tree (represented as a linear array).
(a) Consider using instead a ternary progress tree. Is the complexity of the algorithm affected? Give the details of the modified algorithm (including an allocation strategy) and analyze its work complexity.
(b) Using the intuition gained in (a), analyze the algorithm for any q-ary progress tree, $q > 3$ being a constant.

4.7. Consider the same questions as in Exercise 4.1 for algorithm X.

4.8. Algorithm X solves the *Do-All* problem with asynchronous processors.
(a) Discuss algorithmic modifications needed to solve the *Do-All* problem with synchronous processors under detectable crashes and restarts. In this model, a processor that crashes may recover, and it is aware of the crash. Furthermore, a restarted processor can join the computation at a predefined step (to resynchronize such processor with other processors).
(b) Show that work complexity of the algorithm remains the same.

4.9. Write a detailed pseudocode for Algorithm *Groote*.

4.10. Consider the same questions as in Exercise 4.1 for algorithm AW^T.

4.11. What algorithmic paradigm(s) (Section 3.1) does algorithm $\text{TLAW}(q, t)$ implement? What technique(s) (Section 3.2) does it use for this purpose? Explain your answers.

4.7   BIBLIOGRAPHICAL NOTES

Algorithm W of Kanellakis and Shvartsman [54, 55], is the first *Do-All* algorithm in the shared-memory model. Martel proved the tightest upper bound (Lemma 4.4) for algorithm W. Kedem, Palem, Raghunathan, and Spirakis [57] present a variation of algorithm W that has the same upper bound and that uses additional data structures to enable local optimizations. Georgiou, Russell, and Shvartsman [38] presented a failure-sensitive analysis of algorithm W that shows precisely how the number of crashes $f < p$ relates with the efficiency of the algorithm. In particular, they showed that algorithm W has work $S = O(n + \log n \log p / \log(p/f))$ when $f \leq p \log p$, and work $S = O(n + \log n \log p / \log \log p)$ when $f > p \log p$. The presentation of Algorithm W in Section 4.1 follows that of Kanellakis and Shvartsman in [55].

Kanellakis, Michailidis, and Shvartsman [53] developed a deterministic synchronous algorithm, called algorithm $W_{\mathrm{CR/W}}^{\mathrm{opt}}$, that solves *Do-All* under processor crashes while controlling the read and write memory access concurrency. The algorithm uses the same data structures as algorithm W, but it introduces and uses two additional data structures to control the memory access concurrency: (a) *processor priority trees* are used to determine which processors are allowed to read or write each shared location that has to be accessed concurrently by more than one processor, and (b) *broadcast arrays* are used to disseminate values among readers and writers. The write concurrency, denoted ω, measures the redundant write memory accesses as follows: Consider a step of a synchronous parallel computation, where a particular location is written by $x \leq p$ processors. Then $x - 1$ of these writes are "redundant", because a single write should suffice. Hence, the write concurrency for this step is $x - 1$. The read concurrency, denoted ρ, is measured in a similar manner. Algorithm $W_{\mathrm{CR/W}}^{\mathrm{opt}}$ was shown to have work $S = O(n + p \log^2 n \log^2 p / \log \log n)$, write concurrency $\omega \leq f$ and read concurrency $\rho \leq f \log n$, f being the number of crashes. Later, Georgiou, Russell, and Shvartsman [40] presented a failure-sensitive analysis on the work of algorithm $W_{\mathrm{CR/W}}^{\mathrm{opt}}$. They showed that the algorithm achieves work $S = O(n + p \log^2 n \log^2 p / \log(p/f))$ when $f \leq p / \log p$, and work $S = O(n + p \log^2 n \log^2 p / \log \log p)$ when $f > p / \log p$.

Buss, Kanellakis, Ragde, and Shvartsman [16] present algorithm X in the fail-stop model with detectable restarts and asynchronous settings. López-Ortiz [68] showed the best known lower bound of $S = \Omega(n \log^2 n / \log \log n)$ for algorithm X in the fail-stop no-restart model. The presentation of Algorithm X in Section 4.2 follows that of Kanellakis and Shvartsman in [55].

Algorithm AW^T is named after Anderson and Woll [10], who developed several efficient algorithms for the asynchronous model. They formulate the permutation-based approach to solving the *Do-All* problem, proposing the notion of *contention* of permutations. Showing the existence of suitable permutations, they proved that the work of algorithm AW^T is $O(n^{1+\varepsilon})$ for any $\varepsilon > 0$. Naor and Roth [78] show how to construct such permutations. The notion of *left-to-right* (or *right-to-left*) maxima is due to Knuth [59] (page 13). The presentation of Algorithm AW^T in Section 4.4 follows that of Kanellakis and Shvartsman in [55].

Groote, Hesselink, Mauw, and Vermeulen [47] present an algorithm, which we call algorithm *Groote* in Section 4.3, that has work $S = O(np^{\log(\frac{x+1}{x})})$ where $x = n^{\frac{1}{\log p}}$. The authors argue that their algorithm performs better than $\mathrm{AW^T}$ under practical circumstances where $p \ll n$, e.g., when $n = p^2$. Here we presented a simpler analysis of this algorithm.

Given that work optimality for *Do-All* cannot be achieved when $p = \Theta(n)$, Malewicz [70] presents the first qualitative advancement in the search for optimality by exhibiting a deterministic asynchronous algorithm that has work $S = O(n + p^4 \log n)$ using $p < n$. The algorithm obtains optimal work for a non-trivial number p of processors, where $p = \sqrt[4]{n/\log n}$. This compares favorably to all previously known deterministic algorithms that require as much as $\omega(n)$ work when $p = n^{1/c}$, for any fixed $c > 1$. (The algorithm uses Test-And-Set instructions, as opposed to the previous algorithms that used only atomic Read/Write instructions.)

Using different techniques, Kowalski and Shvartsman [66] exhibited an algorithm, presented as algorithm *TwoLevelAW* in Section 4.5, that has work complexity $S = O(n + p^{2+\varepsilon})$, achieving optimality for an even larger range of processors, specifically for $p = O(n^{1/(2+\varepsilon)})$. (The algorithm uses only atomic Read/Write instructions.)

CHAPTER 5

Message-Passing Algorithms

In this chapter, we consider the *Do-All* problem in the message-passing model. We start by showing how to solve *Do-All* by emulating shared memory in message-passing systems, then present algorithms that solve *Do-All* using message passing directly. In particular, we present the following algorithms:

- Algorithms X_{MP} and AW_{MP}^T: These algorithms emulate the asynchronous shared-memory algorithms X (Section 4.2) and AW^T (Section 4.4), respectively, in the message-passing model with processor crashes. The algorithms follow a hybrid local/global allocation paradigm depending on the type of local information. Algorithm X_{MP} solves the *Do-All* problem for $1 \leq p \leq n$ with work $O(\max\{r, d, a\}\, n\, p^{\log_2(3/2)})$ and message complexity $O(r\, n\, p^{\log_2(3/2)})$, where $r \leq p$ is an emulation parameter, d is a bound on the message delay, and a is a bound on the processors message response delay (d and a are unknown to the processors). Algorithm AW_{MP}^T solves the *Do-All* problem for $1 \leq p \leq n$ and any $\varepsilon > 0$ with work $O(\max\{r, d, a\}\, n\, p^{\varepsilon})$ and message complexity $O(r\, n\, p^{\varepsilon})$.

- Algorithm *AN*: This is an algorithm in the global allocation paradigm for synchronous systems with processor crashes. It solves the *Do-All* problem for $1 \leq p \leq n$ with work $O((n + p \log p / \log \log p) \log f)$ and message complexity $O(n + p \log p / \log \log p + fp)$, where $f < p$ is a bound on the number of processor crashes. The correctness and efficiency of the algorithm rely on the assumption of reliable multicast.

- Algorithm *GKS*: This is another algorithm for synchronous systems with processor crashes. This algorithm has work complexity $O(n + p \log^3 p)$ and message complexity $O(p^{1+2\varepsilon})$ for any $\varepsilon > 0$. Unlike algorithm *AN*, it does not rely on reliable multicast. Instead, it implements a combination of the global allocation paradigm and the hashed allocation paradigm for efficiently sharing information among processors; it uses a gossip algorithm as a building block and makes use of permutations and expander graphs.

- Algorithms KS_{AW} and KS_{PA}: These algorithms solve *Do-All* in asynchronous systems with processor crashes. The algorithms in the family KS_{AW} are modeled after the shared-memory algorithm AW^T (Section 4.4) and use permutations in the same way. Given any constant $\varepsilon > 0$, there is an algorithm in the family KS_{AW} that solves *Do-All* for $1 \leq p \leq n$ with work $S = O(np^{\varepsilon} + p\, d\lceil n/d\rceil^{\varepsilon})$ and message complexity $O(p \cdot S)$, where d is a bound on the message delay. Algorithm KS_{PA} relies directly on permutation schedules, as opposed to the algorithms in the family KS_{AW} that rely indirectly through algorithm AW^T. Algorithm KS_{PA} solves

Do-All for $1 \leq p \leq n$ with work $S = O(n \log p + p \min\{n, d\} \log(2 + n/d))$ and message complexity $O(p \cdot S)$.

5.1   SOLVING DO-ALL THROUGH SHARED-MEMORY EMULATION

The two major multiprocessor computation paradigms are the shared-memory paradigm and the message-passing paradigm. Developing efficient algorithms that can tolerate component failures and timing delays for these models has been a goal for algorithm designers for a long time. It has been observed that, in many cases, it is easier to develop algorithms for the shared-memory model than for the message-passing model. Consequently, in such cases, there is value in developing an algorithm first for the shared-memory model (such as algorithms in Chapter 4) and then automatically converting it to run in the message-passing model.

Among the important results in this area are the algorithms of Attiya, Bar-Noy, and Dolev who showed that it is possible to emulate shared memory robustly in message-passing systems. It was shown that any wait-free algorithm for the shared-memory model that uses atomic single-writer/multi-reader registers can be emulated in the message-passing model where processors or links are subject to crash failures. The construction is based on replicating shared-memory locations among the processors, then using processor majorities to guarantee consistency. Thus, this approach is able to tolerate scenarios where any minority of processors are disabled or are unable to communicate. The emulation uses a procedure that broadcasts messages and collects responses from any majority of processors.

In this section, we present an approach to constructing algorithms for *Do-All* that is based on shared-memory algorithms layered over a quorum-based emulation of shared-memory in message-passing systems. We demonstrate this approach by obtaining and analyzing the emulations of shared-memory algorithm X (Section 4.2) and algorithm AW^T (Section 4.4) in message-passing systems.

5.1.1   MESSAGE-PASSING SETTING, QUORUMS, AND ADVERSITY

Our distributed system consists of p asynchronous processors with unique processor identifiers (PID) from the set $\mathcal{P} = \{0, \ldots, p - 1\}$. Processors communicate by passing messages and have no access to shared memory. Message delivery is unreliable and unordered, but messages are not corrupted. If a system delivers multiple messages to a processor, it can process these messages in one local time step. Similarly, if a processor has several messages to send, the messages can be sent during a single local time step.

Quorums.   We are going to provide a shared-memory abstraction in message-passing systems using *quorum configurations*. A quorum configuration (or system) is a collection of sets, called *quorums*, where every pair of sets intersect. Quorums can be seen as generalized majorities whose intersection property can be used to provide data consistency.

Definition 5.1   Let $C = \{Q_i\}$ be a collection of subsets of processor identifiers, such that for all $Q_i, Q_j \in C$, we have $Q_i \cap Q_j \neq \emptyset$. Then C is a *quorum configuration*. We use $mem(C) = \cup Q_i$ to denote the set of processor identifiers appearing in read and write quorums, and $size(C)$ to denote the total number of identifiers, that is, $size(C) = |mem(C)|$.

We note that to ensure liveness in algorithms using quorums, at least one quorum must be available to the computation.

Adversity.   The adversary may cause message loss, delays (asynchrony), and processor crash failures.

Note that with the standard assumption that initially all tasks are known to all processors, the *Do-All* problem can be solved by a communication-oblivious algorithm where each processor performs all tasks. Such a solution has work $S = \Theta(n \cdot p)$, and requires no communication. However, for an algorithm to be interesting, it must be better than the oblivious algorithm, and in particular, it must have subquadratic work complexity. However, if messages can be delayed for a "long time" (e.g., $\Theta(n)$ time), then the processors cannot coordinate their activities, leading to an immediate lower bound on work of $\Omega(p \cdot n)$.

Given these observations, we are interested in settings where processors are asynchronous, but where there is an upper bound d on message delay. Additionally, we assume that when a processor receives a message requiring a reply, it can send the reply in at most a time units. The bounds d and a need not be constant, and they are unknown to the processors—the algorithms must be correct for any d and a.

We constrain the adversary in two ways:
(1) the adversary must respect the bounds d and a defined above; we call it (d, a)-adversary, and
(2) when an algorithm uses a quorum configuration C, the adversary can cause any processor crashes as long as the processors of at least one quorum $Q \in C$ remains operational and are able to communicate; we call this adversary($\{C\}$).

Let $Q = \{C_i\}$ be the set of all quorum configurations C_i used by an algorithm. We denote by (d, a)-adversary(Q) the adversary that respects the above two constraints for each configuration C_i. When Q is implied by the context, we use the simplified notation (d, a)-adversary.

Remark 5.2   Our definition of the adversary is somewhat involved for several reasons. If the adversary is allowed to cause arbitrary message delays, then communication is impossible and work complexity of any algorithm becomes trivially quadratic. Hence, we posit an upper bound on message delays. If the adversary is allowed to prevent processors from sending replies expediently, then a similar situation results. Hence, we posit an upper bound on the time it takes a processor to send a reply. Lastly, our approach relies on the use of quorum systems. If the adversary is allowed to cause failures that disable the quorum systems used by the algorithms, then shared memory cannot be emulated, again leading to processors acting in isolation and performing quadratic work. Hence, we assume that quorum systems are not disabled.

5.1.2   SHARED-MEMORY EMULATION SERVICE AM

We now present an atomic memory service that we call AM. The algorithm implements multi-reader/multi-writer shared memory in asynchronous message-passing systems that are prone to message loss and processor crashes. In order to achieve fault-tolerance and availability, we replicate memory cells at several network locations. In order to maintain memory consistency, the algorithm uses quorum configurations. We now describe the implementation of the service.

For an emulated shared location z, we use the quorum configuration $C_z = \{Q_i\}$. Every processor $i \in mem(C_z)$ maintains a replica of the value of z, $value_{i,z}$ and a tag associated with the replica, $tag_{i,z} = \langle seq, pid \rangle$, where seq is a sequence number and pid is the id of the processor that performed the write of that value to z. Tags are compared lexicographically. Each new write assigns a unique tag, where the originating process id is used to break ties. These tags are used to determine an ordering of the write operations, and therefore determine the values that subsequent read operations return.

Read and write operations consist of two phases, a Get phase and a Put phase, each of which obtains information from some quorum of replicas. The pseudocode is given in Figure 5.1. The protocol of each phase is formulated in terms of point-to-point messages. First, the messages are sent to the members of the quorum configuration, then the replies are collected until a complete quorum responds.

$read_\rho(z, v)$

Get: Broadcast $\langle get, z, \rho \rangle$ to $mem(C_z)$.
Await responses $\langle z, val, tag \rangle$ from all members of some $Q \in C_z$.
Let v be the value that corresponds to the maximum tag $maxtag$ received from Q.

Put: Broadcast $\langle put, z, v, maxtag, \rho \rangle$ to $mem(C_z)$
Await responses $\langle ack, z, val, maxtag \rangle$ from all members of some $Q \in C_z$.
Return v.

end.

Upon $receive(\langle get, z, \rho \rangle)$ at replica i
Send $\langle z, value_{i,z}, tag_{i,z} \rangle$ to ρ.

$write_w(z, v)$

Get: Broadcast $\langle get, z, w \rangle$ to $mem(C_z)$.
Await responses $\langle z, val, tag \rangle$ from all members of some $Q \in C_z$.
Let $maxtag = \langle seq, pid \rangle$ be the maximim tag received from Q.

Put: Let $newtag = \langle seq + 1, w \rangle$.
Broadcast $\langle put, z, v, newtag, w \rangle$ to $mem(C_z)$
Await responses $\langle ack, z, val, newtag \rangle$ from all members of some $Q \in C_z$.

end.

Upon $receive(\langle put, z, v, t, \rho \rangle)$ at replica i
if $t > tag_{i,z}$ **then**
Set $val_{i,z}$ to v and $tag_{i,z}$ to t. **fi**
Send $\langle ack, z, v, t \rangle$ to ρ.

Figure 5.1: Atomic memory service AM.

The read and write operations are similar. Assume that a read operation is initiated at node ρ. First, in the Get phase, node ρ broadcasts a request to the members of the configuration and awaits responses from at least one quorum. It then determines the most recent available tag and its associated value. In the Put phase, node ρ broadcasts another message, containing the value it obtained and awaits acknowledgments from any quorum. Thus, the second phase of a read operation propagates the latest tag and value discovered in the first phase to some quorum.

If the operation is a write operation, the main difference is in the Put phase. The writing node w chooses a new tag by incrementing the maximum sequence number and using its own identifier w. Node w then propagates the new tag, along with the new value to some quorum.

The correctness (atomicity) of the protocol follows from the use of quorums, specifically using the property that any two quorums intersect. Thus, in the Get phase, read and write operations obtain the tag that is at least as large as any tag of a complete write. In the Put phase, read and write operations wait until the value (to be returned by the read and to be written by the write, respectively) becomes known to the members of a complete quorum. This guarantees that all writes are ordered by their tags, and that reads return the value of the immediately preceding complete write. The atomicity of the implementation follows.

Each of the two phases of the read or write operations, accesses quorums of processors, incurring a round-trip message delay. Assuming that there is an upper bound d on message delays and that local processing is negligible, this means that each phase can take at most $2d$ time. Given that all operations consist of two phases, each operation takes at most $4d$ time.

5.1.3   THE MESSAGE-PASSING ALGORITHM X_{MP}

We now present the emulation of the shared-memory algorithm X (Section 4.2) in the message-passing model. We call this algorithm X_{MP}. The new algorithm follows a hybrid local/global allocation paradigm depending on the type of local information. When the locally available information indicates that certain progress was made globally by the algorithm, then this local information is used. However, when performing activities that a processor believes have not been done elsewhere (based on local information), then the new knowledge is propagated globally by means of shared-memory emulation.

In algorithm X_{MP}, the data that used to be stored in shared memory by algorithm X is replicated among the processors. Each processor has a local progress tree containing the replicas of the vertices used by the shared-memory algorithm. Specific vertices are additionally *owned* by certain designated processors as described below (each processor has a replica of each vertex, but not all processors are owners).

Memory Management.   The progress tree is stored in the array $done[1, \ldots, 2p-1]$. This array is replicated at each processor.

We use the index x to denote the vertex $done[x]$ of the progress tree. For each x, we define $own(x)$ to be some non-empty subset of processor identifiers that will act as the *owners* of the vertex $done[x]$. These processors are responsible for maintaining consistent (atomic) replicas of the vertex by participating in memory service AM. For this purpose we posit, for each x, a quorum configuration $\mathcal{C}_x$, such that $mem(\mathcal{C}_x) = own(x)$. For a set Y containing some indices of the progress tree, we let $own(Y) = \cup_{x \in Y} own(x)$.

When a processor needs to access the global copy of a vertex x within the progress tree, it uses the memory service AM with quorum configuration $\mathcal{C}_x$ as described in Section 5.1.2. Alternatively, when the algorithm determines that accessing the local value in the progress tree is sufficient, it uses this local value. We next explain this in detail.

Algorithm Description. Algorithm X_{MP} for each processor has the structure identical to algorithm X, except that each processor has a local copy of the progress tree and may use memory service AM to access the vertices of the tree. The processors access the progress tree vertices as follows:

- If a processor needs to read vertex x, and its local value is 0, it uses AM to obtain a fresh copy of x.

- If a processor needs to read vertex x, and its local value is 1 (i.e., done), the processor uses this value—this is safe because once a progress tree vertex is marked done, it is never unmarked.

- If a processor needs to write (always value 1 according to the algorithm) to vertex x, and its local value is 0, it uses AM to write to x, and it updates the local value accordingly.

- If a processor needs to write vertex x, and its local value is already 1, the processor does not need to write—once a progress tree vertex is marked done, it is never unmarked.

The tasks are known to all processors and are associated with the leaves of the tree (as in algorithm X). Initially, the values stored in each local tree are all zeros. Each processor starts at the leaf of its local tree according to its PID, and it continues executing the algorithm until the root of its local tree is set to 1.

Algorithm AW^T (Section 4.4) can be emulated in the message-passing system using the memory service AM in essentially the same way. Recall that the main distinction is that algorithm X uses a binary tree, while algorithm AW^T uses a q-ary tree.

Correctness. We claim that algorithm X_{MP} correctly solves the *Do-All* problem. This follows from the correctness of algorithm X with the following additional observations:

(1) The correctness of the memory service AM implies that if a vertex of the progress tree is ever determined to be 1, it must be previously set to 1.

(2) A processor sets a vertex of the progress tree to 1 if and only if it verifies that its children (if any) are set to 1, or the processor performed the task(s) associated with the vertex when it is a leaf.

(3) A processor leaves a subtree if and only if the subtree contains no unfinished work and its root is marked accordingly.

Identical argument is used to show the correctness of the q-ary tree algorithm based on algorithm AW^T.

Quorum Configuration Parameterization. We use the size of the *owner* sets, $|own(\cdot)|$, to parameterize algorithm X_{MP}. This will allow us later to study the trade-off between the algorithm efficiency and fault-tolerance.

For a specific algorithm instance that uses the set of data objects Y (e.g., the nodes of the progress tree), we assume for each object $x \in Y$ a *quorum configuration* C_x with $mem(C_x) = own(x)$ as discussed before. We let r to be the size of the largest quorum configuration, that is, $r = \max_x\{|own(x)|\}$.

We define $\mathcal{Q}$ to be the set of all quorum configurations used by the algorithm, that is $\mathcal{Q} = \{C_x : x \in Y\}$.

We now discuss some specific assignment of vertices to owners in algorithm X_{MP}. We assume that all *owner* sets in the system have the same size (this is done for simplicity of analysis only—the algorithm is correct for any quorum configurations and with owner sets of different sizes). Each vertex of the progress tree is thus owned by r processors. This results in $\binom{p}{r}^{2n-1}$ combinations of "owned" replica placements. Examples 5.3 and 5.4 illustrate two possible placements, when $n = p$.

Example 5.3 Let n and r be powers of 2. The processors are divided into n/r segments with contiguous PIDs. Each segment owns the leaves of the progress tree corresponding to its processors' PIDs along with the vertices in the subtree of the owned leaves. Moreover, each vertex at the height greater than $\log r$ is owned by the owner of its left child. It is not hard to show that the processors with $PID = 0, \ldots, r-1$ (the first segment) own $2r - 1 + \log(n/r)$ vertices but processors with $PID = n - r, \ldots, n - 1$ (the last segment) own $2r - 1$ vertices. (Therefore, the first segment processors are more likely to be busier than other processors responding to messages as replica owners). Figure 5.1.3 illustrates this example where $n = 16$ and $r = 4$. Here, $\mu(\{1,2,4,8,9,16,17,18,19\}) = \{P_0, P_1, P_2, P_3\}, \mu(\{5, 10, 11, 20, 21, 22, 23\}) = \{P_4, P_5, P_6, P_7\}$, etc. (to avoid confusion between tree indices and PIDs, we use P_i to denote the processor with PID i).

Example 5.4 The processors are divided into n/r segments, and each segment has r processors with contiguous PIDs. Vertex i of the progress tree is owned by the $j + 1^{th}$ segment, where $i \overset{r}{\equiv} j$. Since there are $2n - 1$ vertices in the progress tree, each processor owns either $\lfloor r(2n - 1)/n \rfloor$ or $\lceil r(2n - 1)/n \rceil$ vertices. Hence, there is an almost uniform distribution of vertices among the owners.

5.1.4 ALGORITHM ANALYSIS

We assess the efficiency of our algorithm against the (d, a)-adversary$(\mathcal{Q})$ (that respects the delays d and a, and that does not disable the quorum system $\mathcal{Q}$). We start with the following lemma about the cost of reads and writes.

Lemma 5.5 *Using the memory service AM, each read or write operation contributes at most $4(r + d) + 2a$ to the work complexity and at most $4r$ to the total number of messages.*

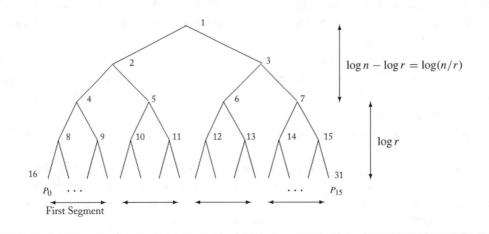

Figure 5.2: Owners for $n = 16$ and $r = 4$ (in Example 5.3).

Proof. The processor performing a read or a write operation uses the service AM with quorum configurations of size at most r. Thus, each quorum consists of no more than r processors. In a single phase (see the overview of the service AM in Section 5.1.2), it takes no more than r units of work to send messages to r processors. After sending the last message, the processor may have to wait additional $2d + a$ time steps to receive the responses. If some r' responses are received, then it takes at most r units of work to process them (since $r' \leq r$). Thus, it takes time $2r + 2d + a$ to process a single phase. The second phase similarly takes time $2r + 2d + a$. Thus, the two phases of an operation take time $4(r + d) + 2a$.

Each stage involves sending r messages and receiving no more than r responses. The total number of messages is no more than $4r$. □

Now we present the work and communication analyses.

Theorem 5.6   Algorithm X_{MP} solves *Do-All* of size n with $p \leq n$ processors, for (d, a)-adversary($\mathcal{Q}$), with work $S(n, p) = O(\max\{r, d, a\}n\, p^{\log_2 \frac{3}{2}})$ and message complexity $M(n, p) = O(r\, n\, p^{\log_2 \frac{3}{2}})$.

Proof. Recall that the work of algorithm X is $S_X = O(n\, p^{\log_2 \frac{3}{2}})$, counting local operations, and shared-memory read/write operations. In algorithm X_{MP}, each local operation takes one local time step, and each read or write operation takes time $4(r + d) + 2a$ by Lemma 5.5. Thus, the total work is $S(n, p) = (4(r + d) + 2a) \cdot S_X = (4(r + d) + 2a) \cdot O(n\, p^{\log_2 \frac{3}{2}}) = O(\max\{r, d, a\}p\, n^{\log_2 \frac{3}{2}})$.

From the analysis of algorithm X, we note that the vertices of the progress tree are updated by the processors a total of $O(n\, p^{\log_2 \frac{3}{2}})$ times. In algorithm X_{MP}, by Lemma 5.5, each update contributes $4r$ messages to the message complexity. Thus, the total number of messages is $M_{n,p} = 4r \cdot S_x = O(r\ n\ p^{\log_2 \frac{3}{2}})$. □

The above analysis approach is applied in the same way when using algorithm AW^T as the basis, together with the same memory emulation approach. Call the resulting algorithm AW^T_{MP}. Given that work complexity of algorithm AW^T is $O(n\ p^\varepsilon)$, the following result follows.

Theorem 5.7   Algorithm AW^T_{MP} solves *Do-All* of size n with $p \leq n$ processors, for (d, a)-adversary$(\mathcal{Q})$, with work $S(n, p) = O(\max\{r, d, a\}\ n\ p^\varepsilon)$, and with message complexity $M(n, p) = O(r\ n\ p^\varepsilon)$, for any $\varepsilon > 0$.

In order to give an explicit result regarding the magnitude of processor crashes, we use majority quorum systems. Given r, we use quorum systems with all majorities of size $\lceil (r + 1)/2 \rceil$, so that we can tolerate the crashes of any minority of processors in a configuration. The next result follows immediately.

Theorem 5.8   Algorithm X_{MP} tolerates any pattern of f failures, for $f \leq \lfloor (r - 1)/2 \rfloor$.

We make the following observations regarding the trade-off between efficiency and fault-tolerance. The algorithm is most efficient when $r = 1$, that is when each shared memory location has a single owner; unfortunately, this is not fault-tolerant at all. Thus, we are interested in parameter-izations that achieve *subquadratic* work and communication, while maximizing the fault-tolerance of the algorithm. We obtain this by constraining r on the basis of Theorem 5.6 in the following corollary.

Corollary 5.9   *Algorithm X_{MP} solves Do-All of size n, with $p \leq n$ processors, and for any (d, a)-adversary$(\mathcal{Q})$, with subquadratic (in n and p) work and message complexity of $O(n\ p^\delta)$ with $\log_2 \frac{3}{2} < \delta < 1$, when the parameter r is $O(p^{\delta - \log_2 \frac{3}{2}})$, and when $d, a = O(r)$.*

Note that if δ is chosen to be close to $\log_2 3/2$ (≈ 0.59), the algorithm tolerates only a constant number of failures, but it is as work-efficient as its shared-memory counterpart. As δ approaches 1, the complexity remains subquadratic, while the fault-tolerance of the algorithm improves. In particular, when δ is close to 1, the algorithm is able to tolerate about $O(p^{0.41})$ crashes.

Of a more theoretical importance is the following corollary, specializing Theorem 5.7 to obtain subquadratic work and message complexity.

Corollary 5.10   *There exists an algorithm that solves Do-All of size n, with $p \leq n$ processors, and for any (d, a)-adversary$(\mathcal{Q})$, with subquadratic (in n and p) work and message complexity of $O(n\ p^\delta)$ with $0 < \varepsilon < \delta < 1$, when the parameter r is $O(p^{\delta - \varepsilon})$, and when $d, a = O(r)$.*

Here we observe that to improve work we need to reduce δ and thus ε. The trade-off is that smaller δ (and ε) diminishes r and thus lowers the number of failures that can be tolerated. (We also note that diminishing ε leads to increasingly large constants hidden in the big-O expression for work of algorithm AW^T and thus also in the work of its emulation.)

5.2   ALGORITHM *AN*

In this section, we present and analyze a synchronous algorithm for the *Do-All* problem that uses crash-prone message-passing processors. The algorithm, called Algorithm *AN*, combines local data structures and the multiple-coordinator technique, as discussed in Section 3.3 to accumulate, approximating the global allocation paradigm, the knowledge about the progress of the computation.

Recall from Section 3.3, that the multiple-coordinator technique uses an aggressive coordination paradigm that permits multiple processors to act as coordinators concurrently. The number of coordinators is managed adaptively. When failures of coordinators disrupt the progress of the computation, the number of coordinators is increased; when the failures subside, a single coordinator is appointed. As discussed, this technique is effective when communication is reliable. If a processor sends a message to another operational processor and when the message arrives at the destination, the processor is still operational, then the message is received. Moreover, if an operational processor sends a multicast message and then fails, then either the message is sent to all destinations or to none at all (that is, reliable multicast is available). Such multicast is received by all operational processors.

There are several reasons for considering solutions with such reliable multicast. First of all, in a distributed setting where processors cooperate closely, it becomes increasingly important to assume the ability to perform efficient and reliable broadcast or multicast. This assumption might not hold for extant WANs, but broadcast LANs (e.g., Ethernet and bypass rings) have the property that if the sender is transmitting a multicast message, then the message is sent to all destinations. Of course, this does not guarantee that such multicast will be received; however, when a processor is unable to receive or process a message, e.g., due to unavailable buffer space or failure of the network interface hardware at the destination, this can be interpreted as a failure of the receiver.

Algorithm *AN* is tolerant of f crash-failures ($f < p$) and has work complexity $S = O((n + p \log p / \log \log p) \log f)$ and message complexity $M = O(n + p \log p / \log \log p + fp)$. We note that Algorithm *AN* forms the basis for another algorithm for crash-prone processors that are able to restart (see Bibliographic Notes).

5.2.1   DATA STRUCTURES AND PHASES OF ALGORITHM *AN*

Algorithm *AN* proceeds in a *loop* that is repeated until all the tasks are executed. A single iteration of the loop is called a *phase*. A phase consists of three consecutive *stages*. Each stage consists of three steps (thus a phase consists of 9 steps). In each stage, processors use the first step to receive messages sent in the previous stage, the second step to perform local computation, and the third step to send messages. We refer to these three steps as the *receive* substage, the *compute* substage, and the *send* substage.

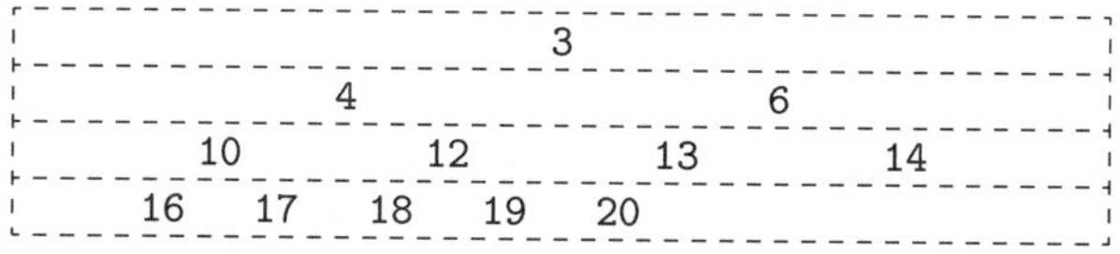

Figure 5.3: A local view for phase $\ell + 2$.

Coordinators and workers. A processor can be a *coordinator* of a given phase. All processors (including coordinators) are *workers* in a given phase. Coordinators are responsible for recording progress, while workers perform tasks and report on that to the coordinators. In the first phase, one processor acts as the coordinator. There may be multiple coordinators in subsequent phases.

The number of processors that assume the coordinator role is determined by the *martingale principle*: if none of the expected coordinators survive through the entire phase, then the number of coordinators for the next phase is doubled. Whenever at least one coordinator survives a given phase, the number of coordinators for the next phase is reduced to one.

If at least one processor acts as a coordinator during a phase and it completes the phase without failing, we say that the phase is *attended*, the phase is *unattended* otherwise.

Local views. Processors assume the role of a coordinator based on their local knowledge. During the computation, each processor w maintains a list $L_w = \langle q_1, q_2, ..., q_k \rangle$ of supposed live processors. We call such list a *local view*. The processors in L_w are partitioned into *layers* consisting of consecutive sublists of L_w: $L_w = \langle \Lambda^0, \Lambda^1, ..., \Lambda^j \rangle^1$. The number of processors in layer Λ^{i+1}, for $i = 0, 1, ..., j - 1$, is the double of the number of processors in layer Λ^i. Layer Λ^j may contain less processors. When $\Lambda^0 = \langle q_1 \rangle$, the local view can be visualized as a binary tree rooted at processor q_1, where nodes are placed from left to right with respect to the linear order given by L_w. Thus, in a tree-like local view, layer Λ^0 consists of processor q_1, layer Λ^i consists of 2^i consecutive processors starting at processor q_{2^i} and ending at processor $q_{2^{i+1}-1}$, with the exception of the very last layer that may contain a smaller number of processors.

Example 5.11 Suppose that we have a system of $p = 31$ processors. Assume that for phase ℓ, all processors are in the local view of a worker w, in order of processor identifier, and that the view is a tree-like view (e.g., at the beginning of the computation, for $\ell = 0$). If in phase ℓ, processors $1, 5, 7, 8, 21, 22, 23, 24, 31$ fail (hence phase ℓ is unattended) and in phase $\ell + 1$, processors $2, 9, 11, 15, 25, 26, 27, 28, 29, 30$ fail (phase $\ell + 1$ is attended by processor 3), then the view of processor w for phase $\ell + 2$ is the one in Figure 5.3. ∎

The local view is used to implement the martingale principle of appointing coordinators as follows. Let $L_{\ell,w} = \langle \Lambda^0, \Lambda^1, ..., \Lambda^j \rangle$ be the local view of worker w at the beginning of phase

---

^{1} For sequences $L = \langle e_1, ..., e_n \rangle$ and $K = \langle d_1, ..., d_m \rangle$, we define $\langle L, K \rangle$ to be the sequence $\langle e_1, ..., e_n, d_1, ..., d_m \rangle$.

ℓ. Processor w expects processors in layer Λ^0 to coordinate phase ℓ; if no processor in layer Λ^0 completes phase ℓ, then processor w expects processors in layer Λ^1 to coordinate phase $\ell + 1$; in general, processor w expects processors in layer Λ^i to coordinate phase $\ell + i$ if processors in all previous layers Λ^k, $\ell \le k < \ell + i$, did not complete phase $\ell + k$. The local view is updated at the end of each phase.

Phase structure and task allocation. The structure of a phase of the algorithm is as follows. Each processor w keeps its local information about the set of tasks already performed, denoted D_w, and the set of live processors, denoted P_w, as known by processor w. Set D_w is always an underestimate of the set of tasks actually done, and P_w is always an overestimate of the set of processors that are "available" from the start of the phase. We denote by U_w the set of *unaccounted* tasks, i.e., whose done status is unknown to w. Sets U_w and D_w are related by $U_w = \mathcal{T} \setminus D_w$, where $\mathcal{T}$ is the set of all the tasks. Given a phase ℓ, we use $P_{\ell,w}$, $U_{\ell,w}$ and $D_{\ell,w}$ to denote the values of the corresponding sets at the beginning of phase ℓ.

   Computation starts with phase 0, and any processor q has all processors in $L_{0,q}$ and has $D_{0,q}$ empty. At the beginning of phase ℓ, each worker (that is, each processor) w performs one task according to its local view $L_{\ell,w}$ and its knowledge of the set $U_{\ell,w}$ of unaccounted tasks, using the following *load balancing rule*. Worker w executes the task whose rank is $(i \bmod |U_{\ell,w}|)^{th}$ in the set $U_{\ell,w}$ of unaccounted tasks, where i is the rank of processor w in the local view $L_{\ell,w}$. Then the worker reports the execution of the task to all the processors that, according to the worker's local view, are supposed to be coordinators of phase ℓ. For simplicity, we assume that a processor sends a message to itself when it is both worker and coordinator. Any processor c that, according to its local view, is supposed to be coordinator, gathers reports from the workers, updates its information about $P_{\ell,c}$ and $U_{\ell,c}$ and broadcasts this new information causing the local views to be reorganized.

   We will see that at the beginning of any phase ℓ all live processors have the same local view L_ℓ and the same set U_ℓ of unaccounted tasks and that accounted tasks have been actually executed. A new phase starts if U_ℓ is not empty.

5.2.2   DETAILS OF ALGORITHM *AN*

We now present algorithm *AN* in detail. The algorithm follows the algorithmic structure described in the previous section. The computation starts with phase number 0 and proceeds in a loop until all tasks are known to have been executed. The detailed description of a phase is given in Figure 5.4.

Local view update rule. In phase 0, the local view $L_{0,w}$ of any processor w is a tree-like view containing all the processors in $\mathcal{P}$ ordered by their PIDs. Let $L_{\ell,w} = \langle \Lambda^0, \Lambda^1, ..., \Lambda^j \rangle$ be the local view of processor w for phase ℓ. We distinguish two possible cases.

Case 1: Phase ℓ is unattended. Then the local view of processor w for phase $\ell + 1$ is $L_{\ell+1,w} = \langle \Lambda^1, ..., \Lambda^j \rangle$.

Case 2: Phase ℓ is attended. Then processor w receives `summary` messages from some coordinator in Λ^0. Processor w computes its set P_w as described in stage 3 (we will see that all processors compute

Phase ℓ of algorithm *AN*:

STAGE 1.

RECEIVE: The receive substage is not used.

COMPUTE: Processor w performs task z according to the load balancing rule.

SEND: Processor w sends report(z) to all coordinators, that is, to all processors in layer Λ^0 of its local view $L_{\ell,w}$.

STAGE 2.

RECEIVE: : If processor w is coordinator c, it gathers report messages. For any coordinator c, let $Z = \{z^{r_1}, \ldots, z^{r_k}\}$ be the set of TIDs received from processors $R = \{r_1, \ldots, r_k\}$, respectively.

COMPUTE: Coordinator c sets $D_c \leftarrow D_c \cup Z$ and $P_c \leftarrow R$.

SEND: Coordinator c multicasts summary(D_c, P_c) to processors in P_c.

STAGE 3.

RECEIVE: Processor w receives some set $\{$summary(D^i, P^i)$\}$ of messages (we will see in the analysis that these messages are in fact identical).

COMPUTE: Processor w sets $D_w \leftarrow D^i$ and $P_w \leftarrow P^i$ for an arbitrary i and updates its local view $L_{\ell,w}$ (the update rule is described in detail in the text).

SEND: The send substage is not used.

Figure 5.4: Algorithm *AN*: phase ℓ of processor w.

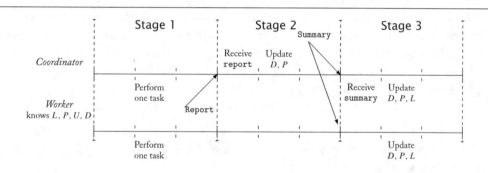

Figure 5.5: One phase of algorithm *AN*.

the same set P_w). The local view $L_{\ell+1,w}$ of w for phase $\ell + 1$ is a tree-like local view containing the processors in P_w ordered by their PIDs.

Figure 5.5 gives a pictorial description of a single phase of algorithm *AN* with its three stages, each consisting of receive, compute, and send substages.

5.2.3   ANALYSIS OF ALGORITHM *AN*

Before we analyze the performance of algorithm *AN*, we argue that the algorithm correctly solves the *Do-All* problem with crash-prone processors and under the assumption of reliable multicast.

Correctness of Algorithm *AN*. Given an execution of the algorithm, we enumerate the phases. We denote the attended phases of the execution by $\alpha_1, \alpha_2, \ldots$, etc. We denote by π_i the sequence of unattended phases between the attended phases α_i and α_{i+1}. We refer to π_i as the ith (unattended) period; an unattended period can be empty. Hence, the computation proceeds as follows: unattended period π_0, attended phase α_1, unattended period π_1, attended phase α_2, and so on.

To show correctness, one needs to argue that after a finite number of attended phases, the algorithm terminates. That is, if the algorithm correctly solves the problem, it must be the case that there are no tasks left unaccounted after a certain phase α_τ.

We first argue that at the beginning of each (attended) phase, every live processor has consistent knowledge of the ongoing computation.

Lemma 5.12   *In any execution of algorithm AN, for any two processors w, v alive at the beginning of phase ℓ, we have that $L_{\ell,w} = L_{\ell,v}$ and that $U_{\ell,w} = U_{\ell,v}$.*

The above can be shown by induction on the number of phases. Because of Lemma 5.12, we can define $L_\ell = L_{\ell,w}$ for any live processor w as the view at the beginning of phase ℓ, $P_\ell = P_{\ell,w}$ as the set of live processors, $D_\ell = D_{\ell,w}$ as the set of done tasks and $U_\ell = U_{\ell,w}$ as the set of unaccounted tasks at the beginning of phase ℓ. Furthermore, we denote by p_ℓ the cardinality of the set of live processors computed for phase ℓ, i.e., $p_\ell = |P_\ell|$, and by u_ℓ the cardinality of the set of unaccounted tasks for phase ℓ, i.e., $u_\ell = |U_\ell|$. We have $p_1 = p$ and $u_0 = n$.

We now argue that the processor and task accounting is accurate.

Lemma 5.13   *In any execution of algorithm AN, if a processor w is alive during the first two stages of phase ℓ, then processor w belongs to P_ℓ.*

Lemma 5.14   *In any execution of algorithm AN, if a task z does not belong to U_ℓ, then it has been executed in one of the phases $1, 2, ..., \ell - 1$.*

Both lemmas can be proved by careful investigation of the code of the algorithm. We next show progress (task execution) properties, which imply the correctness of the algorithm. The first progress property follows for the observation that no task is added to U_ℓ.

Lemma 5.15   *In any execution of algorithm AN, for any phase ℓ, we have that $u_{\ell+1} \leq u_\ell$.*

We now argue that global progress is made in attended phases. This follows from Lemmas 5.13 and 5.15, the definition of an attended phase and the assumption of reliable multicast.

Lemma 5.16   *In any execution of algorithm AN, for any attended phase ℓ, we have that $u_{\ell+1} < u_\ell$.*

The layered structure of the local views, together with the doubling of the coordinators in unattended periods, yield the following result.

Lemma 5.17   *In any execution of algorithm AN, any unattended period consists of at most $\log f$ phases.*

Putting all lemmas together, we get the correctness of Algorithm *AN*.

Theorem 5.18   In any execution of algorithm *AN*, the algorithm terminates with all tasks performed after at most $O(n \log f)$ phases.

Complexity Analysis of Algorithm *AN*. We now analyze the performance of algorithm *AN* in terms of work S and message complexity M.

To assess work S, we consider separately all the attended phases and all the unattended phases of the execution. Let S_a be the part of S spent during all the attended phases and S_u be the part of S spent during all the unattended phases. Hence, we have $S = S_a + S_u$.

Lemma 5.19   *In any execution of algorithm AN with $f < p$, we have $S_a = O(n + p \log p / \log \log p)$.*

Proof. We consider all the attended phases $\alpha_1, \alpha_2, ..., \alpha_\tau$ by subdividing them into two cases.

Case 1: All attended phases α_i such that $p_{\alpha_i} \le u_{\alpha_i}$. The load balancing rule assures that at most one processor is assigned to a task. Hence, the available processor steps used in this case can be charged to the number of tasks executed which is at most $n + f \le n + p$. Hence, $S_1 = O(n + p)$.

Case 2: All attended phases in which $p_{\alpha_i} > u_{\alpha_i}$. We let $d(p)$ stand for $\log p / \log \log p$. We consider the following two subcases.

Subcase 2.1: All attended phases α_i after which $u_{\alpha_{i+1}} < u_{\alpha_i}/d(p)$. Since $u_{\alpha_{i+1}} < u_{\alpha_i} < p_{\alpha_i} < p$ and phase α_τ is the last phase for which $u_\tau > 0$, it follows that subcase 2.1 occurs $O(\log_{d(p)} p)$ times. The quantity $O(\log_{d(p)} p)$ is $O(d(p))$ because $d(p)^{d(p)} = \Theta(p)$. No more than p processors complete such phases; therefore, the part $S_{2.1}$ of S_a spent in this case is

$$S_{2.1} = O\left(p \frac{\log p}{\log \log p}\right).$$

Subcase 2.2: All attended phases α_i after which $u_{\alpha_{i+1}} \ge u_{\alpha_i}/d(p)$. Consider a particular phase α_i. Since in this case $p_{\alpha_i} > u_{\alpha_i}$, by the load balancing rule at least $\lfloor \frac{p_{\alpha_i}}{u_{\alpha_i}} \rfloor$ but no more than $\lceil \frac{p_{\alpha_i}}{u_{\alpha_i}} \rceil$

processors are assigned to each of the u_{α_i} unaccounted tasks. Since $u_{\alpha_{i+1}}$ tasks remain unaccounted after phase α_i, the number of processors that failed during this phase is at least

$$u_{\alpha_{i+1}} \left\lfloor \frac{p_{\alpha_i}}{u_{\alpha_i}} \right\rfloor \geq \frac{u_{\alpha_i}}{d(p)} \cdot \frac{p_{\alpha_i}}{2u_{\alpha_i}} = \frac{p_{\alpha_i}}{2d(p)} .$$

Hence, the number of processors that proceed to phase α_{i+1} is no more than

$$p_{\alpha_i} - \frac{p_{\alpha_i}}{2d(p)} = p_{\alpha_i}\left(1 - \frac{1}{2d(p)}\right) .$$

Let $\alpha_{i_0}, \alpha_{i_1}, \ldots, \alpha_{i_k}$ be the attended phases in this subcase. Since the number of processors in phase α_{i_0} is at most p, the number of processors alive in phase α_{i_j} for $j > 0$ is at most $p(1 - \frac{1}{2d(p)})^j$. Therefore, the part $S_{2.2}$ of S_a spent in this case is bounded as follows:

$$S_{2.2} \leq \sum_{j=0}^{k} p\left(1 - \frac{1}{2d(p)}\right)^j \leq \frac{p}{1 - (1 - \frac{1}{2d(p)})} = p \cdot 2d(p) = O(p \cdot d(p)) .$$

Summing up the contributions of all the cases considered we get S_a:

$$S_a = S_1 + S_{2.1} + S_{2.2} = O\left(n + p\frac{\log p}{\log \log p}\right) ,$$

as desired. □

Lemma 5.20   *In any execution of algorithm AN with $f < p$, we have $S_u = O(S_a \log f)$.*

Proof. The number of processors alive in a phase of the unattended period π_i is at most p_{α_i}, that is the number of processors alive in the attended phase immediately preceding π_i. To cover the case when π_0 is not empty, we let $\alpha_0 = 0$ and $p_{\alpha_0} = |\mathcal{P}| = p$. By Lemma 5.17, the number of phases in period π_i is at most $\log f$. Hence, the part of S_u spent in period π_i is at most $p_{\alpha_i} \log f$. We have

$$S_u \leq \sum_{i=0}^{\tau}(p_{\alpha_i} \log f) = \log f \cdot \sum_{i=1}^{\tau} p_{\alpha_i} \leq (p + S_a)\log f = O(S_a \log f) ,$$

as desired. □

The analysis of algorithm AN can be refined for the range of crashes $f \leq \frac{p}{\log p}$.

Lemma 5.21   *In any execution of algorithm AN with $f \leq \frac{p}{\log p}$, we have $S_a = O\left(n + p\log_{\frac{p}{f}} p\right)$.*

Proof. In the correctness analysis (Lemma 5.12), we have argued that at the beginning of an attended phase α_i the processors have consistent information on the identities and the number of surviving processors p_{α_i}, and the identities and the number of remaining tasks u_{α_i}. Hence, the processors in attended phases can perform perfect load balancing. Therefore, focusing only on the attended phases (and assuming that in the worst case no progress is made in unattended phases), we can obtain the desired result by induction on the number of remaining tasks. □

We now combine the results of the key lemmas to obtain the work complexity of algorithm *AN*.

Theorem 5.22 In any execution of algorithm *AN*, its work complexity is

$$S = O\left(\log f\left(n + p\frac{\log p}{\log(p/f)}\right)\right) \text{ when } f \leq \frac{p}{\log p}, \text{ and}$$

$$S = O\left(\log f\left(n + p\frac{\log p}{\log\log p}\right)\right) \text{ when } \frac{p}{\log p} < f < p.$$

Proof. The total work S is given by $S = S_a + S_u$. The theorem follows from Lemmas 5.19 and 5.20 for $f < p$, and from Lemma 5.21 for $\frac{p}{\log p} < f < p$. □

We now assess the message complexity (recall that each multicast costs as much as sending point-to-point messages to each destination). First, remember that the computation proceeds as follows: $\pi_0, \alpha_1, \pi_1, \alpha_2, \ldots, \pi_{\tau-1}, \alpha_\tau$. In order to count the total number of messages, we distinguish between the attended phases preceded by a nonempty unattended period and the attended phases which are not preceded by unattended periods. Formally, we let M_u be the number of messages sent in $\pi_{i-1}\alpha_i$, for all those i's such that π_{i-1} is nonempty, and we let M_a be the number of messages sent in $\pi_{i-1}\alpha_i$, for all those i's such that π_{i-1} is empty (clearly, in these cases, we have $\pi_{i-1}\alpha_i = \alpha_i$). Next we compute M_a and M_u and thus the message complexity M of algorithm *AN*.

Lemma 5.23 *In any execution of algorithm AN with $f < p$, we have $M_a = O(S_a)$.*

Proof. First, notice that in a phase ℓ where there is a unique coordinator, the number of messages sent is $2p_\ell$. By the definition of M_a, messages counted in M_a are messages sent in a phase α_i such that π_{i-1} is empty. This means that the phase previous to α_i is α_{i-1} which, by definition, is attended. Hence, by the local view update rule of attended phases, we have that α_i has a unique coordinator. Thus, phase α_i gives a contribution of at most $2p_{\alpha_i}$ messages to M_a. It is possible that some of the attended phases do not contribute to M_a; however, counting all the attended phases as contributing to M_a, we have that $M_a \leq \sum_{i=1}^{\tau} 2p_{\alpha_i} = 2S_a$. □

Lemma 5.24 *In any execution of algorithm AN with $f < p$, we have $M_u = O(fp)$.*

Proof. First, we notice that in any phase the number of messages sent is $O(cp)$ where c is the number of coordinators for that phase. Hence, to estimate M_u, we simply count all the supposed coordinators in the phases included in $\pi_{i-1}\alpha_i$, where π_{i-1} is nonempty.

Let i be such that π_{i-1} is not empty. Since the number of processors doubles in each consecutive layer of the local view according to the martingale principle, we have that the total number of supposed coordinators in all the phases of $\pi_{i-1}\alpha_i$ is $2f_{i-1} + 1 = O(f_{i-1})$, where f_{i-1} is the number of failures during π_{i-1}. Hence, the total number of supposed coordinators, in all of the phases contributing to M_u, is $\sum_{i=1}^{\tau} O(f_{i-1}) = O(f)$.

Hence, the total number of messages counted in M_u is $O(fp)$. $\square$

We now give the message complexity of algorithm *AN*.

Theorem 5.25   In any execution of algorithm *AN*, we have

$$M = O\left(n + p\frac{\log p}{\log(p/f)} + fp\right) \text{ when } f \leq \frac{p}{\log p}, \text{ and}$$

$$M = O\left(n + p\frac{\log p}{\log\log p} + fp\right) \text{ when } \frac{p}{\log p} < f < p.$$

Proof. The total number of messages sent is $M = M_a + M_u$. The theorem follows from Lemmas 5.23 and 5.24, and Lemmas 5.19 and 5.21.
$\square$

5.3   ALGORITHM *GKS*

We now study the *Do-All* problem for the setting where processors use point-to-point messaging, without resorting to reliable multicast used by algorithm *AN* from the previous section. As one would expect in this setting, the problem becomes more challenging and new techniques are needed to obtain efficient work.

We again consider the *Do-All* problem for n tasks, p processors, and up to f processor crashes. The key in developing efficient deterministic algorithms for *Do-All* in this setting lies in the ability to share knowledge among processors efficiently. As we discussed in Section 3.3, algorithms that rely on a single-coordinator mechanism necessarily have lower bound on work of $\Omega(n + fp)$ for f crashes. Algorithm *AN* beats this lower bound by using multiple coordinators; however, it uses reliable multicast. Therefore, we are interested in developing algorithms that do not use coordinators or reliable multicast and that are efficient, especially for large f.

We present a synchronous, message-passing, deterministic *Do-All* algorithm that we call algorithm *GKS*. This algorithm uses point-to-point messaging and has work complexity $S = O(n + p\log^3 p)$ and message complexity $M = O(p^{1+2\varepsilon})$, for any $\varepsilon > 0$. Thus, the work complexity of this algorithm beats the single-coordinator lower bound (for $f = \omega(\log^3 p)$), and the work is comparable to that of algorithm *AN*. The algorithm implements a combination of the global allocation paradigm and the hashed allocation paradigm for efficiently sharing information among processors. In particular, the algorithm deploys a gossip-based coordination technique (see Section 3.3.1 – paragraph "Gossip-based Coordination") where processors share information using an algorithm developed to solve the *gossip problem* in synchronous message-passing systems with processor crashes. To achieve messaging efficiency, the point-to-point messaging is constrained by the use of expander graphs (Section 3.3.2, paragraph "Expander Graphs and Multicast"), that is, communication graphs that represent a certain subset of the edges in a complete communication network. Furthermore, processors send messages based on permutations (Section 3.3.1, paragraph "Permutations") with certain properties.

Before we present algorithm *GKS*, we first define the *Gossip* problem and describe a *Gossip* algorithm that algorithm *GKS* uses as a building block for the efficient coordination of processors.

5.3.1 THE GOSSIP PROBLEM

The *Gossip* problem is considered one of the fundamental problems in distributed computing and it is normally stated as follows: each processor has a distinct piece of information, called a *rumor*, and the goal is for each processor to learn all rumors. In our setting, where we consider processor crashes, it might not always be possible to learn the rumor of a processor that crashed, since all the processors that have learned the rumor of that processor might have also crashed in the course of the computation. Hence, we consider a variation of the traditional gossip problem:

> Gossip: *Given a set of p crash-prone processors, where initially each processor has a rumor, all non-faulty processor must learn the rumors of all non-faulty processors and for every failed processor v, every non-faulty processor must either learn the rumor of v or that v has crashed.*

It is important to note that it is not required for the non-faulty processors to reach agreement: if a processor crashes then some of the non-faulty processors may get to learn its rumor while others may only learn that it has crashed.

We now define the measures of efficiency we use in studying the complexity of the synchronous *Gossip* problem. We measure the efficiency of a *Gossip* algorithm in terms of its *time complexity* and *message complexity*. Time complexity is naturally measured as the number of parallel steps taken by the processors until the *Gossip* problem is solved. More formally:

Definition 5.26 Let A be an algorithm that solves a problem with p processors under adversary $\mathcal{A}$. For execution $\xi \in \mathcal{E}(A, \mathcal{A})$, if algorithm A solves the problem by time $\tau(\xi)$ (according to the external clock), then the *time complexity* T of algorithm A is as follows:

$$T = T_A(p) = \max_{\xi \in \mathcal{E}(A, \mathcal{A})} \{\tau(\xi)\}.$$

The message complexity is defined as in Definition 2.3 where the size of the problem is p: it is measured as the total number of point-to-point messages sent by the processors until the problem is solved. As before, when a processor communicates using a multicast, its cost is the total number of point-to-point messages.

5.3.2   COMBINATORIAL TOOLS

We now present tools used to control the message complexity of the *Gossip* algorithm (and the *Do-All* algorithm) presented in the next section.

Expander Graphs. The algorithm deploys expander communication graphs, that is, conceptual graphs that are used to constrain the communication depending on the processor crashes that occur during the computation. Details on the use of expander graphs are discussed in Paragraph "Expander Graphs and Multicast" in Section 3.3.

We now present the properties that the expander graphs deployed by the *Gossip* algorithm satisfy. We first give necessary terminology and notation.

Let $G = (V, E)$ be a (undirected) graph, with V the set of nodes (representing processors, $|V| = p$) and E the set of edges (representing communication links). For a subgraph G_Q of G induced by Q ($Q \subseteq V$), we define $N_G(Q)$ to be the subset of V consisting of all the nodes in Q and their neighbors in G. The maximum node degree of graph G is denoted by Δ. Let G_{V_i} be the subgraph of G induced by the sets V_i of nodes. Each set V_i corresponds to the set of processors that haven't crashed by step i of a given execution. Hence, $V_{i+1} \subseteq V_i$ (since the processors do not restart). Also, each $|V_i| \geq p - f$, since no more than $f < p$ processors may crash in a given execution. Let G_{Q_i} denote a component of G_{V_i} where $Q_i \subseteq V_i$. Then:

Definition 5.27   Graph $G = (V, E)$ has the *Compact Chain Property* $CCP(p, f, \varepsilon)$, if:

  I. The maximum degree of G is at most $\left(\frac{p}{p-f}\right)^{1+\varepsilon}$,

  II. For a given sequence $V_1 \supseteq \ldots \supseteq V_k$ ($V = V_1$), where $|V_k| \geq p - f$, there is a sequence $Q_1 \supseteq \ldots \supseteq Q_k$ such that for every $i = 1, \ldots, k$:
  - **(a)** $Q_i \subseteq V_i$,
  - **(b)** $|Q_i| \geq |V_i|/7$, and
  - **(c)** the diameter of G_{Q_i} is at most $31 \log p$.

The following shows existence of graphs satisfying *CCP* for some parameters.

Lemma 5.28   *For $p > 2$, every $f < p$, and constant $\varepsilon > 0$, there is a graph G of $O(p)$ nodes satisfying property $CCP(p, f, \varepsilon)$.*

Sets of Permutations. We now deal with sets of permutations that satisfy certain properties. These permutations are used by the processors in the gossip algorithm to decide to what subset of processors they send their rumor in each step of a given execution. We extend the notion of "contention" presented in Section 4.4.1 to that of "(d, q)-contention".

Consider the symmetric group $\mathcal{S}_t$ of all permutations on set $\{1, \ldots, t\}$, with the composition operation $\circ$, and identity $\mathbf{e}_t$ (t is a positive integer). For permutation $\pi = \langle \pi(1), \ldots, \pi(t) \rangle$ in $\mathcal{S}_t$, we say that $\pi(i)$ is a d-left-to-right maximum, if there are less than d previous elements in π of value greater than $\pi(i)$, i.e., $|\{\pi(j) : \pi(j) > \pi(i) \wedge j < i\}| < d$. For a given permutation π, let (d)-$lrm(\pi)$ denote the number of d-left-to-right maxima in π.

Let Υ and Ψ, $\Upsilon \subseteq \Psi$, be two sets containing permutations from $\mathcal{S}_t$. For every σ in $\mathcal{S}_t$, let $\sigma \circ \Upsilon$ denote the set of permutations $\{\sigma \circ \pi : \pi \in \Upsilon\}$. For a given Υ and permutation $\sigma \in \mathcal{S}_t$, let $(d, |\Upsilon|)$-$\mathrm{Cont}(\Upsilon, \sigma)$ be equal to $\sum_{\pi \in \Upsilon} (d)$-$lrm(\sigma^{-1} \circ \pi)$. We then define the (d, q)-contention of set Ψ as (d, q)-$\mathrm{Cont}(\Psi) = \max\{(d, q)$-$\mathrm{Surf}(\Upsilon, \sigma) : \Upsilon \subseteq \Psi \wedge |\Upsilon| = q \wedge \sigma \in \mathcal{S}_t\}$.

The following result is known for (d, q)-contention.

Fact 5.29   There is a set of p permutations Ψ from $\mathcal{S}_t$ such that, for every positive integers d and $q \leq p$, (d, q)-$\mathrm{Cont}(\Psi) \leq t \ln t + 10qd \ln(t + p)$.

The efficiency of the gossip algorithm (and hence the efficiency of a *Do-All* algorithm that uses such gossip) relies on the existence of permutations of the above fact (however, the algorithm is correct for any set of permutations). These permutations can be efficiently constructed (see Bibliographic Notes).

5.3.3   THE GOSSIP ALGORITHM

We now present the gossip algorithm, called $\mathrm{Gossip}_\varepsilon$ (ε is a given constant).

DESCRIPTION OF ALGORITHM $\mathrm{Gossip}_\varepsilon$

Suppose constant $0 < \varepsilon < 1/3$ is given. The algorithm proceeds in a loop that is repeated until each non-faulty processor v learns either the rumor of every processor w or that w has failed. A single iteration of the loop is called an *epoch*. The algorithm terminates after $\lceil 1/\varepsilon \rceil - 1$ epochs. Each of the first $\lceil 1/\varepsilon \rceil - 2$ epochs consists of $\alpha \log^2 p$ *phases*, where α is such that $\alpha \log^2 p$ is the smallest integer that is larger than $341 \log^2 p$. Each phase is divided into two *stages*, the *update* stage, and the *communication* stage. In the update stage, each processor updates its local knowledge regarding other processors' rumors (known/unknown) and conditions (failed/operational). In the communication stage processors exchange their local knowledge (more momentarily). We say that processor v *heard about processor w* if either v knows the rumor of w or it knows that w has failed. Epoch $\lceil 1/\varepsilon \rceil - 1$ is the terminating epoch where each processor sends a message to all the processors that it has not heard about, requesting their rumor.

The pseudocode of the algorithm is given in Figure 5.6. The details of the algorithm are explained in the rest of this section.

Initialization

$status_v = $ collector;

$\text{ACTIVE}_v = \langle 1, 2, \ldots, p \rangle;$

$\text{BUSY}_v = \langle \pi_v(1), \pi_v(2), \ldots, \pi_v(p) \rangle;$

$\text{WAITING}_v = \langle \pi_v(1), \pi_v(2), \ldots, \pi_v(p) \rangle \setminus \langle v \rangle;$

$\text{RUMORS}_v = \langle (v, rumor_v) \rangle;$

$\text{NEIGHB}_v = N_{G_1}(v) \setminus \{v\};$

$\text{CALLING}_v = \{\};$

$\text{ANSWER}_v = \{\};$

Iterating epochs

for $\ell = 1$ **to** $\lceil 1/\varepsilon \rceil - 2$ **do**

if BUSY_v is empty **then** set $status_v$ to idle; **fi**

$\text{NEIGHB}_v = \{w : w \in \text{ACTIVE}_v \wedge w \in N_{G_\ell}(v) \setminus \{v\}\};$

repeat $\alpha \log^2 p$ times $-\!\!-$ *iterating phases*

update stage;

communication stage;

end repeat

od

Terminating epoch $(\lceil 1/\varepsilon \rceil - 1)$

update stage;

if $status_v = $ collector **then**

send $\langle \text{ACTIVE}_v, \text{BUSY}_v, \text{RUMORS}_v, $ call$\rangle$ to each processor in $\text{WAITING}_v;$

fi

receive messages;

send $\langle \text{ACTIVE}_v, \text{BUSY}_v, \text{RUMORS}_v, $ reply$\rangle$ to each processor in $\text{ANSWER}_v;$

receive messages;

update $\text{RUMORS}_v;$

Figure 5.6: Algorithm $\text{GOSSIP}_\varepsilon$, stated for processor v; $\pi_v(i)$ denotes the ith element of permutation π_v.

Local knowledge and messages. Initially, each processor v has its *rumor$_v$* and permutation π_v from a set Ψ of permutations on $[p]$, such that Ψ satisfies the thesis of Fact 5.29. Moreover, each processor v is associated with the variable $status_v$. Initially, $status_v = $ collector (and we say that v is a collector), meaning that v has not heard from all processors yet. Once v hears from all other processors, then $status_v$ is set to informer (and we say that v is an informer), meaning that now v will inform the other processors of its status and knowledge. When processor v learns that all non-faulty processors w also have $status_w = $ informer, then at the beginning of the next epoch, *status$_v$* becomes idle (and we say that v *idles*), meaning that v idles until termination, but it might send responses to messages (see call-messages below).

Each processor maintains several lists and sets. We now describe the lists maintained by processor v:

- List ACTIVE$_v$: it contains the pids of the processors that v considers to be non-faulty. Initially, list ACTIVE$_v$ contains all p pids.

- List BUSY$_v$: it contains the pids of the processors that v consider as collectors. Initially, list BUSY$_v$ contains all pids, *permuted according to π_v*.

- List WAITING$_v$: it contains the pids of the processors that v did not hear from. Initially, list WAITING$_v$ contains all pids except from v, *permuted according to π_v*.

- List RUMORS$_v$: it contains pairs of the form $(w, rumor_w)$ or $(w, \perp)$. The pair $(w, rumor_w)$ denotes the fact that processor v knows processor w's rumor and the pair $(w, \perp)$ means that v does not know w's rumor, but it knows that w has failed. Initially, list RUMORS$_v$ contains the pair $(v, rumor_v)$.

A processor can send a message to any other processor, but to lower the message complexity, in some cases (see communication stage), we require processors to communicate according to a conceptual communication graph $G_\ell, \ell \leq \lceil 1/\varepsilon \rceil - 2$, that satisfies property $CCP(p, p - p^{1-\ell\varepsilon}, \varepsilon)$ (see Definition 5.27 and Lemma 5.28). When processor v sends a message m to another processor w, m contains lists ACTIVE$_v$, BUSY$_v$ RUMORS$_v$, and the variable *type*. When *type* = call, processor v requires an answer from processor w, and we refer to such a message as a *call-message*. When *type* = reply, no answer is required—this message is sent as a response to a call-message.

We now present the sets maintained by processor v.

- Set ANSWER$_v$: it contains the pids of the processors that v received a call-message. Initially, set ANSWER$_v$ is empty.

- Set CALLING$_v$: it contains the pids of the processors that v will send a call-message. Initially, CALLING$_v$ is empty.

- Set NEIGHB$_v$: it contains the pids of the processors that are in ACTIVE$_v$ and that according to the communication graph G_ℓ, for a given epoch ℓ, are neighbors of v (NEIGHB$_v$ = $\{w : w \in$ ACTIVE$_v \wedge w \in N_{G_\ell}(v)\}$). Initially, NEIGHB$_v$ contains all neighbors of v (all nodes in $N_{G_1}(v)$).

Communication stage. In this stage, the processors communicate in an attempt to obtain information from other processors. This stage contains *four sub-stages*:

- First sub-stage: every processor v that is either a collector or an informer (i.e., *status$_v$* ≠ idle) sends a message ⟨ACTIVE$_v$, BUSY$_v$, RUMORS$_v$, call⟩ to every processor in CALLING$_v$. The idle processors do not send any messages in this sub-stage.

- Second sub-stage: all processors (collectors, informers, and idling) collect the information sent by other processors in the previous sub-stage. Specifically, processor v collects lists ACTIVE_w, BUSY_w, and RUMORS_w, of every processor w that it received a call-message from, and v inserts w in set ANSWER_v.

- Third sub-stage: every processor (regardless of its status) responds to each processor that it received a call-message from. Specifically, processor v sends a message $\langle \text{ACTIVE}_v, \text{BUSY}_v, \text{RUMORS}_v, \text{reply} \rangle$ to the processors in ANSWER_v and empties ANSWER_v.

- Fourth sub-stage: the processors receive the responses to their call-messages.

Update stage. In this stage, each processor v updates its local knowledge based on the messages it received in the *last communication stage*[2]. If $status_v = \text{idle}$, then v idles. We now present the six **update rules** and their processing. Note that the rules are not disjoint, but we apply them in the order from (r1) to (r6):

(r1) Updating BUSY_v or RUMORS_v: For every processor w in CALLING_v (i) if v is an informer, it removes w from BUSY_v, (ii) if v is a collector and RUMORS_w was included in one of the messages that v received, then v adds the pair $(w, rumor_w)$ in RUMORS_v, and (iii) if v is a collector but RUMORS_w was not included in one of the messages that v received, then v adds the pair $(w, \perp)$ in RUMORS_v.

(r2) Updating RUMORS_v and WAITING_v: For every processor w in $[p]$, (i) if $(w, rumor_w)$ is not in RUMORS_v and v learns the rumor of w from some other processor that it received a message from, then v adds $(w, rumor_w)$ in RUMORS_v, (ii) if both $(w, rumor_w)$ and $(w, \perp)$ are in RUMORS_v, then v removes $(w, \perp)$ from RUMORS_v, and (iii) if either of $(w, rumor_w)$ or $(w, \perp)$ is in RUMORS_v and w is in WAITING_v, then v removes w from WAITING_v.

(r3) Updating BUSY_v: For every processor w in BUSY_v, if v receives a message from processor v' so that w is not in $\text{BUSY}_{v'}$, then v removes w from BUSY_v.

(r4) Updating ACTIVE_v and NEIGHB_v: For every processor w in ACTIVE_v (i) if w is not in NEIGHB_v and v received a message from processor v' so that w is not in $\text{ACTIVE}_{v'}$, then v removes w from ACTIVE_v, (ii) if w is in NEIGHB_v and v did not receive a message from w, then v removes w from ACTIVE_v and NEIGHB_v, and (iii) if w is in CALLING_v and v did not receive a message from w, then v removes w from ACTIVE_v.

(r5) Changing status: If the size of RUMORS_v is equal to p and v is a collector, then v becomes an informer.

---

[2]In the first update stage of the first phase of epoch 1, where no communication has yet to occur, no update of the list or sets takes place.

(r6) Updating CALLING$_v$: Processor v empties CALLING$_v$ and (i) if v is a collector then it updates set CALLING$_v$ to contain the first $p^{(\ell+1)\varepsilon}$ pids of list WAITING$_v$ (or all pids of WAITING$_v$ if *sizeof*(WAITING$_v$) $< p^{(\ell+1)\varepsilon}$) and all pids of set NEIGHB$_v$, and (ii) if v is an informer then it updates set CALLING$_v$ to contain the first $p^{(\ell+1)\varepsilon}$ pids of list BUSY$_v$ (or all pids of BUSY$_v$ if *sizeof*(BUSY$_v$) $< p^{(\ell+1)\varepsilon}$) and all pids of set NEIGHB$_v$.

Terminating epoch. Epoch $\lceil 1/\varepsilon \rceil - 1$ is the last epoch of the algorithm. In this epoch, each processor v updates its local information based on the messages it received in the last communication stage of epoch $\lceil 1/\varepsilon \rceil - 2$. If after this update processor v is still a collector, then it sends a call-message to every processor that is in WAITING$_v$ (list WAITING$_v$ contains the pids of the processors that v does not know their rumor or does not know whether they have crashed). Then every processor v receives the call-messages sent by the other processors (set ANSWER$_v$ is updated to include the senders). Next, every processor v that received a call-message sends its local knowledge to the sender (i.e. to the members of set ANSWER$_v$). Finally, each processor v updates RUMORS$_v$ based on any received information. More specifically, if a processor w responded to v's call-message (meaning that v now learns the rumor of w), then v adds $(w, rumor_w)$ in RUMORS$_v$. If w did not respond to v's call-message, and $(w, rumor_w)$ is not in RUMORS$_v$ (it is possible for processor v to learn the rumor of w from some other processor v' that learned the rumor of w before processor w crashed), then v knows that w has crashed and adds $(w, \perp)$ in RUMORS$_v$.

ANALYSIS OF ALGORITHM GOSSIP$_\varepsilon$

Before we analyze the performance of algorithm GOSSIP$_\varepsilon$, we argue that the algorithm correctly solves the *Gossip* problem, meaning that by the end of epoch $\lceil 1/\varepsilon \rceil - 1$, each non-faulty processor has heard about all other $p - 1$ processors.

Correctness of Algorithm GOSSIP$_\varepsilon$. First, we show that no non-faulty processor is removed from a processor's list of active processors.

Lemma 5.30 *In any execution of algorithm* GOSSIP$_\varepsilon$, *if processors v and w are non-faulty by the end of any epoch $\ell < \lceil 1/\varepsilon \rceil - 1$, then w is in* ACTIVE$_v$.

The above can be shown by induction on the number of epochs. Next, we show that if a non-faulty processor w has not heard from all processors yet, then no non-faulty processor v removes w from its list of busy processors. This can also be shown by induction on the number of epochs.

Lemma 5.31 *In any execution of algorithm* GOSSIP$_\varepsilon$ *and any epoch $\ell < \lceil 1/\varepsilon \rceil - 1$, if processors v and w are non-faulty by the end of epoch ℓ and $status_w$ = collector, then w is in* BUSY$_v$.

We now show that each processor's list of rumors is updated correctly. This can be shown by induction on the number of epochs together with careful investigation of the code of the algorithm.

Lemma 5.32   *In any execution of algorithm* $\text{GOSSIP}_\varepsilon$ *and any epoch* $\ell < \lceil 1/\varepsilon \rceil - 1$,
(i) *if processors* v *and* w *are non-faulty by the end of epoch* ℓ *and* w *is not in* WAITING_v, *then* $(w, rumor_w)$ *is in* RUMORS_v, *and*
(ii) *if processor* v *is non-faulty by the end of epoch* ℓ *and* $(w, \perp)$ *is in* RUMORS_v, *then* w *is not in* ACTIVE_v.

We are now ready to show the correctness of algorithm $\text{GOSSIP}_\varepsilon$.

Theorem 5.33   By the end of epoch $\lceil 1/\varepsilon \rceil - 1$ of any execution of algorithm $\text{GOSSIP}_\varepsilon$, every non-faulty processor v either knows the rumor of processor w or it knows that w has crashed.

Proof. The result follows by the observation that the claims of Lemmas 5.30, 5.31, and 5.32 also hold after the end of the update stage of the terminating epoch and by close investigation of the code following the update stage of the terminating epoch.   □

Note from the above that the correctness of algorithm $\text{GOSSIP}_\varepsilon$ does not depend on whether the set of permutations Ψ satisfies the conditions of Fact 5.29. The algorithm is correct for any set of permutations of $[p]$.

Complexity Analysis of Algorithm $\text{GOSSIP}_\varepsilon$. We now analyze the complexity of algorithm $\text{GOSSIP}_\varepsilon$ in terms of its time and message complexity.

Consider some set $V_\ell, |V_\ell| \geq p^{1-\ell\varepsilon}$, of processors that are not idle at the beginning of epoch ℓ and do not fail by the end of epoch ℓ. Let $Q_\ell \subseteq V_\ell$ be such that $|Q_\ell| \geq |V_\ell|/7$ and the diameter of the subgraph induced by Q_ℓ is at most $31 \log p$. Q_ℓ exists because of Lemma 5.28 applied to graph G_ℓ and set V_ℓ.

For any processor v, let $\text{CALL}_v = \text{CALLING}_v \setminus \text{NEIGHB}_v$. Recall that the size of CALL is equal to $p^{(\ell+1)\varepsilon}$ (or less if list WAITING, or BUSY, is shorter than $p^{(\ell+1)\varepsilon}$) and the size of NEIGHB is at most $p^{(\ell+1)\varepsilon}$. We refer to the call-messages sent to the processors whose pids are in CALL as *progress-messages*. If processor v sends a progress-message to processor w, it will remove w from list WAITING_v (or BUSY_v) by the end of current stage. Let $d = (31 \log p + 1)p^{(\ell+1)\varepsilon}$. Note that $d \geq (31 \log p + 1) \cdot |\text{CALL}|$.

We begin the analysis of the gossip algorithm with a bound on the number of progress-messages sent under certain conditions.

Lemma 5.34   *The total number of progress-messages sent by processors in* Q_ℓ *from the beginning of epoch* ℓ *until the first processor in* Q_ℓ *will have its list* WAITING *(or list* BUSY*) empty, is at most* $(d, |Q_\ell|)\text{-Cont}(\Psi)$.

We now define an invariant, that we call I_ℓ, for $\ell = 1, \ldots, \lceil 1/\varepsilon \rceil - 2$:

$\mathbf{I}_\ell$: There are at most $p^{1-\ell\varepsilon}$ non-faulty processors having status collector or informer in any step after the end of epoch ℓ.

Using Lemma 5.34 and Fact 5.29, we can show the following:

Lemma 5.35 *In any execution of algorithm* GOSSIP$_\varepsilon$, *the invariant I_ℓ holds for any epoch $\ell = 1, \ldots, \lceil 1/\varepsilon \rceil - 2$.*

We are now ready to show the time and message complexity of algorithm GOSSIP$_\varepsilon$.

Theorem 5.36 Algorithm GOSSIP$_\varepsilon$ solves the *Gossip* problem using p crash-prone processors with time complexity $T = O(\log^2 p)$ and message complexity $M = O(p^{1+3\varepsilon})$.

Proof. First, we show the bound on time. Observe that each update and communication stage takes $O(1)$ time. Therefore, each of the first $\lceil 1/\varepsilon \rceil - 2$ epochs takes $O(\log^2 p)$ time. The last epoch takes $O(1)$ time. From this and the fact that ε is a constant, we have that the time complexity of the algorithm is in the worse case $O(\log^2 p)$.

We now show the bound on messages. From Lemma 5.35, we have that for every $1 \le \ell < \lceil 1/\varepsilon \rceil - 2$, during epoch $\ell + 1$, there are at most $p^{1-\ell\varepsilon}$ processors sending at most $2p^{(\ell+2)\varepsilon}$ messages in every communication stage. The remaining processors are either faulty (hence they do not send any messages) or have status idle—these processors only respond to call-messages and their total impact on the message complexity in epoch $\ell + 1$ is at most as large as the others. Consequently, the message complexity during epoch $\ell + 1$ is at most $4(\alpha \log^2 p) \cdot (p^{1-\ell\varepsilon} p^{(\ell+2)\varepsilon}) \le 4\alpha p^{1+2\varepsilon} \log^2 p \le 4\alpha p^{1+3\varepsilon}$. After epoch $\lceil 1/\varepsilon \rceil - 2$ there are, per $I_{\lceil 1/\varepsilon \rceil - 2}$, at most $p^{2\varepsilon}$ processors having list WAITING not empty. In epoch $\lceil 1/\varepsilon \rceil - 1$, each of these processors sends a message to at most p processors twice, hence the message complexity in this epoch is bounded by $2p \cdot p^{2\varepsilon}$. From the above and the fact that ε is a constant, we have that the message complexity of the algorithm is $O(p^{1+3\varepsilon})$. $\square$

5.3.4 THE DO-ALL ALGORITHM

We now put the gossip algorithm to use by constructing a robust *Do-All* algorithm, called algorithm GKS$_\varepsilon$ (as with algorithm GOSSIP$_\varepsilon$, ε is a given constant).

DESCRIPTION OF ALGORITHM GKS$_\varepsilon$

The algorithm proceeds in a loop that is repeated until all the tasks are executed, and all non-faulty processors are aware of this. A single iteration of the loop is called an *epoch*. Each epoch consists of $\beta \log p + 1$ *phases*, where $\beta > 0$ is a constant integer. We show that the algorithm is correct for any integer $\beta > 0$, but the complexity analysis of the algorithm depends on specific values of β that we show to exist. Each phase is divided into two *stages*, the *work* stage and the *gossip* stage. In the work stage, processors perform tasks, and in the gossip stage, processors execute an instance of the GOSSIP$_{\varepsilon/3}$ algorithm to exchange information regarding completed tasks and non-faulty processors (more details momentarily). Computation starts with epoch 1. We note that (unlike in algorithm $\text{GOSSIP}_\varepsilon$) the non-faulty processors may stop executing at different steps. Hence, we need to argue about the termination decision that the processors must take. This is done in the paragraph "Termination decision".

The pseudocode for a phase of epoch ℓ of the algorithm is given in Figure 5.7. The details are explained in the rest of this section.

Initialization
    $done_v = $ false;
    $\text{TASK}_v = \langle \pi_v(1), \pi_v(2), \ldots, \pi_v(p) \rangle$;
    $\text{PROC}_v = \langle 1, 2, \ldots, p \rangle$;

Epoch ℓ
    repeat $\beta \log p + 1$ times   -- *iterating phases of epoch ℓ*

        repeat $T_\ell = \lceil \frac{n + p \log^3 p}{\frac{p}{2^\ell} \log p} \rceil$ times   -- *work stage begins*
          if TASK_v not empty **then**
              perform task whose id is first in TASK_v;
              remove task's id from TASK_v;
          elseif TASK_v empty and $done_v = $ false **then**
              set $done_v$ to true;
          fi
        end repeat
        if TASK_v empty and $done_v = $ false **then**
          set $done_v$ to true;
        fi
        run $\text{GOSSIP}_{\varepsilon/3}$ with $rumor_v = (\text{TASK}_v, \text{PROC}_v, done_v)$;   -- *gossip stage begins*
        if $done_v = $ true and $done_w = $ true for all w received rumor from **then**
          TERMINATE;
        else
          update TASK_v and PROC_v;
        fi
    end repeat

Figure 5.7: Algorithm GKS_ε, stated for processor v; $\pi_v(i)$ denotes the ith element of permutation π_v.

Local knowledge. Each processor v maintains a list of tasks TASK_v it believes not to be done, and a list of processors PROC_v it believes to be non-faulty. Initially, $\text{TASK}_v = \langle 1, \ldots, n \rangle$ and $\text{PROC}_v = \langle 1, \ldots, p \rangle$. The processor also has a boolean variable $done_v$ that describes the knowledge of v regarding the completion of the tasks. Initially, $done_v$ is set to false, and when processor v is assured that all tasks are completed, $done_v$ is set to true.

Task allocation. Each processor v is equipped with a permutation π_v from a set Ψ of permutations on $[n]$. (This is distinct from the set of permutation on $[p]$ required by the gossip algorithm.) We show that the algorithm is correct for any set of permutations on $[n]$, but its complexity analysis depends on specific set of permutations Ψ that we show to exist. These permutations can be constructed efficiently.

Initially TASK$_v$ is permuted according to π_v and then processor v performs tasks according to the ordering of the tids in TASK$_v$. In the course of the computation, when processor v learns that task z is performed (either by performing the task itself or by obtaining this information from some other processor), it removes z from TASK$_v$ while preserving the permutation order.

Work stage. For epoch ℓ, each work stage consists of $T_\ell = \left\lceil \frac{n + p \log^3 p}{\frac{p}{2^\ell} \log p} \right\rceil$ work *sub-stages*. In each sub-stage, each processor v performs a task according to TASK$_v$. Hence, in each work stage of a phase of epoch ℓ, processor v must perform the first T_ℓ tasks of TASK$_v$. However, if TASK$_v$ becomes empty at a sub-stage prior to sub-state T_ℓ, then v performs no-ops in the remaining sub-stages (each no-op operation takes the same time as performing a task). Once TASK$_v$ becomes empty, $done_v$ is set to true.

Gossip stage. Here processors execute algorithm GOSSIP$_{\varepsilon/3}$ using their local knowledge as the rumor, i.e., for processor v, $rumor_v = (\text{TASK}_v, \text{PROC}_v, done_v)$. At the end of the stage, each processor v updates its local knowledge based on the rumors it received. The **update rule** is as follows: (a) If v does not receive the rumor of processor w, then v learns that w has failed (guaranteed by the correctness of GOSSIP$_{\varepsilon/3}$). In this case, v removes w from PROC$_v$. (b) If v receives the rumor of processor w, then it compares TASK$_v$ and PROC$_v$ with TASK$_w$ and PROC$_w$, respectively, and updates its lists accordingly—it removes the tasks that w knows are already completed and the processors that w knows that have crashed. Note that if TASK$_v$ becomes empty after this update, variable $done_v$ remains false. It will be set to true in the next work stage. This is needed for the correctness of the algorithm (see Lemma 5.41).

Termination decision. We would like all non-faulty processors to learn that the tasks are done. Hence, it would not be sufficient for a processor to terminate once the value of its *done* variable is set to true. It has to be assured that all other non-faulty processors' *done* variables are set to true as well, and then terminate. This is achieved as follows: If processor v starts the gossip stage of a phase of epoch ℓ with $done_v =$ true, and all rumors it receives suggest that all other non-faulty processors know that all tasks are done (their *done* variables are set to true), then processor v terminates. If at least one processor's *done* variable is set to false, then v continues to the next phase of epoch ℓ (or to the first phase of epoch $\ell + 1$ if the previous phase was the last of epoch ℓ).

Remark 5.37 In the complexity analysis of the algorithm, we first assume that $n \leq p^2$ and then we show how to extend the analysis for the case $n > p^2$. In order to do so, we assume that when $n > p^2$, before the start of algorithm GKS$_\varepsilon$, the tasks are partitioned into $n' = p^2$ chunks, where each chunk contains at most $\lceil n/p^2 \rceil$ tasks. In this case, it is understood that in the above description of the algorithm, n is actually n', and when we refer to a task, we really mean a chunk of tasks.

ANALYSIS OF ALGORITHM GKS_ε

Before we analyze the performance of algorithm GKS_ε, we argue that the algorithm correctly solves the *Do-All* problem, meaning that the algorithm terminates with all tasks performed, and all non-faulty processors are aware of this. (Note that this is a stronger correctness condition than the one required by the definition of *Do-All*.)

Correctness of Algorithm GKS_ε. First, we show that no non-faulty processor is removed from a processor's list of non-faulty processors.

Lemma 5.38   *In any execution of algorithm GKS_ε, if processors v and w are non-faulty by the end of the gossip stage of phase s of epoch ℓ, then processor w is in* $PROC_v$.

Proof. Let v be a processor that is non-faulty by the end of the gossip stage of phase s of epoch ℓ. By the correctness of algorithm $GOSSIP_{\varepsilon/3}$ (called at the gossip stage), processor v receives the rumor of every non-faulty processor w and vice-versa. Since there are no restarts, v and w were alive in all prior phases of epochs $1, 2, \ldots, \ell$, and hence, v and w received each other rumors in all these phases as well. By the update rule, it follows that processor v does not remove processor w from its processor list and vice-versa. Hence, w is in $PROC_v$ and w is in $PROC_v$ by the end of phase s, as desired.   □

Next, we argue that no undone task is removed from a processor's list of undone tasks. This can be shown by induction on the number of epochs.

Lemma 5.39   *In any execution of algorithm GKS_ε, if a task z is not in $TASK_v$ of any processor v at the beginning of the first phase of epoch ℓ, then z has been performed in a phase of one of the epochs $1, 2, \ldots, \ell - 1$.*

Next, we show that under certain conditions, local progress is guaranteed. For processor v, we denote by $TASK_v^{(\ell,s)}$ the list $TASK_v$ at the beginning of phase s of epoch ℓ. Note that if s is the last phase – $(\beta \log^2 p)$th phase – of epoch ℓ, then $TASK_v^{(\ell,s+1)} = TASK_v^{(\ell+1,1)}$, meaning that after phase s processor v enters the first phase of epoch $\ell + 1$.

Lemma 5.40   *In any execution of algorithm GKS_ε, if processor v enters a work stage of a phase s of epoch ℓ with $done_w = $ false, then $sizeof(TASK_v^{(\ell,s+1)}) < sizeof(TASK_v^{(\ell,s)})$.*

Proof. Let v be a processor that starts the work stage of phase s of epoch ℓ with $done_w = $ false. According to the description of the algorithm, the value of variable $done_v$ is initially false, and it is set to true only when $TASK_v$ becomes empty. Hence, at the beginning of the work stage of phase s of epoch ℓ, there is at least one task identifier in $TASK_v^{(\ell,s)}$, and therefore v performs at least one task. From this and the fact that no tid is ever added in a processor's task list, we get that $sizeof(TASK_v^{(\ell,s+1)}) < sizeof(TASK_v^{(\ell,s)})$.   □

We now show that when during a phase s of an epoch ℓ, a processor learns that all tasks are completed and it does not crash during this phase, then the algorithm is guaranteed to terminate by phase $s + 1$ of epoch ℓ; if s is the last phase epoch ℓ, then the algorithm is guaranteed to terminate by the first phase of epoch $\ell + 1$. For simplicity of presentation, in the following lemma, we assume that s is not the last phase of epoch ℓ.

Lemma 5.41   *In any execution of algorithm* GKS_ε, *for any phase s of epoch ℓ and any processor v, if* $done_v$ *is set to* true *during phase s and v is non-faulty by the end of phase s, then the algorithm terminates by phase $s + 1$ of epoch ℓ.*

Proof. Consider phase s of epoch ℓ and processor v. According to the code of the algorithm, the value of variable $done_w$ is updated during the work stage of a phase (the value of the variable is not changed during the gossip stage). Hence, if the value of variable $done_w$ is changed during the phase s of epoch ℓ, this happens before the start of the gossip stage. This means that TASK_v contained in $rumor_v$ in the execution of algorithm $\text{GOSSIP}_{\varepsilon/3}$ is empty. Since v does not fail during phase s, the correctness of algorithm $\text{GOSSIP}_{\varepsilon/3}$ guarantees that all non-faulty processors learn the rumor of v, and consequently they learn that all tasks are performed. This means that all non-faulty processors w start the gossip stage of phase $s + 1$ of epoch ℓ with $done_w = $ true, and all rumors they receive contain the variable $done$ set to true.

The above, in conjunction with the termination guarantees of algorithm $\text{GOSSIP}_{\varepsilon/3}$, leads to the conclusion that all non-faulty processors terminate by phase $s + 1$ (and hence the algorithm terminates by phase $s + 1$ of epoch ℓ).   □

Finally, we show the correctness of algorithm GKS_ε.

Theorem 5.42   In any execution of algorithm GKS_ε, the algorithm terminates with all tasks performed and all non-faulty processors being aware of this.

Proof. By Lemma 5.38, no non-faulty processor leaves the computation, and by our model, at least one processor does not crash ($f < p$). Also from Lemma 5.39, we have that no undone task is removed from the computation. From the code of the algorithm, we get that a processor continues performing tasks until its TASK list becomes empty, and by Lemma 5.40, we have that local progress is guaranteed. The above in conjunction with the correctness of algorithm $\text{GOSSIP}_{\varepsilon/3}$ lead to the conclusion that there exist a phase s of an epoch ℓ and a processor v so that during phase s processor v sets $done_v$ to true, all tasks are indeed performed and v survives phase s. By Lemma 5.41, the algorithm terminates by phase $s + 1$ of epoch ℓ (or by the first phase of epoch $\ell + 1$ if s is the last phase of epoch ℓ). Now, from the definition of T_ℓ, it follows that the algorithm terminates after at most $O(\log p)$ epochs: consider epoch $\log p$; $T_{\log p} = \lceil (n + p \log^3 p)/\log p \rceil = \lceil n/\log p + p \log^2 p \rceil$. Recall that each epoch consists of $\beta \log p + 1$ phases. Say that $\beta = 1$. Then, when a processor reaches epoch $\log p$, it can perform all n tasks in this epoch. Hence, all tasks that are not done until epoch

$\log p - 1$ are guaranteed to be performed by the end of epoch $\log p$, and all non-faulty processors will know that all tasks have been performed. □

Note from the above that the correctness of algorithm GKS_ε does not depend on the set of permutations that processors use to select what tasks to do next. The algorithm works correctly for any set of permutations on $[n]$. It also works for any integer $\beta > 0$.

Complexity Analysis of Algorithm GKS_ε. We now derive the work and message complexities for algorithm GKS_ε. The analysis is based on the following terminology. For the purpose of the analysis, we number globally all phases by positive integers starting from 1. Consider a phase i in epoch ℓ of an execution ξ of algorithm GKS_ε. Let $V_i(\xi)$ denote the set of processors that are non-faulty at the beginning of phase i. Let $p_i(\xi) = |V_i(\xi)|$. Let $U_i(\xi)$ denote the set of tasks z such that z is in some list TASK_v, for some $v \in V_i(\xi)$, at the beginning of phase i. Let $u_i(\xi) = |U_i(\xi)|$.

Now we classify the possibilities for phase i as follows. If at the beginning of phase i, $p_i(\xi) > p/2^{\ell-1}$, we say that phase i is a *majority* phase. Otherwise, phase i is a *minority* phase. If phase i is a minority phase and at the end of i the number of surviving processors is less than $p_i(\xi)/2$, i.e., $p_{i+1}(\xi) < p_i(\xi)/2$, we say that i is an *unreliable* minority phase. If $p_{i+1}(\xi) \geq p_i(\xi)/2$, we say that i is a *reliable* minority phase. If phase i is a reliable minority phase and $u_{i+1}(\xi) \leq u_i(\xi) - \frac{1}{4}p_{i+1}(\xi)T_\ell$, then we say that i is an *optimal* reliable minority phase (the task allocation is optimal – the same task is performed only by a constant number of processors on average). If $u_{i+1}(\xi) \leq \frac{3}{4}u_i(\xi)$, then i is a *fractional* reliable minority phase (a fraction of the undone tasks is performed). Otherwise, we say that i is an *unproductive* reliable minority phase (not much progress is obtained). The classification possibilities for phase i of epoch ℓ are depicted in Figure 5.8.

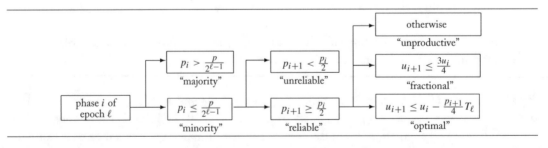

Figure 5.8: Classification of a phase i of epoch ℓ; execution ξ is implied.

Our goal is to choose a set Ψ of permutations and a constant $\beta > 0$ such that for any execution there will be no unproductive and no majority phases. To do this, we analyze sets of random permutations, give certain properties of algorithm GKS_ε for such sets (in Lemmas 5.43 and 5.44), and finally use the probabilistic method to obtain an existential deterministic solution.

We now give the intuition why the phases, with high probability, are neither majority nor minority reliable unproductive. First, in either of such cases, the number of processors crashed during the phase is at most half of all operational processors during the phase. Consider only those majorities of processors that survive the phase and the tasks performed by them. If there are a lot of processors, then all tasks will be performed if the phase is a majority phase, or at least $\min\{u_i(\xi), |Q|T_\ell\}/4$, yet unperformed tasks are performed by the processors if the phase is a minority reliable unproductive phase, all with high probability. Hence, one can derandomize the choice of suitable set of permutations such that for any execution there are neither majority nor minority reliable unproductive phases.

Lemma 5.43 *Let Q be a fixed nonempty subset of processors in phase i of epoch ℓ of algorithm GKS_ε. Then the probability of event "for every execution ξ of algorithm GKS_ε such that $V_{i+1}(\xi) \supseteq Q$ and $u_i(\xi) > 0$, the following inequality holds $u_i(\xi) - u_{i+1}(\xi) \geq \min\{u_i(\xi), |Q|T_\ell\}/4$," is at least $1 - 1/e^{-|Q|T_\ell/8}$.*

Using Lemma 5.43, the following result can be shown.

Lemma 5.44 *Assume $n \leq p^2$ and $p \geq 2^8$. There exists a constant integer $\beta > 0$ such that for every phase i of some epoch $\ell > 1$ of any execution ξ of algorithm GKS_ε, if there is a task unperformed by the beginning of phase i then:*

(a) the probability that phase i is a majority phase is at most $e^{-p \log p}$, and

(b) the probability that phase i is a minority reliable unproductive phase is at most $e^{-T_\ell/16}$.

Recall that epoch ℓ consists of $\beta \log p + 1$ phases for some $\beta > 0$ and that $T_\ell = \lceil \frac{n + p \log^3 p}{(p/2^\ell) \log p} \rceil$. Also by the correctness proof of algorithm GKS_ε (Theorem 5.42), the algorithm terminates in at most $O(\log p)$ epochs; hence, the algorithm terminates in at most $O(\log^2 p)$ phases. Let g_ℓ be the number of steps that each gossip stage takes in epoch ℓ, i.e., $g_\ell = \Theta(\log^2 p)$.

We now show the work and message complexity of algorithm GKS_ε.

Theorem 5.45 *There is a set of permutations Ψ and a constant integer $\beta > 0$ (e.g., $\beta = 9$) such that algorithm GKS_ε, using permutations from Ψ, solves the Do-All problem with work $S = O(n + p \log^3 p)$ and message complexity $M = O(p^{1+2\varepsilon})$.*

Proof. We show that for any execution ξ of algorithm GKS_ε there exists a set of permutations Ψ and an integer $\beta > 0$ so that the complexity bounds are as desired. Let β be from Lemma 5.44. We consider two cases:

Case 1: $n \leq p^2$. Consider phase i of epoch ℓ of execution ξ for randomly chosen set of permutations Ψ. We reason about the probability of phase i belonging to one of the classes illustrated in Figure 5.8, and about the work that phase i contributes to the total work incurred in the execution, depending on its classification. From Lemma 5.44(a), we get that phase i may be a majority phase with probability at least $e^{-p \log p}$, which is a very small probability. More precisely, the probability that for a set of permutations Ψ, in execution ξ obtained for Ψ some phase i is a majority phase, is $O(\log^2 p \cdot$

$e^{-p \log p}) = e^{-\Omega(p \log p)}$, and consequently using the probabilistic method argument, we obtain that for almost any set of permutations Ψ, there is no execution in which there is a majority phase.

Therefore, we focus on minority phases that occur with high probability (per Lemma 5.44(a)). We can not say anything about the probability of a minority phase to be a reliable or unreliable, since this depends on the specific execution. Note however, that by definition, we cannot have more than $O(\log p)$ unreliable minority phases in any execution ξ (at least one processor must remain operational). Moreover, the work incurred in an unreliable minority phase i of an epoch ℓ in any execution ξ is bounded by

$$O(p_i(\xi) \cdot (T_\ell + g_\ell)) = O\left(\frac{p}{2^{\ell-1}} \cdot \left(\frac{n + p \log^3 p}{\frac{p}{2^\ell} \log p} + \log^2 p \right) \right) = O\left(\frac{n}{\log p} + p \log^2 p \right).$$

Thus, the total work incurred by all unreliable minority phases in any execution ξ is $O(n + p \log^3 p)$.

From Lemmas 5.43 and 5.44(b), we get that a reliable minority phase may be fractional or optimal with high probability $1 - e^{-T_\ell/16}$, whereas it may be unproductive with very small probability $e^{-T_\ell/16} \leq e^{-\log^2 p}/16$. Using a similar argument as for majority phases, we get that for almost all sets of permutations Ψ (probability $1 - O(\log^2 p \cdot e^{-T_\ell/16}) \geq 1 - e^{-\Omega(T_\ell)}$) and for every execution ξ, there is no minority reliable unproductive phase. The work incurred by a fractional phase i of an epoch ℓ in any execution ξ, is bounded by $O(p_i(\xi) \cdot (T_\ell + g_\ell)) = O(\frac{n}{\log p} + p \log^2 p)$. Also note that by definition, there can be at most $O(\log_{3/4} n)$ ($= O(\log p)$ since $n \leq p^2$) fractional phases in any execution ξ, and hence, the total work incurred by all fractional reliable minority phases in any execution ξ is $O(n + p \log^3 p)$. We now consider the optimal reliable minority phases for any execution ξ. Here we have an optimal allocation of tasks to processors in $V_i(\xi)$. By definition of optimality, in average one task in $U_i(\xi) \setminus U_{i+1}(\xi)$ is performed by at most *four* processors from $V_{i+1}(\xi)$, and by definition of reliability, by at most *eight* processors in $V_i(\xi)$. Therefore, in optimal phases, each unit of work spent on performing a task results to a unique task completion (within a constant overhead), for any execution ξ. It therefore follows that the work incurred in all optimal reliable minority phases is bounded by $O(n)$ in any execution ξ.

Therefore, from the above, we conclude that when $n \leq p^2$, for random set of permutations Ψ the work complexity of algorithm GKS_ε executed on such set Ψ is $S = O(n + p \log^3 p)$ with probability $1 - e^{-\Omega(p \log p)} - e^{-\Omega(T_\ell)} = 1 - e^{-\Omega(T_\ell)}$ (the probability appears only from analysis of majority and unproductive reliable minority phases). Consequently, such set Ψ exists. Also, from Lemma 5.44 and the above discussion, $\beta > 0$ (e.g., $\beta = 9$) exists. Finally, the bound on messages using selected set Ψ and constant β is obtained as follows: there are $O(\log^2 p)$ executions of gossip stages. Each gossip stage requires $O(p^{1+\varepsilon})$ messages (message complexity of one instance of $\text{GOSSIP}_{\varepsilon/3}$). Thus, $M = O(p^{1+\varepsilon} \log^2 p) = O(p^{1+2\varepsilon})$.

Case 2: $n > p^2$. In this case, the tasks are partitioned into $n' = p^2$ chunks, where each chunk contains at most $\lceil n/p^2 \rceil$ tasks (see Remark 5.37). Using the result of Case 1 and selected set Ψ and constant

β, we get that $S = O(n' + p \log^3 p) \cdot \Theta(n/p^2) = O(p^2 \cdot n/p^2 + n/p^2 \cdot p \log^3 p) = O(n)$. The message complexity is derived with the same way as in Case 1.   □

5.4   ALGORITHMS KS_{AW} AND KS_{PA}

In this section, we consider the *Do-All* problem in the message-passing model subject to processor crashes and asynchrony. Obtaining algorithmic efficiency in asynchronous message-passing models of computation is difficult. For an algorithm to be interesting, it must be better than the oblivious algorithm with work $S = O(n \cdot p)$. However, as we discussed in Section 5.1, if messages are delayed by $\Theta(n)$ time then the trivial lower bound $\Omega(n \cdot p)$ applies. Thus, it is interesting to develop algorithms that are correct for any pattern of asynchrony and failures, and whose efficiency depends on the message latency upper bound, such that work complexity increases gracefully as the latency grows. The quality of the algorithms can be assessed by comparing their work to corresponding *delay-sensitive* lower bounds.

In this section, we present complexity bounds for work-efficient message-passing deterministic algorithms for the *Do-All* problem. The algorithms tolerate any pattern of processor crashes with at least one surviving processor, and achieve subquadratic work in n and p as long as $d = o(n)$. Thus, we pursue *delay-sensitive* analysis of work and message complexity. Noting again that work is necessarily $\Omega(p \cdot n)$ for $d = \Omega(n)$, we give a comprehensive analysis for $d < n$, achieving substantially better work complexity.

We present a family of deterministic algorithms called KS_{AW} and a deterministic algorithm KS_{PA} along with delay-sensitive analyses. First, we formulate the adversarial behavior and provide a delay-sensitive lower bound for deterministic *Do-All* algorithms.

5.4.1   ADVERSARIAL MODEL, COMPLEXITY AND LOWER BOUNDS

Processors communicate over a fully connected network by sending point-to-point messages via reliable asynchronous channels. Messages are subject to delays, but are not corrupted or lost.

We assume an omniscient (on-line) adversary that introduces delays. We call this adversary $\mathcal{A}_D$. The adversary can introduce arbitrary delays between local processor steps and cause processor crashes (crashes can be viewed as infinite delays). The only restriction is that at least one processor is non-faulty. Adversary $\mathcal{A}_D$ also causes arbitrary message delays.

We specialize adversary $\mathcal{A}_D$ by imposing a constraint on message delays. We assume the existence of a global real-timed clock that is unknown to the processors. For convenience, we measure time in terms of units that represent the smallest possible time between consecutive clock-ticks of any processor. We define the delay-constrained adversary as follows. We assume that there exists an integer parameter d, that is not assumed to be a constant and that is *unknown* to the processors, such that messages are delayed by at most d time units. We call this adversary $\mathcal{A}_D^{(d)}$. It is easy to see that $\mathcal{A}_D^{(d)} \subseteq \mathcal{A}_D^{(d+1)}$ for any $d \geq 0$, because increasing the maximum delays introduces new adversarial behaviors. We also note that $\mathcal{A}_D = \bigcup_{d \in \mathbb{N}} \mathcal{A}_D^{(d)}$.

We are interested in algorithms that are correct against adversary $\mathcal{A}_D$, i.e., for any message delays. For the purpose of analysis of such algorithms, we are interested in complexity analysis under adversary $\mathcal{A}_D^{(d)}$, for some specific positive d that is unknown to the algorithm. Note that by the choice of the time units, a processor can take at most d local steps during any global time period of duration d.

We assess the efficiency of algorithms in terms of work and message complexity under adversary $\mathcal{A}_D^{(d)}$. We use the notation $S(n, p, d)$ to denote work, and $M(n, p, d)$ to denote message complexity. That is, we extend the notation introduced in Chapter 2 to include parameter d. (When work or messages complexities do not depend on d, we omit d and use, for example, $S(n, p)$ and $M(n, p)$ for work and message complexity.)

Next, we formulate a proposition leading us to not consider algorithms where a processor may halt voluntarily before learning that all tasks have been performed.

Proposition 5.46   *Let Alg be a Do-All algorithm such that there is some execution ξ of Alg in which there is a processor that (voluntarily) halts before it learns that all tasks have been performed. Then there is an execution ξ' of Alg with unbounded work in which some task is never performed.*

As the result of Proposition 5.46, we only consider algorithms where a processor may voluntarily halt only after it knows that all tasks are complete, i.e., for each task the processor has local knowledge that either it performed the task or that some other processor did.

Note that for large message delays the work of any *Do-All* algorithm is necessarily $\Omega(n \cdot p)$. The following proposition formalizes this lower bound and motivates the delay-sensitive approach.

Proposition 5.47   *Any algorithm that solves the Do-All problem in the presence of adversary $\mathcal{A}_D^{(c \cdot n)}$, for a constant $c > 0$, has work $S(n, p) = \Omega(n \cdot p)$.*

We now show a delay-sensitive lower bound on work for deterministic asynchronous *Do-All* algorithms under adversary adversary $\mathcal{A}_D^{(d)}$, for $d \geq 1$.

Theorem 5.48   Any deterministic algorithm solving *Do-All* with n tasks using p asynchronous message-passing processors against adversary $\mathcal{A}_D^{(d)}$ performs work $S(n, p, d) = \Omega(n + p \min\{d, n\} \log_{d+1}(d + n))$.

Proof. That the required work is at least n is obvious—each task must be performed. We present the analysis for $n > 5$ and n that is divisible by 6 (this is sufficient to prove the lower bound). We present the following adversarial strategy. The adversary partitions computation into stages, each containing $\min\{d, n/6\}$ steps. We assume that the adversary delivers all messages sent to a processor in stage s at the end of stage s (recall that the receiver can process any such message later, according to its own local clock)—this is allowed since the length of stage s is at most d. For stage s, we define the set of processors P_s such that the adversary delays all processors not in P_s. More precisely, each processor in P_s is not delayed during stage s, but any processor not in P_s is delayed, so it does not complete any step during stage s.

Consider stage s. Let $u_s > 0$ be the number of tasks that remain unperformed at the beginning of stage s, and let U_s be the set of such tasks. We now show how to define the set P_s. Suppose first that each processor is not delayed during stage s (with respect to the time unit). Let $J_s(i)$, for every processor i, $i \in \mathcal{P}$ (recall that $\mathcal{P}$ is the set of all processors), denote the set of tasks from U_s (we do not consider tasks not in U_s in the analysis of stage s since they were performed before) which are performed by processor i during stage s (recall that inside stage s processor i does not receive any message from other processors). Note that $|J_s(i)|$ is at most $\min\{d, n/6\}$, which is the length of a stage.

Claim. *There are at least $\frac{u_s}{3\min\{d,n/6\}}$ tasks z such that each of them is contained in at most $2p\min\{d, n/6\}/u_s$ sets in the family $\{J_s(i) \mid i \in \mathcal{P}\}$.*

We prove the claim by the pigeonhole principle. If the claim is not true, then there would be more than $u_s - \frac{u_s}{3\min\{d,t/6\}}$ tasks such that each of them would be contained in more than $2p\min\{d, n/6\}/u_s$ sets in the family $\{J_s(i) \mid i \in \mathcal{P}\}$. This yields a contradiction because the following inequality holds

$$p \min\{d, n/6\} = \sum_{i \in \mathcal{P}} |J_s(i)| \geq \left(u_s - \frac{u_s}{3\min\{d, n/6\}}\right) \cdot \frac{2p\min\{d, n/6\}}{u_s}$$

$$= \left(2 - \frac{2}{3\min\{d, n/6\}}\right) \cdot p\min\{d, n/6\} > p \min\{d, n/6\},$$

since $d \geq 1$ and $n > 4$. This proves the claim.

We denote the set of $\frac{u_s}{3\min\{d,n/6\}}$ tasks from the above claim by J_s. We define P_s to be the set $\{i : J_s \cap J_s(i) = \emptyset\}$. By the definition of tasks $z \in J_s$ we obtain that

$$|P_s| \geq p - \frac{u_s}{3\min\{d, n/6\}} \cdot \frac{2p\min\{d, n/6\}}{u_s} \geq p/3.$$

Since all processors, other that those in P_s, are delayed during the whole stage s, work performed during stage s is at least $\frac{p}{3} \cdot \min\{d, n/6\}$ and all tasks from J_s remains unperformed. Hence, the number u_{s+1} of undone tasks after stage s is still at least $\frac{u_s}{3\min\{d,n/6\}}$.

If $d < n/6$ then work during stage s is at least $p\,d/6$, and there remain at least $\frac{u_s}{3d}$ unperformed tasks. Hence, this process may be continued, starting with n tasks, for at least $\log_{3d} n = \Omega(\log_{d+1}(d + n))$ stages, until all tasks are performed. The total work is then $\Omega(p\,d\log_{d+1}(d + n))$.

If $d \geq n/6$, then during the first stage work performed is at least $p\,n/18 = \Omega(p\,n\log_{d+1}(d + n)) = \Omega(p\,n)$, and at the end of stage 1, at least $\frac{n}{3n/6} = 2$ tasks remain unperformed. Notice that this asymptotic value does not depend on whether the minimum is selected among d and n, or among d and $n/6$. More precisely, the works is

$$\Omega(p\min\{d, n\}\log_{d+1}(d + n)) = \Omega(p\min\{d, n/6\}\log_{d+1}(d + n)),$$

which completes the proof.   □

The above lower bound shows that work grows with d and becomes $\Omega(p\,n)$ as d approaches n.

5.4.2   FAMILY OF DETERMINISTIC ALGORITHMS KS_{AW}

We now present a deterministic solution for the *Do-All* problem with p processors and n tasks. In particular, we develop a family of deterministic algorithms KS_{AW}, such that for any constant $\varepsilon > 0$, there is an algorithm with work $S = O(np^\varepsilon + p\,d\lceil n/d\rceil^\varepsilon)$ and message complexity $M = O(p \cdot S)$.

More precisely, algorithms from the family KS_{AW} are parameterized by a positive integer q and a list Ψ of q permutations on the set $[q] = \{1, \ldots, q\}$, where $2 \leq q < p \leq n$. We show that for any constant $\varepsilon > 0$, there is a constant q and a corresponding set of permutations Ψ, such that the resulting algorithm has work $S = O(np^\varepsilon + p\,d\lceil n/d\rceil^\varepsilon)$ and message complexity $M = O(p \cdot S)$. The work of these algorithms is within a small polynomial factor of the corresponding lower bound of Theorem 5.48.

Algorithms in the family KS_{AW} are modeled after the shared-memory Algorithm AW^T that we studied in Section 4.4 and use a list of q permutations in the same way (satisfying Fact 4.14). The are two main differences:

  (i) instead of maintaining a global data structure representing a q-ary tree, in these algorithms each processor has a local replica of the tree, and

 (ii) instead of using atomic shared memory to access the nodes of the tree, processors read values from the local tree, and instead of writing to the tree, processors multicast the tree; the local data structures are updated when multicast messages are received.

DESCRIPTION OF ALGORITHM $KS_{AW}(q)$

Let q be some constant such that $2 \leq q \leq p$. We assume that the number of tasks n is an integer power of q, specifically let $n = q^h$ for some $h \in \mathbb{N}$. (When the number of tasks is not a power of q, standard padding techniques can be used that do not affect the asymptotic complexity of the algorithm.) We also assume that $\log_q p$ is a positive integer. If it is not, we pad the processors with at most qp "infinitely delayed" processors, so this assumption is satisfied; in this case, the upper bound is increased by a (constant) factor of at most q.

The algorithm uses any list of q permutations $\Psi = \langle \pi_0, \ldots \pi_{q-1} \rangle$ from $\mathcal{S}_q$ such that Ψ has the minimum contention among all such lists (recall discussion on contention of permutations from Section 4.4.1). We define a family of algorithms, where each algorithm is parameterized by q, and a list Ψ with the above contention property. We call this algorithm $KS_{AW}(q)$. In this section, we first present the algorithm for $p \geq n$, then state the parameterization for $p < n$.

Algorithm $KS_{AW}(q)$, utilizes a q-ary boolean *progress tree* with n leaves, where the tasks are associated with the leaves. Initially, all nodes of the tree are 0 (false) indicating that no tasks have been performed. Instead of maintaining a global data structure representing a q-ary tree, in the algorithms each processor has a replica of the tree.

Whenever a processor learns that all tasks in a subtree rooted at a certain node have been performed, it sets the node to 1 (true) and shares the good news with all other processors. This is done by multicasting the processor's progress tree; the local replicas at each processor are updated when multicast messages are received.

Each processor, acting independently, searches for work in the smallest immediate subtree that has remaining unperformed tasks. It then performs any tasks it finds, and moves out of that subtree when all work within it is completed. When exploring the subtrees rooted at an interior node at height m, a processor visits the subtrees in the order given by one of the permutations in Ψ. Specifically, the processor uses the permutation π_s such that s is the value of the m-th digit in the q-ary expansion of the processor's identifier (PID). We now present this in more detail.

Data Structures. Given the n tasks, the progress tree is a q-ary ordered tree of height h, where $n = q^h$. The number of nodes in the progress tree is $l = \sum_{i=0}^{h-1} q^i = (q^{h+1}-1)/(q-1) = (qn-1)/(q-1)$. Each node of the tree is a boolean, indicating whether the subtree rooted at the node is done (value 1) or not (value 0).

The progress tree is stored in a boolean array $Tree[0..l-1]$, where $Tree[0]$ is the root, and the q children of the interior node $Tree[v]$ being the nodes $Tree[qv+1], Tree[qv+2], \ldots, Tree[qv+q]$. The space occupied by the tree is $O(n)$. The n tasks are associated with the leaves of the progress tree, such that the leaf $Tree[v]$ corresponds to the task $Task(v+n+1-l)$.

We represent the PID of each of the p processors in terms of its q-ary expansion. We care only about the h least significant q-ary digits of each PID (thus when $p > n$ several processors may be indistinguishable in the algorithm). The q-ary expansions of each PID is stored in the array $x[0..h-1]$.

Control Flow. The code is given in Figure 5.9. Each of the p processors executes two concurrent threads. One thread (lines 10-14) traverses the local progress tree in search of work, performs the tasks, and broadcasts the updated progress tree. The second thread (lines 20-26) receives messages from other processors and updates the local progress tree. (Each processor is asynchronous, but we assume that its two threads run at approximately the same speed. This is assumed for simplicity only, as it is trivial to explicitly schedule the threads on a single processor.) Note that the updates of the local progress tree *Tree* are always monotone: initially, each node contain 0, then once a node changes its value to 1, it remains 1 forever. Thus, no issues of consistency arise.

The progress tree is traversed using the recursive procedure DOWORK (lines 40-54). The order of traversals within the progress tree is determined by the list of permutations $\Psi = \langle \pi_0, \pi_1, \ldots, \pi_{q-1} \rangle$. Each processor uses, at the node of depth η, the ηth q-ary digit $x[\eta]$ of its PID to select the permutation $\pi_{x[\eta]}$ from Ψ (recall that we use only the h least significant q-ary digits of each PID when representing the PID in line 42). The processor traverses the q subtrees in

```
00    const q -- Arity of the progress tree
01    const Ψ = ⟨π_r | 0 ≤ r < q ∧ π_r ∈ S_q⟩ -- Fixed list of q permutations of [q]
02    const l = (qt−1)/(q−1) -- The size of the progress tree
03    const h = log_q n -- The height of the progress tree
04    type ProgressTree: array [0 .. l − 1] of boolean -- Progress tree

05    for each processor PID = 1 to p begin
06        ProgressTree Tree_PID -- The progress tree at processor PID

10        thread -- Traverse progress tree in search of work
11            integer v init = 0 -- Current node, begin at the root
12            integer η init = 0 -- Current depth in the tree
13            DOWORK(v, η)
14        end

20        thread -- Receive broadcast messages
21            set of ProgressTree B -- Incoming messages
22            while Tree_PID[0] ≠ 1 do -- While not all tasks certified
23                receive B -- Deliver the set of received messages
24                Tree_PID := Tree_PID ∨ (⋁_{b∈B} b) -- Learn progress
25            od
26        end
27    end.
```

```
40    procedure DOWORK(v, η) -- Recursive progress tree traversal
41    -- v : current node index ; η : node depth
42        const array x[0 .. h − 1] = PID_(base q) -- h least significant q-ary digits of PID
43        if Tree_PID[v] = 0 then -- Node not done – still work left
44            if η = h then -- Node v is a leaf
45                perform Task(n − l + v + 1) -- Do the task
46            else -- Node v is not a leaf
47                for r = 1 to q do -- Visit subtrees in the order of π_{x[η]}
48                    DOWORK(qv + π_{x[η]}(r), η + 1)
49                od
50            fi
51            Tree_PID[v] := 1 -- Record completion of the subtree
52            broadcast Tree_PID -- Share the good news
53        fi
54    end.
```

Figure 5.9: The deterministic algorithm $KS_{AW}(q)$ ($p \geq n$).

the order determined by $\pi_{x[\eta]}$ (lines 47-49); the processors starts the traversal of a subtree only if the corresponding bit in the progress tree is not set (line 43).

In other words, each processor PID traverses its progress tree in a post-order fashion using the q-ary digits of its PID and the permutations in Ψ to establish the order of the subtree traversals, except that when the messages from other processors are received, the progress tree of processor PID can be pruned based on the progress of other processors.

Parameterization for Large Number of Tasks. When the number of input tasks n' exceeds the number of processors p, we divide the tasks into *jobs*, where each job consists of at most $\lceil n'/p \rceil$ tasks. The algorithm in Figure 5.9 is then used with the resulting p jobs ($p = n$), where $Task(j)$ now refers to the job number j ($1 \leq j \leq n$). Note that in this case the cost of work corresponding to doing a single job is $\lceil n'/p \rceil$.

ANALYSIS OF ALGORITHM $KS_{AW}(q)$

Before we analyze the complexity of Algorithm $KS_{AW}(q)$, we first show that the algorithm correctly solves the *Do-All* problem.

Correctness of Algorithm $KS_{AW}(q)$. The correctness follows from the observation that a processor leaves a subtree by returning from a recursive call to DOWORK if and only if the subtree contains no unfinished work and its root is marked accordingly. This is formalized as follows.

Lemma 5.49 *In any execution of algorithm $KS_{AW}(q)$, whenever a processor returns from a call to* DOWORK(v, η), *all tasks associated with the leaves that are the descendants of node v have been performed.*

The result follows by code inspection and by induction on η. We now give the main correctness result.

Theorem 5.50 *Any execution of algorithm $KS_{AW}(q)$ terminates in finite time having performed all tasks.*

Proof. The progress tree used by the algorithm has finite number of nodes. By code inspection, each processor executing the algorithm makes at most one recursive call per each node of the tree. Thus, the algorithm terminates in finite time. By Lemma 5.49, whenever a processor returns from the call to DOWORK$(v\,(=0),\ \eta\,(=0))$, all tasks associated with the leaves that are the descendants of the node $v = 0$ are done, and the value of node is set to 1. Since this node is the root of the tree, all tasks are done. $\square$

Complexity Analysis of Algorithm $KS_{AW}(q)$. We start by showing a lemma that relates the work of the algorithm, against adversary $\mathcal{A}_D^{(d)}$ to its recursive structure.

We consider the case $p \geq n$. Let $S(n, p, d)$ denote the work of algorithm $KS_{AW}(q)$ through the first global step in which some processor completes the last remaining task and broadcasts the message containing the progress tree where $T[0] = 1$. Observe that $S(1, p, d) = O(p)$. This is because the progress tree has only one leaf. Each processor makes a single call to DoWork, performs the sole task and broadcasts the completed progress tree.

Lemma 5.51   *For p-processor, n-task algorithm $KS_{AW}(q)$ with $p \geq n$ and n and p divisible by q:*

$$S(n, p, d) = O(\text{Cont}(\Psi) \cdot S(p/q, n/q, d) + p \cdot q \cdot \min\{d, n/q\}) .$$

The result is obtained by close investigation of the code of the algorithm and the properties of contention per Fact 4.14. We now prove the following theorem about the work of algorithm $KS_{AW}(q)$.

Theorem 5.52   Consider algorithm $KS_{AW}(q)$ with p processors and n tasks where $p \geq n$. Let d be the maximum message delay. For any constant $\varepsilon > 0$, there is a constant q such that the algorithm has work $S(n, p, d) = O(p \min\{n, d\} \lceil n/d \rceil^{\varepsilon})$.

Proof. Fix a constant $\varepsilon > 0$; without loss of generality, we can assume that $\varepsilon \leq 1$. Let a be the sufficiently large positive constant "hidden" in the big-oh upper bound for $S(n, p, d)$ in Lemma 5.51. We consider a constant $q > 0$ such that $\log_q(4a \log q) \leq \varepsilon$. Such q exists since $\lim_{q \to \infty} \log_q(4a \log q) = 0$ (however, q is a constant of order $2^{\frac{\log(1/\varepsilon)}{\varepsilon}}$).

First, suppose that $\log_q n$ and $\log_q p$ are positive integers. We prove by induction on p and n that

$$S(n, p, d) \leq q \cdot n^{\log_q(4a \log q)} \cdot p \cdot d^{1-\log_q(4a \log q)} ,$$

For the *base case* of $n = 1$, the statement is correct since $S(1, p, d) = O(p)$. For $n > 1$, we choose the list of permutations Ψ with $\text{Cont}(\Psi) \leq 3q \log q$ per Lemma 4.14. Due to our choice of parameters, $\log_q n$ is an integer and $n \leq p$. Let β stand for $\log_q(4a \log q)$. Using Lemma 5.51 and inductive hypothesis, we obtain

$$\begin{aligned} S(n, p, d) &\leq a \cdot \left(3q \log q \cdot q \cdot \left(\frac{n}{q}\right)^{\beta} \cdot \frac{p}{q} \cdot d^{1-\beta} + p \cdot q \cdot \min\{d, n/q\}\right) \\ &\leq a \cdot \left(\left(q \cdot n^{\beta} \cdot p \cdot d^{1-\beta}\right) \cdot 3 \log q \cdot q^{-\beta} + p \cdot q \cdot \min\{d, n/q\}\right) . \end{aligned}$$

We now consider two cases:

Case 1: $d \leq n/q$. It follows that

$$p \cdot q \cdot \min\{d, n/q\} = p q d \leq p q d^{1-\beta} \cdot \left(\frac{n}{q}\right)^{\beta} .$$

Case 2: $d > n/q$. It follows that

$$p \cdot q \cdot \min\{d, n/q\} = p n \leq p q d^{1-\beta} \cdot \left(\frac{n}{q}\right)^{\beta} .$$

Putting everything together, we obtain the desired inequality

$$S(n, p, d) \leq a \left(\left(q \cdot n^\beta \cdot p \cdot d^{1-\beta} \cdot q^{-\beta} \right) 4 \log q \right) \leq q \cdot n^\beta \cdot p \cdot d^{1-\beta} .$$

To complete the proof, consider any $n \leq p$. We add $n' - n$ new "dummy" tasks, where $n' - n < q\,n - 1$, and $p' - p$ new "virtual" processors, where $p' - p < q\,p - 1$, such that $\log_q n'$ and $\log_q p'$ are positive integers. We assume that all "virtual" crash at the start of the computation (else they can be thought of as delayed to infinity). It follows that

$$S(n, p, d) \leq S(n', p', d) \leq q \cdot (n')^\beta p' \cdot d^{1-\beta} \leq q^{2+\beta} n^\beta p \cdot d^{1-\beta} .$$

Since $\beta \leq \varepsilon$, we obtain that work of algorithm $KS_{AW}(q)$ is $O(\min\{n^\varepsilon p\, d^{1-\varepsilon}, n\ p\}) = O(p \min\{n, d\} \lceil n/d \rceil^\varepsilon)$, which completes the proof of the theorem. $\qquad \square$

Now we consider the case $p < n$. Recall that in this case we divide the n tasks into p jobs of size at most $\lceil n/p \rceil$, and we let the algorithm work with these jobs. It takes a processor $O(n/p)$ work (instead of a constant) to process a single job.

Theorem 5.53   Consider algorithm $KS_{AW}(q)$ with p processors and n tasks where $p < n$. Let d be the maximum message delay. For any constant $\varepsilon > 0$, there is a constant q such that $KS_{AW}(q)$ has work $S(n, p, d) = O(np^\varepsilon + p \min\{n, d\} \lceil n/d \rceil^\varepsilon)$.

Proof. We use Theorem 5.52 with p jobs (instead of n tasks), where a single job takes $O(n/p)$ units of work. The upper bound on the maximal delay for receiving messages about the completion of some job is $d' = \lceil pd/n \rceil = O(1 + pd/n)$ "job units", where a single job unit takes $\Theta(n/p)$ time. We obtain the following bound on work:

$$
\begin{aligned}
O\left(p \min\{p, d'\} \lceil p/d' \rceil^\varepsilon \cdot \frac{n}{p} \right)
&= O\left(\min\left\{ p^2, p^\varepsilon p(d')^{1-\varepsilon} \right\} \cdot \frac{n}{p} \right) \\
&= O\left(\min\left\{ n\,p, n\,p^\varepsilon + pn^\varepsilon d^{1-\varepsilon} \right\} \right) \\
&= O\left(n\,p^\varepsilon + p \min\{n, d\} \left\lceil \frac{n}{d} \right\rceil^\varepsilon \right),
\end{aligned}
$$

as desired. $\qquad \square$

Finally, we consider the message complexity of the algorithm.

Theorem 5.54   Algorithm $KS_{AW}(q)$ with p processors and n tasks has message complexity $M(n, p, d) = O(p \cdot S(n, p, d))$.

Proof. In each step, a processor broadcasts at most one message to $p - 1$ other processors. $\qquad \square$

5.4.3   ALGORITHM KS_{PA}

We now present and analyze a deterministic algorithm that is simpler than algorithms KS_{AW}. The algorithm, called KS_{PA}, relies *directly* on permutation schedules (as opposed to algorithms KS_{AW} that rely indirectly through algorithm AW^T). Before we describe the algorithm, we first generalize the notion of contention (of Section 4.4.1) to the notion of *d-contention*.

GENERALIZED CONTENTION

For a schedule $\pi = \langle \pi(1), \ldots, \pi(n) \rangle$, an element $\pi(j)$ of π is a *d-left-to-right maximum* (or d-lrm for short) if the number the elements in π preceding and greater than $\pi(j)$ is less than d, i.e., $|\{i : i < j \wedge \pi(i) > \pi(j)\}| < d$.

   Given a n-schedule π, we define (d) - $\mathrm{LRM}(\pi)$ as the number of d-lrm's in the schedule π. For a list $\Psi = \langle \pi_0, \ldots, \pi_{p-1} \rangle$ of permutations from $\mathcal{S}_n$ and a permutation δ in $\mathcal{S}_n$, the d-contention of Ψ with respect to δ is defined as

$$(d)\text{-Cont}(\Psi, \delta) = \sum_{u=0}^{p-1} (d) \text{ - } \mathrm{LRM}(\delta^{-1} \circ \pi_u) .$$

The *d-contention of the list of schedules* Ψ is defined as

$$(d)\text{-Cont}(\Psi) = \max_{\delta \in \mathcal{S}_n} \{(d)\text{-Cont}(\Psi, \delta)\} .$$

   Then, the following is known for d-contention.

Fact 5.55   There is a list of p schedules Ψ from $\mathcal{S}_n$ such that $(d)\text{-Cont}(\Psi) \leq n \log n + 8pd \ln(e + n/d)$, for every positive integer d.

DESCRIPTION OF ALGORITHM KS_{PA}

The main operation of the algorithm is that each processor, while it has not ascertained that all tasks are complete, performs a specific task from its local list based on a permutation over tasks and broadcasts this fact to other processors. The known complete tasks are removed from the list. We assume the existence of the list of permutations Ψ chosen per Fact 5.55. Each processor pid permutes its list of tasks according to the local permutation $\pi_{\mathrm{PID}} \in \Psi$. The code is given in Figure 5.10.

   As with algorithms KS_{AW}, we initially consider the case of $p \geq n$. The case of $p < n$ is obtained by dividing the n tasks into p jobs, each of size at most $\lceil n/p \rceil$. In this case, we deal with jobs instead of tasks in the code of the algorithm.

ANALYSIS OF ALGORITHM KS_{PA}

The correctness of the algorithm is derived from the proofs of the complexity analysis. Hence, we proceed to the complexity analysis of the algorithm.

```
00      type TaskId : [n]
01      type TaskList : list of TaskId
02      type MsgBuff : set of TaskList
03      const list Ψ = ⟨TaskList πᵣ | 1 ≤ r ≤ p ∧ πᵣ ∈ Sₙ⟩ -- Ψ is a fixed list of p permutations
10      for each processor PID = 1 to p begin
11          TaskList Tasks_PID initially [n]
12          MsgBuf B -- Incoming messages
13          TaskId tid -- Task id; next to done
20          ORDER(Tasks_PID)
21          while Tasks_PID ≠ ∅ do
22              receive B -- Deliver the set of received messages
23              Tasks_PID := Tasks_PID − (⋃_{b∈B} b) -- Remove tasks
24              tid := SELECT(Tasks_PID) -- Select next task
25              perform Task(tid)
26              Tasks_PID := Tasks_PID − {tid} -- Remove done task
27              broadcast Tasks_PID -- Share the news
28          od
29      end.

40      procedure ORDER(T) begin  T := π_PID  end.
41      TaskId function SELECT(T) begin  return(T(1))  end.
```

Figure 5.10: Algorithm KS_{PA} ($p \geq n$).

In the analysis, we use the quantity t defined as $t = \min\{n, p\}$. When $n < p$, t represents the number of tasks to be performed. When $n \geq p$, t represents the number of jobs (of size at most $\lceil n/p \rceil$) to be performed; in this case, each task in Figure 5.10 represents a single job. In the sequel, we continue referring to "tasks" only—from the combinatorial perspective there is no distinction between a task and a job, and the only accounting difference is that a task costs $\Theta(1)$ work, while a job costs $\Theta(\lceil n/p \rceil)$ work.

Recall that we measure global time units according to the time steps defined to be the smallest time between any two clock-ticks of any processor (Section 5.4.1). Thus, during any d global time steps, no processor can take more than d local steps.

For the purpose of the next lemma, we introduce the notion of adversary $\mathcal{A}_D^{(d,\sigma)}$, where σ is a permutation of n tasks. This is a specialization of adversary $\mathcal{A}_D^{(d)}$ that schedules the asynchronous processors so that each of the n tasks is performed for the first time in the order given by σ. More precisely, if the execution of the task σ_i is completed for the first time by some processor at the global time τ_i (unknown to the processor), and the task σ_j, for any $1 \leq i < j \leq n$, is completed for the first time by some processor at time τ_j, then $\tau_i \leq \tau_j$. Note that any execution of an algorithm solving the *Do-All* problem against adversary $\mathcal{A}_D^{(d)}$ corresponds to the execution against some adversary $\mathcal{A}_D^{(d,\sigma)}$ for the specific σ.

Lemma 5.56   *The work S of algorithm KS_{PA} is at most (d)-Cont(Ψ) against adversary $\mathcal{A}_D^{(d)}$.*

Proof. Suppose processor i starts performing task z at (real) time τ. By the definition of adversary $\mathcal{A}_D^{(d)}$, no other processor successfully performed task z and broadcast its message by time $(\tau - d)$. Consider adversary $\mathcal{A}_D^{(d,\sigma)}$, for any permutation $\sigma \in \mathcal{S}_n$.

For each processor i, let J_i contain all pairs (i, r) such that i performs task $\pi_i(r)$ during the computation. We construct function L from the pairs in the set $\bigcup_i J_i$ to the set of all d-lrm's of the list $\sigma^{-1} \circ \Psi$ and show that L is a bijection. We do the construction independently for each processor i. It is obvious that $(i, 1) \in J_i$, and we let $L(i, 1) = 1$. Suppose that $(i, r) \in J_i$ and we defined function L for all elements from J_i less than (i, r) in lexicographic order. We define $L(i, r)$ as the first $s \leq r$ such that $(\sigma^{-1} \circ \pi_i)(s)$ is a d-lrm not assigned by L to any element in J_i.

Claim. *For every* $(i, r) \in J_i$, $L(i, r)$ *is well defined.*

For $r = 1$, we have $L(i, 1) = 1$. For the (lexicographically) first d elements in J_i, this is also easy to show. Suppose L is well defined for all elements in J_i less than (i, r), and (i, r) is at least the $(d + 1)$st element in J_i. We show that $L(i, r)$ is also well defined. Suppose, to the contrary, that there is no position $s \leq r$ such that $(\sigma^{-1} \circ \pi_i)(s)$ is a d-lrm and s is not assigned by L before the step of the construction for $(i, r) \in J_i$. Let $(i, s_1) < \ldots < (i, s_d)$ be the elements of J_i less than (i, r) such that $(\sigma^{-1} \circ \pi_i)(L(i, s_1)), \ldots, (\sigma^{-1} \circ \pi_i)(L(i, s_d))$ are greater than $(\sigma^{-1} \circ \pi_i)(r)$. They exist from the fact, that $(\sigma^{-1} \circ \pi_i)(r)$ is not a d-lrm and all "previous" d-lrm's are assigned by L. Let τ_r be the global time when task $\pi_i(r)$ is performed by i. Obviously, task $\pi_i(L(i, s_1))$ has been performed at time that is at least $d + 1$ local steps (and hence also global time units) before τ_r. It follows from this and the definition of adversary $\mathcal{A}_D^{(d,\sigma)}$ that task $\pi_i(r)$ has been performed by some other processor in a local step, which ended also at least $(d + 1)$ time units before τ_r. This contradicts the observation made at the beginning of the proof of lemma. This proves the claim.

That L is a bijection follows directly from the definition of L. It follows that the number of performances of tasks – equal to the total number of local steps until completion of all tasks – is at most (d)-Cont(Ψ, σ), against any adversary $\mathcal{A}_D^{(d,\sigma)}$. Hence, total work is at most (d)-Cont(Ψ) against adversary $\mathcal{A}_D^{(d)}$. $\qquad\square$

We are now ready to give the main complexity result for algorithm KS_{PA}.

Theorem 5.57   There exists a deterministic list of schedules Ψ such that algorithm KS_{PA}, under adversary $\mathcal{A}_D^{(d)}$, performs work
$$S(n, p, d) = O(n \log t + p \min\{n, d\} \log(2 + n/d))$$
and has message complexity
$$M(n, p, d) = O(n\, p \log t + p^2 \min\{n, d\} \log(2 + n/d)) .$$

Proof. The work complexity follows from using the set Ψ from Fact 5.55 together with Lemma 5.56 and some algebraic manipulation. The message complexity follows from the fact that in every local step, each processor sends $p - 1$ messages. $\qquad\square$

5.5   EXERCISES

5.1. In Section 5.1, it is shown how to emulate shared-memory *Do-All* algorithms X and AW^T from Chapter 4 in the message-passing model. Using the same approach, give an overview of how algorithm *Groote* from Section 4.3 can be emulated in the message-passing model. What are the resulting work and message complexities?

5.2. Prove Lemma 5.12. Use induction on the number of attended phases.

5.3. Prove that the processor and task accounting of algorithm *AN* is accurate. That is, prove Lemmas 5.13 and 5.14.

5.4. Algorithm *AN* relies on reliable broadcast. Show that if instead of reliable broadcast the coordinators use separate point-to-point messages, the set of participating processors may partition into two or more groups in such a way that the processors in one group consider all other processors as crashed.

5.5. Analyze work complexity of algorithm *AN* under the assumption that the broadcast is not reliable, when the set of processors partitions into g similarly sized groups, each of size $O(p/g)$, after which failures cease.

5.6. Prove the lower bound on work of $\Omega(n + fp)$ for any single coordinator p-processor message-passing (point-to-point) n-task *Do-All* algorithm that is subject to at most $f < p$ processor crashes.

5.7. Prove Lemma 5.32. Use induction on the number of epochs.

5.8. Prove Lemma 5.39. Use induction on the number of epochs.

5.9. Prove Proposition 5.46. For the proof assume a stronger model of computation where in one local step any processor can learn the complete state of another processor, including, in particular, the complete computation history of the other processor.

5.10. Prove Proposition 5.46. For the proof define a certain adversarial strategy of adversary $\mathcal{A}_D^{(c \cdot n)}$ and show that any *Do-All* algorithm under this strategy incurs the claimed work bound.

5.11. What algorithmic paradigm (from Section 3.1) do the algorithms of the family KS_{AW} implement? Explain your answer.

5.12. Prove Lemma 5.49. Use induction on η.

5.13. What algorithmic paradigm (from Section 3.1) does algorithm KS_{PA} implement? Explain your answer.

5.6   BIBLIOGRAPHICAL NOTES

Dwork, Halpern, and Waarts [28] introduced and studied the *Do-All* problem in the message-passing model. They developed several deterministic algorithms for the *Do-All* problem with synchronous crash-prone processors. Several subsequent works pursued the development of new algorithms for the same setting, see for example the works of De Prisco, Mayer, and Yung [83], Galil, Mayer, and Yung [33], and Chlebus, Gasieniec, Kowalski, and Shvartsman [18]. A comprehensive presentation of the *Do-All* problem in the message-passing setting can be found in [41].

The authors in [83] show the lower bound of $S = \Omega(n + (f + 1)p)$ for any algorithm that uses the stage-checkpoint strategy; note that this bound is quadratic in p for f comparable with p. Moreover, any protocol with at most one active coordinator (that is, a protocol that uses a single coordinator paradigm) is bound to have $S = \Omega(n + (f + 1)p)$. As we have seen in this chapter, algorithm *AN* beats this lower bound by using a multiple coordinators and reliable multicast. There are several algorithms for implementing reliable multicast, for example, see the presentation by Hadzilacos and Toueg in [48]. Algorithm GKS_ε also presented in this chapter beats this lower bound without using checkpointing and single coordinators; instead, it uses a gossip algorithm for the dissemination of information.

Attiya, Bar-Noy, and Dolev [13] were the first to show how to emulate an atomic Single-Writer Multi-Reader (SWMR) shared register in the message-passing model under processor crashes or link failures. Many works followed considering emulations of SWMR or MWMR registers under various failure models. For an overview see the survey of Attiya [12]. The emulation of shared-memory *Do-All* algorithms in the message-passing model in Section 5.1 is based on the work of Kowalski, Momenzadeh, and Shvartsman [62]. The atomic memory service AM is based on the reconfigurable atomic memory service of Gilbert, Lynch, and Shvartsman [45]. Memory service AM is a simplified version that uses a single quorum configuration for each object and does not use reconfiguration. The correctness of the algorithm and its performance properties follow directly from [45]. Quorum systems are well-known mathematical tools used for coordination in distributed systems [35, 44, 82].

Algorithm *AN* in Section 5.2 is based on a paper by Chlebus, De Prisco, and Shvartsman [17]. Missing proofs in that section appear there. The proof of Lemma 5.21 that refines the work complexity of algorithm *AN* for a small number of failures is due to Georgiou, Russell, and Shvartsman [38]. The authors in [17] present algorithm AR that solves the *Do-All* problem with synchronous crash-prone processors that are able to restart. The algorithm has work complexity $S = O((n + p \log p + f) \cdot \min\{\log p, \log f\})$ and message complexity $M = O(n + p \log p + fp)$, where f is the number of crashes and restarts (note that f can be unbounded). Algorithm AR is an extension of algorithm *AN*. The difference is that there are added messages to handle the restart of processors; in the absence of restarts, the two algorithms behave identically.

Algorithms $\text{GOSSIP}_\varepsilon$ and GKS_ε in Section 5.3 are based on the work of Georgiou, Kowalski, and Shvartsman [37] (algorithm GKS_ε is called DOALL_ε in that paper). Missing proofs from the section appear there. The complexity results presented in Section 5.3 involve the use of conceptual communication graphs (expander graphs) and sets of permutations with specific combinatorial properties. Expander graphs have been considered in various settings, see for example [8, 9, 18, 69, 90]. The notion of *contention* of permutations was proposed and studied by Anderson and Woll [10]. The notion of the *left-to-right maximum* is due to Knuth [59] (p. 13). Kowalski, Musial, and Shvartsman [63] explore ways of efficiently constructing permutations with low contention; they show that such permutations can be constructed deterministically in polynomial time; however, the efficiency of the algorithms using these constructions is slightly detuned.

Observe that the complexity bounds presented in Section 5.3 do not show how work and message complexities depend on f, the maximum number of crashes. In fact, it is possible to subject the algorithm to "failure-sensitivity-training" and obtain better results. Georgiou, Kowalski, and Shvartsman [37] show how this can be achieved and present a modified version of algorithm GKS_ε (that uses a modified version of algorithm $GOSSIP_\varepsilon$) that has work $S = O(n + p \cdot \min\{f + 1, \log^3 p\})$ and message complexity $M = O(fp^\varepsilon + p \min\{f + 1, \log p\})$, for any $\varepsilon > 0$.

Chlebus and Kowalski [19] were the first to define and study the *Gossip* problem for synchronous message-passing processors under an adaptive adversary that causes processor crashes (this is the version of the *Gossip* problem considered in Section 5.3.1). They give an efficient gossip algorithm and use it as a building block to obtain an efficient synchronous algorithm for the consensus problem with crashes. In a later work [20], Chlebus and Kowalski present another algorithm for the synchronous *Gossip* problem with crashes and use it to obtain an efficient early-stopping consensus algorithm for the same setting. More details of the work on gossip in fault-prone distributed message-passing systems can be found in the survey of Pelc [81] and the book of Hromkovic, Klasing, Pelc, Ruzicka, and Unger [49].

Kowalski and Shvartsman present a delay-sensitive study of *Do-All* in [65] and develop asynchronous algorithms achieving, for the first time, *subquadratic* work as long as the message delay d is $o(n)$ (that is, the work complexity is $o(p^2 + p\, n)$, with the usual assumption that $p \leq n$). The message complexity is somewhat higher than quadratic in some executions. The authors posed the question whether it is possible to construct asynchronous algorithms that simultaneously achieve subquadratic work and communication. It appears that in order to do so, one must strengthen the model assumptions, e.g., impose upper bounds on delays and constrain the failure patterns that may occur during the execution. The presentation in Section 5.4 of the asynchronous message-passing *Do-All* problem is based on the paper by Kowalski and Shvartsman [65] (the family of algorithms KS_{AW} is called DA and algorithm KS_{PA} is called PaDet in the paper). Missing proofs appear there. The algorithms in the family KS_{AW} are inspired by the shared-memory algorithm AW^T of Anderson and Woll [10].

CHAPTER 6

The *Do-All* Problem in Other Settings

In this final chapter, we survey selected additional research topics that deal with the *Do-All* problem in the following distributed message-passing settings:

- Message-passing processors subject to Byzantine failures (Section 6.1),

- Broadcast multiple access channels and crash-prone processors (Section 6.2),

- Partitionable networks (Section 6.3), and

- Prolonged absence of communication (Section 6.4).

6.1 DO-ALL WITH BYZANTINE PROCESSORS

The *Do-All* problem in a synchronous message-passing setting with processors subject to Byzantine faults is considered by Fernandez, Georgiou, Russell, and Shvartsman [31]. When a processor experiences a Byzantine fault [67], it may perform arbitrary actions, including those that interfere with the ongoing computation (see Section 2.3). For such a system with p synchronous processors, f of which may be faulty, the authors in [31] present upper and lower bounds on the complexity of *Do-All* with n tasks under the following modeling alternatives: (a) the maximum number of faulty processors f is known, (b) the maximum number of failures is unknown, (c) correct task execution can be verified without re-executing the task, and (d) task executions cannot be verified. The efficiency of algorithms is evaluated in terms of work S and message complexity M. Given the virulent nature of Byzantine failures, it is not surprising that in some cases obtaining work $\Theta(n \cdot p)$ is the best one can do; that is, each of the p processors must perform all of the n tasks. For some cases, it is also shown that communication cannot help improve work efficiency.

We begin the overview these results by first considering the setting where *verification is not available*; that is, a processor cannot verify whether or not a task was correctly performed. Thus, a faulty processor can lie about doing a task without any other processor being able to detect it.

For the case with known f, the lower bound for the *Do-All* problem is shown to be $S = \Omega(n(f+1))$. This lower bound has a matching upper bound obtained by a simple algorithm where every task is performed by $f + 1$ processors. Since there are at most f failures, this guarantees that each task is performed at least once. Since this algorithm is optimal with respect to the lower bound, an additional conclusion for this setting is that no amount of communication can help obtain better work efficiency.

For the case with unknown f (where $f < p$), the lower bound on work is shown to be $S = \Omega(n \cdot p)$. Thus, in the setting where task verification is not possible and f is unknown, the trivial algorithm where each processor performs all tasks is optimal.

Now consider the case where a task execution *can be verified* without re-executing the task. Here the study of the *Do-All* problem is more interesting as the verification mechanism enables a correct processor to detect a faulty processor that lies about performing a task: the correct processor can verify the execution of the task (without performing it). Of course, this is helpful only when verifying a task is inexpensive compared to performing the task. Thus, an assumption is made that up to v tasks, $1 \leq v \leq n$, can be verified by a processor in one unit of time. Here performing a task and verifying v tasks consume one unit of work. Furthermore, the messages used to verify tasks are not counted in the message complexity of the *Do-All* problem, as this depends on the implementation of verification (which in [31] leaves as an abstraction).

For the case with known f, the lower bound for *Do-All*, in the presence of $\phi \leq f$ actual Byzantine failures, is $S = \Omega(n + nf/v + p \log_{p/\phi} p)$ when $\phi \leq p/\log p$, and $S = \Omega(n + nf/v + p \log p/\log \log p)$ when $p/\log p < \phi < p$. In this setting, the authors present algorithms *Minority* and *Majority*. Algorithm *Minority* is designed to solve the *Do-All* problem when at most half of the processors are guaranteed not to fail (i.e., $f \geq p/2$) and Algorithm *Majority* when the majority of the processors does not fail (i.e., $f < n/2$).

Algorithm *Minority* proceeds in a loop. In each iteration of the loop, each (non-faulty) processor performs a task based on an allocation function and verifies a certain number of tasks allocated to other processes. In this way, processors may detect faulty processors and estimate the number of remaining tasks. This information is used by the allocation function in the next iteration. In this algorithm, no communication is used for coordination; since with a majority of faulty processors, it is impossible to rely on the validity of information received in messages. Algorithm *Minority* has work $S = O(n + np/v + p \log_{p/\phi} p)$ when $\phi \leq p/\log p$, and work $S = O(n + np/v + p \log p/\log \log p)$ when $p/\log p < \phi < p$.

Algorithm *Majority* also proceeds in a loop. In each iteration of the loop, each (non-faulty) processor is given a set of tasks to performs and a set of identifiers of processors whose tasks it has to verify, based on some allocation function. The processor executes its tasks and verifies the tasks of its set of processors, detecting faulty processors. Then a check-pointing algorithm is executed in which all non-faulty processors agree on a set of processors identified as faulty in this iteration (this is possible since, by assumption, the majority of the processors is non-faulty), and update their information of completed tasks and non-faulty processors accordingly. Algorithm *Majority* has work $S = O(n + nf/v + p(1 + f/p) \cdot \min\{\phi + 1, \log p\})$ and message complexity $M = O(p(f + 1) \cdot \min\{\phi + 1, \log p\})$.

Algorithm *Complete* is then obtained by combining algorithms *Minority* and *Majority* that deal with different ranges of f. Since f is known, depending on its value, algorithm *Complete* either calls the routine "Minority" or the routine "Majority" that are based on the corresponding algorithms. The new algorithm efficiently solves the *Do-All* problem for the entire range of f.

For the case with unknown f, where task verification is available, it is shown that the same lower bound holds for work as for the case with known f, but with $f = p - 1$. Hence, by fixing $f = p - 1$, algorithm *Minority* has optimal work in this setting, again implying that in this setting communication does not help obtaining better work efficiency.

A related work by Fernandez, Georgiou, Lopez, and Santos [30] considers an asynchronous distributed system formed by a master processor and a collection of p worker processors that execute tasks on behalf of the master and that may act maliciously by deliberately returning fallacious results (i.e., workers are Byzantine) . The master decides on the correctness of the results by assigning the same task to several workers. The master is charged one work-unit for each task assigned to a worker. The goal is to have the master accept the correct result of each task with high probability and with the smallest possible amount of work. This problem abstracts Master-Worker Internet-based computations such as SETI@home [4, 61] (recall the discussion in Chapter 2). This work considers two ways of constraining the number of faulty processors: (a) by imposing a fixed bound $f < p/2$ on the maximum number of workers that may fail, and (b) by positing a probability $q < 1/2$ of any processor to be faulty. Here either f or q are known to the master processor. Furthermore, processors can be slow, and messages can get lost or arrive late; these assumptions are modeled by assuming a known probability d (that may depend on p) of the master receiving the reply from a given worker on time.

This work demonstrates that it is possible for the master to accept correct results, with high probability, and achieve efficient work complexity. For the two ways of constraining the number of malicious workers, lower bounds are established on the minimum amount of (expected) work for any algorithm that accepts the correct result with probability of success $1 - \varepsilon$, where $\varepsilon \ll 1$ (e.g., $1/p$). To complement the lower bounds, two algorithms are presented, each using a different decision strategy. Both algorithms obtain the same probability of success $1 - \varepsilon$, and in doing so, obtain similar upper bounds on the (expected) work. Furthermore, under certain conditions, these upper bounds are shown to be asymptotically optimal with respect to the lower bounds.

Konwar, Rajasekaran, and Shvartsman [60] have studied an extension of the problem in which there are p workers and p tasks to be performed. Here the computational model is somewhat stronger than the one considered in [30], as this work assumes a synchronous system in which the result of a task assigned to a non-faulty worker is always received by the master on time. On the other hand, this work does not assume the knowledge of the maximum number of faulty processors f, or the probability q with which a worker may provide an incorrect result. More specifically, the failure model is defined in terms of f-fraction, $0 < f < 1/2$, of the workers that provide faulty results with probability $0 < q < 1/2$, where the master has no prior knowledge of f and q. For this model, an algorithm is given for estimating f and q with customizable accuracy in logarithmic time. A randomized algorithm is also given for detecting faulty processors with high probability in logarithmic time. Ultimately, a randomized algorithm is presented that performs p tasks with high probability, also in logarithmic time. The work of this algorithm is $O(p \log p)$, and it comes within a multiplicative logarithm of the corresponding lower bound, since it is shown that linear work cannot be achieved in this setting.

Fernandez, Georgiou, and Mosteiro [11] extend the work in [30] by considering Master-Worker computations where some workers may act maliciously (as in [30]) and other workers may be *rational* [6] and act on their *self-interest*. Malicious workers have a predefined "bad" behavior which results in reporting an incorrect result to the master. Rational or selfish workers do not have an *a priori* established behavior; they decide on how to act (i.e., compute and truthfully report the correct task result or report a bogus result) in an attempt to increase their own benefit (a quantified measure). For such workers, incentives that increase their benefit must be given for them to act truthfully. For this purpose, an algorithmic mechanism is designed that combines traditional voting techniques to tolerate malicious workers (similar to those in [30]) with game-theoretic techniques [6, 79] for providing the necessary incentives so that the master obtains the correct task result with high probability. Recently, this work was extended to additionally cope with the possibility that the communication between the workers and the master is not reliable [23].

6.2 DO-ALL WITH BROADCAST CHANNELS

Chlebus, Kowalski, and Lingas [21] studied the *Do-All* problem in the setting of broadcast networks where crash-prone processors (or stations as they call them) communicate over a multiple access channel [34], synchronized by a global clock. In such networks, if exactly one processor broadcasts at a time, then the message is delivered to all processors. If more than one processor broadcasts then a *collision* occurs and no message is delivered.

The authors provide randomized and deterministic solutions with and without collision detection, and for various size-bounded adversaries causing crashes. An adversary is f-bounded if it may crash at most $f < p$ processors. If f is a constant fraction of p, then the adversary is called linearly bounded. An f-bounded adversary is weakly adaptive if it selects prior to the start of the computation a subset of processors that might crash at any time during the computation. An f-bounded adversary is strongly adaptive if the upper bound f on the number of crashes is the only restriction on failure occurrences in a computation.

First, the authors prove that $\Omega(n + p\sqrt{n})$ work is required for any (deterministic or randomized) *Do-All* algorithm even when no crashes occur.

For the channel where collision detection, is available, they develop an optimal deterministic *Do-All* algorithm, called Groups-Together, that achieves work $O(n + p\sqrt{n})$ against the f-bounded adversary. The authors also show that randomization does not help to improve efficiency of deterministic algorithms under any adversary.

For the channel with collision detection, a deterministic *Do-All* algorithm, called Two-Lists, is presented that achieves work $O(n + p\sqrt{n} + p \min\{f, n\})$ against the f-bounded adversary. The algorithm is shown to be optimal by providing a matching lower bound for the strongly-adaptive f-bounded adversary. It is shown that randomization does not help improve efficiency of deterministic algorithms under the strongly-adaptive f-bounded adversary. However, a randomized algorithm, called MIX-RAND, is given that achieves expected work $O(n + p\sqrt{n})$ against certain weakly-adaptive size-bounded adversaries. This demonstrates that randomization can help when collision detection is not available and the adversary is sufficiently weak.

Finally, the authors show that if $f = p(1 - o(1/\sqrt{n}))$ and $n = o(p^2)$, then a weakly-adaptive f-bounded adversary can force any *Do-All* algorithm for the channel with collision detection to perform asymptotically more than $\Omega(n + p\sqrt{n})$ work.

Clementi, Monti, and Silvestri [24] consider the *Do-All* problem in broadcast networks without collision detection under an omniscient f-bounded crash-causing adversary, while assuming that the maximum number of crashes f is *known* to the processors. This work introduces the notion of f-*reliability*: a *Do-All* algorithm is f-reliable if it solves the problem against any f-bounded adversary for a known f. Note that the work of Chlebus et al. [21] considers $(p-1)$-reliable algorithms, as f was not be known and the algorithms are designed to work even in the case that up to $p-1$ processors crash (here f is the actual number of processor crashes in a given execution).

The work [24] gives tight bounds on the completion time (total time for the *Do-All* problem to be solved) and work of f-reliable algorithms. In particular, it is shown that the completion time of f-reliable algorithms in broadcast networks without collision detection is $\Theta(\frac{n}{p-f} + \min\{\frac{nf}{p}, f + \sqrt{n}\})$ and the work is $\Theta(n + f \cdot \min\{n, f\})$. The algorithm yielding the upper bound for work is based on a version of algorithm TWO-LISTS of Chlebus et al. [21], modified to exploit the knowledge of f. It is noted that the two lower bounds on completion time and work hold even when crashes take place at the very beginning of the algorithm execution.

6.3 *DO-ALL* IN PARTITIONABLE NETWORKS

Dolev, Segala, and Shvartsman [26] introduced the *Do-All* problem for partitionable networks. As discussed in Section 2.3, partitionable networks may undergo dynamic changes in the network topology that partition the processors into non-overlapping *groups*, where communication is only possible for processors within the same group. For partitionable network settings, it is not always sufficient to learn that all tasks are complete (e.g., to solve the *Do-All* problem). Here it may also be necessary for the processors in each group to learn the results of the task completion. Such *Do-All* problem in partitionable networks, also called *Omni-Do* [42], is stated as follows:

> *Omni-Do: Given a set of n tasks and p message-passing processors, perform all tasks, ensuring that each processor learns the results of all tasks.*

In this setting, no amount of algorithmic sophistication can compensate for the possibility of groups of processors or even individual processors becoming disconnected during the computation. In general, an adversary that is able to partition the network into g components will cause any task-performing algorithm to have work $\Omega(n \cdot g)$ even if each group of processors performs no more than the optimal number of $\Theta(n)$ tasks. In the extreme case where all processors are isolated from the beginning, the work of any algorithm is $\Omega(n \cdot p)$.

Even given this pessimistic work lower bound of $\Omega(n \cdot p)$, it is desirable to design and analyze efficient algorithmic approaches that can be shown to be better than the oblivious approach where each processor or each group performs all tasks. In particular, it is important to develop complexity bounds that are *failure-sensitive*, namely that capture the dependence of work complexity on the nature of network partitions. We note that the work complexity used in the study of the *Omni-Do* problem is the *task-oriented work* that measures the total number of tasks, including multiplicity, performed by the processors in the entire computation. This work measure, denoted here by W, was first introduced by Dwork, Halpern, and Waarts [28]. Task-oriented work is relevant in the settings where the cost of locally executing a task dominates any local computation spent on coordination, bookkeeping, and waiting, or where the local resources can be assigned to other (not necessarily related) activities. (Note that work S is always an upper bound for task-oriented work W because it includes all steps dedicated by the processors to performing tasks, and so we have $W = O(S)$. This means that any lower bound result for W is also a lower bound result for S.)

Dolev et al. [26] present the following results for the asynchronous *Omni-Do* problem, under the assumption that $p = n$:

(*a*) For the case of arbitrary dynamic group changes, they show that the termination time of any on-line task assignment algorithm is greater than the termination time of an off-line task assignment algorithm that has *a priori* knowledge of the pattern of group changes by a factor greater than $n/12$.

(*b*) Here the *Omni-Do* problem is studied for the model of failures that involves *fragmentations* of the initial group of processors into new groups. The work complexity is expressed as a function of n and the *fragmentation-number* f, where f is the increase in the number of groups as the result of network partitions. A *fragmentation* is the partition of a group into two or more groups. The fragmentation-number of a single fragmentation is the number of new groups created due to this fragmentation minus one. The fragmentation-number f of a computation is the sum of all fragmentation-numbers of all the fragmentations occurred in the computation; thus $f < n$. The authors present a load balancing algorithm, called AF, that solves the *Omni-Do* problem under group fragmentations, with the assumption that initially all processors belong to a single group. The algorithm has work complexity $W = O(n + f \cdot n)$. The basic idea of algorithm AF is the following: each processor performs undone tasks according to a certain load balancing rule until it learns the results of all tasks. The algorithm uses an abstract *Group Communication Service* (GCS) to handle group memberships and communication within groups. GCSs enable the application components at different processors to operate collectively as a group, using the service to multicast messages [15, 22].

Georgiou and Shvartsman [42] extended the fragmentation model [26] by considering an adversary that causes any pattern of *fragmentations and merges*, and evaluate both message complexity and work complexity of solving the *Omni-Do* problem. In this work, a *fragmentation* is defined as the partition of a group into one or more groups; this allows (cf. [26]) a group to be reconfigured into a new group with the same members (considering this a different group, as done with some Group Communication Services). A *merge* is defined in a natural way where a collection of disjoint groups merge to form a new group containing all processors of the merged groups). The authors present a robust algorithm, called algorithm AX, that solves the *Omni-Do* problem for asynchronous processors under group fragmentations and merges. As with algorithm AF, algorithm AX uses a group communication service (GCS) to provide membership and communication services to the groups of processors. The algorithm uses a coordinator-based approach for load-balancing the tasks within each group of processors. To analyze the algorithm, the authors introduce *view-graphs* that are directed acyclic graphs used to represent the partially-ordered view (group) history witnessed by the processors (the group changes that processors undergo during the computation). Using view-graphs, it is shown that algorithm AX solves the *Omni-Do* problem for n tasks, p processors and any pattern of group fragmentations and merges with task-oriented work $W < \min\{n\ f_r + n, n\ p\}$ and message complexity $M < 4(n\ f_r + n + p\ f_m)$, where f_r denotes the number of new groups created due to fragmentations and f_m the number of new groups created due to merges. (For comparison, we note that f [26] and f_r measure fragmentations differently, but it is shown in [42] that these measures are within a constant factor not exceeding 2.)

An *Omni-Do* algorithm and its efficiency can only be partially understood through its worst case work analysis. This is because the resulting worst case bound might depend on unusual or extreme patterns of group reconfigurations where all algorithms perform poorly (for example, observe that algorithms AF and AX are optimal with respect to worst case work complexity). In such cases, worst case work may not be the best way to compare the efficiency of algorithms. Hence, in order to understand better the practical implications of performing work in partitionable settings, Georgiou, Russell, and Shvartsman [39] treat the *Omni-Do* problem as an on-line problem, pursuing *competitive analysis* [87] that compares the efficiency of a given algorithm to the efficiency of an off-line algorithm that has full knowledge of future changes in the communication medium. They consider asynchronous processors under arbitrary patterns of network reconfiguration (including, but not limited to, fragmentation and merges) orchestrated by an oblivious/off-line adversary. Processors in the same group can share their knowledge of completed tasks, thus avoiding redundant work. The challenge in this setting is to avoid redundant work "globally", in the sense that processors should be performing tasks with anticipation of future changes in the network topology. An optimal algorithm, with full knowledge of the future regroupings, can schedule the execution of the tasks in each group in to minimize the overall task-oriented work.

The authors present a simple randomized algorithm, called algorithm RS, where each processor (or group) determines the next task to complete by randomly selecting the task from the set of tasks this group does not know to be completed. In order to analyze the competitiveness of this algorithm the authors represent the *computation* in the presence of reconfigurations by means of a directed acyclic graph. Here each vertex corresponds to a group g of processors that exists at some point of the computation, and a directed edge is placed from group g to group g' if at least one processor is a member of both groups and g' is formed by a partition involving processors in g. Two groups g and g' are *independent* if the graph contains no directed path from one to another. Then, for a given computation C, the *computation width* of C, denoted by $cw(C)$, is the maximum number of independent groups reachable (along directed paths) in the graph representing C from any vertex (said informally, the computation width associates a natural number with a history of changes in the communication medium). The authors derive upper and lower bounds on competitiveness in terms of the computation width. Specifically, they show that algorithm RS obtains, for any computation C, the competitive ratio $(1 + cw(C)/e)$, where e is the base of the natural logarithm ($e = 2.7182...$); they also show that this ratio is tight by exhibiting a matching lower bound (for randomized and deterministic algorithms). Note that for a given computation C, if $r(C)$ is the number of groups created due to reconfigurations in C, then $cw(C) \leq r(C)$, and there can be an arbitrary gap between $cw(C)$ and $r(C)$. Hence, cw captures precisely the effect of network reconfigurations on the efficiency of the computation.

Kari, Russell, and Shashidhar [56] additionally consider tasks that have dependencies, as defined by task dependency graphs that are k-partite graphs. Here each partition of the vertices (tasks) of the graph is said to belong to a *level*. Independent tasks belong to the first level, tasks dependent on the first level tasks are at the second level and so on. The k-partite graphs considered in this work are a special kind of task graphs where every task at level ℓ_{i+1} is dependent on every task at level ℓ_i, $i = 1, \ldots, k - 1$ (there is a complete set of directed edges from level ℓ_i to level ℓ_{i+1}, $i = 1, \ldots, k - 1$). The authors present an algorithm, called Modified-RS, whose competitive ratio depends both on the computation width and the dependencies defined by the task graph. The main difference between algorithms RS and Modified-RS is that in the latter each processor (or group) determines the next task to perform by randomly selecting a task τ from the set of tasks this group does not know to be completed such that all tasks that τ depends on have been performed (and the results are known to the group). By first considering 2-level bipartite task graphs (where every task at level 2 depends on every task at level 1), it is shown that algorithm Modified-RS obtains the competitive ratio $(1 + cw(1 - \alpha + \alpha/(e^{\frac{1-\alpha}{\alpha}c+1})))$, where cw is the computation width, $\alpha \in (0, 1]$ denotes the fraction of tasks in the first level ℓ_1 and $c = \frac{1}{1/e+1}$. It is furthermore shown that this result is tight by showing a matching lower bound. Then the analysis is extended to show that algorithm Modified-RS has the competitive ratio $(1 + cw(1 - \alpha_1 + \alpha_1/(e^{\frac{\alpha_k}{\alpha_1}c^{\beta_k}+\beta_k})))$ under any pattern of regroupings and for any k-level task graph, where $\alpha_i \in (0, 1]$ is the fraction of tasks at level ℓ_i, $i = 1, \ldots, k$, $c = \frac{1}{1/e+1}$, and β_i, $i = 1, \ldots, k - 1$, is a sequence defined as follows: $\beta_1 = 1$, $\beta_{i+1} = \frac{\alpha_i}{\alpha_1}c^{\beta_i} + \beta_i$. This result is shown to be tight. Observe that when all tasks are independent, i.e., the task dependency graph has only one level ($\alpha = 1$) the competitive ratio collapses to $(1 + cw/e)$, matching the result in [39].

6.4 *DO-ALL* IN THE ABSENCE OF COMMUNICATION

The final topic we survey deals with the *Omni-Do* (and *Do-All*) problem in the extreme setting where processors need to collaborate *without communication*. Here one needs to understand the extent to which efficient collaboration is possible in the absence of communication. As discussed in Section 2.3, there are in fact cases where such an extreme situation is not a matter of choice: the network may fail, the mobile nodes may have intermittent connectivity, and when communication is unavailable, it may take a long time to (re)establish connectivity. Thus, it is important to characterize the ability of isolated processors to collaborate on a known collection of independent tasks by means of local scheduling decisions that require no communication and that achieve low redundant work in task executions.

To illustrate the challenges in this setting, consider a system where initially isolated processors communicate by means of a *rendezvous*, i.e., two processors that are able to communicate can perform state exchange; this is similar to group merges. The processors that are not able to communicate via rendezvous have no choice but to perform all n tasks. Consider the computation with a single rendezvous: there are $p - 2$ processors that are unable to communicate, and they collectively must perform exactly $n \cdot (p - 2)$ work units to learn all results. Now what about the remaining pair of processors that are able to rendezvous? In the worst case, they rendezvous after performing all tasks individually. In this case, no savings in work are realized. Suppose they rendezvous having performed $n/2$ tasks each. In the best case, the two processors performed mutually-exclusive subsets of tasks and they learn the complete set of results as a consequence of the rendezvous. In particular, if these two processors know that they will be able to rendezvous in the future, they could schedule their work as follows: one processor performs the tasks in the order $1, 2, \ldots, n$, the other in the order $n, n - 1, \ldots, 1$. No matter when they happen to rendezvous, the number of tasks they both perform is minimized. Of course, the processors do not know *a priori* what pair will be able to rendezvous. Thus, it is interesting to produce task execution schedules for *all processors*, such that upon the first rendezvous of any two processors the number of tasks performed redundantly is minimized.

This problem was introduced by Dolev, Segala, and Shvartsman [26], who develop an effective scheduling strategy for minimizing the *task execution redundancy* between any two processors that eventually are able to communicate during the computation. The task execution redundancy is defined as follows. Consider two processors, i and j, and let T_i be the set of task identifiers of the tasks that processor i performed before the communication is established, and similarly let T_j be the set of task identifiers for processor i. The task execution redundancy is defined as $|T_i \cap T_j|$. (Hence, if processors i and j performed different tasks before they are able to communicate, then the task execution redundancy is zero.) They show that for if initially all processors are isolated, then the number of redundant tasks performed by any two processors is at most 1 if the communication is first established when no processor has executed more than $\Theta(n^{1/3})$ tasks.

Malewicz, Russell, and Shvartsman [72] generalized the notion of task execution redundancy, calling the new metric k-*waste*: it measures the worst-case redundant work performed by k groups (or processors) that initially work in isolation and ultimately merge into a single group. In this work, randomized and deterministic schedules are constructed such that task redundancy increases gracefully as the number of tasks performed in isolation increases. It is observed that bounds on pairwise waste (2-waste) can be naturally extended to bounds on k-waste; hence, the authors focus on the investigation of pairwise waste. It is shown that when two processors rendezvous after one performs a tasks and the other b tasks, where $a \leq b$, then the waste is at least $\frac{pa^2}{(p-1)(n-b+a)} - \frac{a}{p-1}$. Then they show that the natural randomized solution, where any disconnected processor randomly selects its next task among the tasks remaining to be done is quite effective in avoiding redundant work. In particular, it is shown that with probability at least $1 - 1/(pn)$, 2-waste is at most $\frac{ab}{n} + 11\sqrt{\frac{ab}{n} \ln(2pn)}$. Asymptotically, this result is near-optimal with respect to the lower bound. The authors also extend the analysis of random schedules to k-waste ($k \geq 2$): they show that with probability at least $1 - \frac{1}{p}$, waste incurred by any k processors that establish communication after having performed a tasks each, is within a lower order summand of $(2k+1)\sqrt{a \ln p}$ from the expected waste of $\sum_{i=2}^{k} (-1)^i \binom{k}{i} \frac{a^i}{n^{i-1}}$.

Finally, two techniques are given for deterministic schedule construction: one for the case when there are more tasks than processors, the other for the (uncommon) case where there are more processors than tasks. In the first construction ($p \leq n$), it is shown how processors can schedule their computation such that pairwise waste is at most a $1 + 22p^{-1/4}$ fraction of the lower bound, when any two processors rendezvous after performing a tasks each (unless a is small compared to n). This construction uses tools from mathematical design theory [50]. In the second construction ($p > n$), schedules are designed such that 2-waste is at most $(2 \log_n p - 1)\sqrt{n} + \frac{4ab}{n}$, where a is the number of tasks performed by one processor and b by the other prior to rendezvous. This construction is based on polynomials over finite fields.

Other approaches for dealing with limited communication have also been explored. Papadimitriou and Yannakakis [80] study how limited patterns of communication affect load-balancing. They consider a problem where there are 3 agents, each of which has a job of a size drawn uniformly at random from [0, 1], and this distribution of job sizes is known to every agent. Any agent A can learn the sizes of jobs of some other agents as given by a directed graph of three nodes. Based on this information, each agent has to decide to which of the two servers its job is sent for processing. Each server has capacity 1, and it may happen that when two or more agents decide to send their jobs to the same server the server will be overloaded. The goal is to devise cooperative strategies for agents that minimize the chances of overloading any server. The authors present several strategies. They show that adding an edge to a graph can improve load balancing. These strategies depend on the communication topology. This problem is similar to the problem as studied in [72]: here sending a job to server number $x \in \{0, 1\}$ resembles doing task number x in *Omni-Do*. The goal of avoiding server overload resembles avoiding overlaps among task sets. The problem of Papadimitriou and Yannakakis is different because in *Omni-Do* we are interested in structuring job execution where the number of tasks n can be arbitrary.

Georgiades, Mavronicolas, and Spirakis [36] study a similar load-balancing problem. On the one hand their treatment is more general in the sense that they consider arbitrary number of agents p and arbitrary computable decision algorithms. However, it is more restrictive in the sense that they consider only one type of communication topology where there is no communication between processors whatsoever. The two servers that process jobs have some given capacity that is not necessarily 1. They study two families of decision algorithms: algorithms that cannot see the size of jobs before making a decision to which server to direct a job for processing, and algorithms that can make decisions based on the size of the job. They completely settle these cases by showing that their decision protocols minimize the chances of overloading any server.

Bibliography

[1] Distributed.net. http://www.distributed.net/. Cited on page(s) 1

[2] FightAIDS@home. http://fightaidsathome.scripps.edu/. Cited on page(s) 1

[3] Internet primenet server. http://mersenne.org/ips/stats.html. Cited on page(s) 1

[4] SETI@home. http://setiathome.ssl.berkeley.edu/. Cited on page(s) 1, 131

[5] M. Abdelguerfi and S. Lavington. *Emerging Trends in Database and Knowledge-Base Machines: The Application of Parallel Architectures to Smart Information Systems.* IEEE Press, 1995. Cited on page(s) 2, 20

[6] I. Abraham, D. Dolev, R. Goden, and J.Y. Halpern. Distributed computing meets game theory: Robust mechanisms for rational secret sharing and multiparty computation. In *Proceedings of the 25th ACM Symposium on Principles of Distributed Computing (PODC 2006)*, pages 53–62, 2006. DOI: 10.1145/1146381.1146393 Cited on page(s) 132

[7] C. Aguirre, J. Martinez-Munoz, F. Corbacho, and R. Huerta. Small-world topology for multi-agent collaboration. In *Proceedings of the 11th International Workshop on Database and Expert Systems Applications*, pages 231–235, 2000. DOI: 10.1109/DEXA.2000.875032 Cited on page(s) 20

[8] N. Alon and F.R.K. Chung. Explicit construction of linear sized tolerant networks. *Discrete Mathematics*, 72:15–19, 1988. DOI: 10.1016/0012-365X(88)90189-6 Cited on page(s) 40, 127

[9] N. Alon, H. Kaplan, M. Krivelevich, D. Malkhi, and J. Stern. Scalable secure storage when half the system is faulty. In *Proceedings of the 27th International Colloquium on Automata, Languages and Programming (ICALP 2000)*, pages 577–587, 2000. DOI: 10.1006/inco.2002.3148 Cited on page(s) 40, 127

[10] R.J. Anderson and H. Woll. Algorithms for the certified Write-All problem. *SIAM Journal of Computing*, 26(5):1277–1283, 1997. DOI: 10.1137/S0097539794319126 Cited on page(s) 19, 40, 76, 127

[11] A. Fernandez Anta, Ch. Georgiou, and M. Mosteiro. Algorithmic mechanisms for internet-based master-worker computing with untrusted and selfish workers. In *Proceedings of the 24th IEEE International Parallel and Distributed Processing Symposium (IPDPS 2010)*, 2010. DOI: 10.1109/IPDPS.2010.5470409 Cited on page(s) 132

142 BIBLIOGRAPHY

[12] H. Attiya. Robust simulation of shared memory: 20 years after. *Bulletin of the EATCS – Distributed Computing Column*, 100:99–113, 2010. Cited on page(s) 126

[13] H. Attiya, A. Bar-Noy, and D. Dolev. Sharing memory robustly in message-passing systems. *Journal of the ACM*, 42(1):124–142, 1995. DOI: 10.1145/200836.200869 Cited on page(s) 126

[14] S. Ben-David, A. Borodin, R. Karp, G. Tardos, and A. Wigderson. On the power of randomization in on-line algorithms. *Algorithmica*, 11(1):2–14, 1994. DOI: 10.1007/BF01294260 Cited on page(s) 20

[15] K.P. Birman and R. van Renesse. *Reliable Distributed Computing with the Isis Toolkit*. IEEE Computer Society Press, 1994. DOI: 10.1109/M-PDT.1996.532142 Cited on page(s) 134

[16] J. Buss, P.C. Kanellakis, P. Ragde, and A.A. Shvartsman. Parallel algorithms with processor failures and delays. *Journal of Algorithms*, 20(1):45–86, 1996. DOI: 10.1006/jagm.1996.0003 Cited on page(s) 20, 40, 76

[17] B. Chlebus, R. De Prisco, and A.A. Shvartsman. Performing tasks on restartable message-passing processors. *Distributed Computing*, 14(1):49–64, 2001. A preliminary version has appeared in WDAG 1997. DOI: 10.1007/PL00008926 Cited on page(s) 19, 40, 126

[18] B.S. Chlebus, L. Gasieniec, D.R. Kowalski, and A.A. Shvartsman. Bounding work and communication in robust cooperative computation. In *Proceedings of the 16th International Symposium on Distributed Computing (DISC 2002)*, pages 295–310, 2002. DOI: 10.1007/3-540-36108-1_20 Cited on page(s) 40, 126, 127

[19] B.S. Chlebus and D.R. Kowalski. Robust gossiping with an application to consensus. *Journal of Computer and System Sciences*, 72(8):1262–1281, 2006. A preliminary version appeared as "Gossiping to reach consensus" in SPAA 2002. DOI: 10.1016/j.jcss.2006.08.001 Cited on page(s) 127

[20] B.S. Chlebus and D.R. Kowalski. Time and communication efficient consensus for crash failures. In *Proceedings of the 20th International Symposium on Distributed Computing (DISC 2006)*, pages 314–328, 2006. DOI: 10.1007/11864219_22 Cited on page(s) 127

[21] B.S. Chlebus, D.R. Kowalski, and A. Lingas. The Do-All problem in broadcast networks. *Distributed Computing*, 18(6):435–451, 2006. A preliminary version appeared in PODC 2001. DOI: 10.1007/s00446-005-0153-4 Cited on page(s) 19, 132, 133

[22] G.V. Chockler, I. Keidar, and R. Vitenberg. Group communication specifications: A comprehensive study. *ACM Computing Surveys*, 33(4):1–43, 2001. DOI: 10.1145/503112.503113 Cited on page(s) 134

[23] E. Christoforou, A. Fernández, Ch. Georgiou, and M. Mosteiro. Algorithmic mechanisms for internet supercomputing under unreliable communication. In *Proceedings of the* 10th *IEEE International Symposium on Network Computing and Applications (NCA 2011)*, 2011. Cited on page(s) 132

[24] A.E.F. Clementi, A. Monti, and R. Silvestri. Optimal F-reliable protocols for the Do-All problem on single-hop wireless networks. In *Proceedings of the* 13*th International Symposium on Algorithms and Computation (ISAAC 2002)*, pages 320–331, 2002. DOI: 10.1007/3-540-36136-7_29 Cited on page(s) 133

[25] P. Dasgupta, Z. Kedem, and M. Rabin. Parallel processing on networks of workstation: A fault-tolerant, high performance approach. In *Proceedings of the* 15th *IEEE International Conference on Distributed Computer Systems (ICDCS 1995)*, pages 467–474, 1995. DOI: 10.1109/ICDCS.1995.500052 Cited on page(s) 19

[26] S. Dolev, R. Segala, and A.A. Shvartsman. Dynamic load balancing with group communication. *Theoretical Computer Science*, 369(1–3):348–360, 2006. A preliminary version appeared in SIROCCO 1999. DOI: 10.1016/j.tcs.2006.09.020 Cited on page(s) 19, 133, 134, 135, 137

[27] M. Dubash. Moore's law is dead, says Gordon Moore. http://news.techworld.com/operating-systems/3477/, April 2005. Cited on page(s) 1

[28] C. Dwork, J. Halpern, and O. Waarts. Performing work efficiently in the presence of faults. *SIAM Journal on Computing*, 27(5):1457–1491, 1998. A preliminary version appears in the *Proceedings of the* 11th *ACM Symposium on Principles of Distributed Computing (PODC 1992)*, pages 91–102, 1992. DOI: 10.1137/S0097539793255527 Cited on page(s) 19, 126, 134

[29] R. Elmasri and S.B. Navathe. *Fundamentals of Database Systems*. Addison-Wesley publishing company, second edition, 1994. Cited on page(s) 2, 20

[30] A. Fernández, Ch. Georgiou, L. Lopez, and A. Santos. Reliably executing tasks in the presence of untrusted entities. In *Proceedings of the* 25th *IEEE Symposium on Reliable Distributed Systems (SRDS 2006)*, pages 39–50, 2006. DOI: 10.1109/SRDS.2006.40 Cited on page(s) 131, 132

[31] A. Fernández, Ch. Georgiou, A. Russell, and A.A. Shvartsman. The Do-All problem with byzantine processor failures. *Theoretical Computer Science*, 333(3):433–454, 2005. A preliminary version appeared in SIROCCO 2003. DOI: 10.1016/j.tcs.2004.06.034 Cited on page(s) 129, 130

[32] J.D. Foley, A. van Dam, S.K. Feiner, and J.F. Hughes. *Computer Graphics: Principle and Practice*. Addison-Wesley publishing company, second edition, 1996. Cited on page(s) 2, 20

[33] Z. Galil, A. Mayer, and M. Yung. Resolving message complexity of byzantine agreement and beyond. In *Proceedings of the* 36th *IEEE Symposium on Foundations of Computer Science (FOCS 1995)*, pages 724–733, 1995. DOI: 10.1109/SFCS.1995.492674 Cited on page(s) 19, 126

[34] G.R. Gallager. A perspective on multi-access channels. *IEEE Transactions on Information Theory*, 31(2):124–142, 1985. DOI: 10.1109/TIT.1985.1057022 Cited on page(s) 132

[35] H. Garcia-Molina and D. Barbara. How to assign votes in a distributed system. *Journal of the ACM*, 32(4):841–860, 1985. DOI: 10.1145/4221.4223 Cited on page(s) 126

[36] S. Georgiades, M. Mavronicolas, and P. Spirakis. Optimal, distributed decision-making: The case of no communication. In *Proceedings of the 12th International Symposium on Fundamentals of Computation Theory (FCT 1999)*, pages 293–303, 1999. DOI: 10.1007/3-540-48321-7_24 Cited on page(s) 138

[37] Ch. Georgiou, D.R. Kowalski, and A.A. Shvartsman. Efficient gossip and robust distributed computation. *Theoretical Computer Science*, 347(1):130–166, 2005. A preliminary version appeared in DISC 2003. DOI: 10.1016/j.tcs.2005.05.019 Cited on page(s) 40, 126, 127

[38] Ch. Georgiou, A. Russell, and A.A. Shvartsman. The complexity of synchronous iterative Do-All with crashes. *Distributed Computing*, 17:47–63, 2004. A preliminary version appeared in DISC 2001. DOI: 10.1007/s00446-003-0099-3 Cited on page(s) 19, 20, 76, 126

[39] Ch. Georgiou, A. Russell, and A.A. Shvartsman. Work-competitive scheduling for cooperative computing with dynamic groups. *SIAM Journal on Computing*, 34(4):848–862, 2005. A preliminary version appeared in STOC 2003. DOI: 10.1137/S0097539704440442 Cited on page(s) 135, 136

[40] Ch. Georgiou, A. Russell, and A.A. Shvartsman. Failure-sensitive analysis of parallel algorithms with controlled memory access concurrency. *Parallel Processing Letters*, 17(2):153–168, 2007. A preliminary version appeared in OPODIS 2002. DOI: 10.1142/S0129626407002946 Cited on page(s) 76

[41] Ch. Georgiou and A. A. Shvartsman. *Do-All Computing in Distributed Systems: Cooperation in the Presence of Adversity*. Springer-Verlag, 2008. Cited on page(s) 126

[42] Ch. Georgiou and A.A. Shvartsman. Cooperative computing with fragmentable and mergeable groups. *Journal of Discrete Algorithms*, 1(2):211–235, 2003. A preliminary version appeared in SIROCCO 2000. DOI: 10.1016/S1570-8667(03)00026-1 Cited on page(s) 19, 133, 134, 135

[43] A. Gharakhani and A.F. Ghoniem. Massively parallel implementation of a 3D vortex-boundary element method. In *Proceedings of the European Series in Applied and Industrial Mathematics*, volume 1, pages 213–223, 1996. DOI: 10.1051/proc:1996011 Cited on page(s) 2, 20

[44] D. K. Gifford. Weighted voting for replicated data. In *Proceedings of the 7th ACM symposium on Operating systems principles (SOSP)*, pages 150–162, 1979. DOI: 10.1145/800215.806583 Cited on page(s) 126

[45] S. Gilbert, N. A. Lynch, and A. A. Shvartsman. RAMBO: A robust, reconfigurable atomic memory service for dynamic networks. *Distributed Computing*, 23(4):225–272, 2010. DOI: 10.1007/s00446-010-0117-1 Cited on page(s) 126

[46] S.A. Green. *Parallel Processing for Computer Graphics*. MIT Press/Pitman Publishing, 1991. Cited on page(s) 2, 20

[47] J.F. Groote, W.H. Hesselink, S. Mauw, and R. Vermeulen. An algorithm for the asynchronous Write-All problem based on process collision. *Distributed Computing*, 14(2):75–81, 2001. DOI: 10.1007/PL00008930 Cited on page(s) 19, 40, 76

[48] V. Hadzilacos and S. Toueg. Fault-tolerant broadcasts and related problems. In *Distributed Systems*, chapter 5, pages 97–145. ACM Press/Addison-Wesley, 1993. Cited on page(s) 126

[49] J. Hromkovic, R. Klasing, A. Pelc, P. Ruzicka, and W. Unger. *Dissemination of Information in Communication Networks: Broadcasting, Gossiping, Leader Election, and Fault-Tolerance*. Springer, 2005. Cited on page(s) 127

[50] D.R. Hughes and F.C. Piper. *Design Theory*. Cambridge University Press, 1985. Cited on page(s) 138

[51] J. Jaja. *An Introduction to Parallel Algorithms*. Addison-Wesley, 1992. Cited on page(s) 40

[52] C.B. Jenssen. *Parallel Computational Fluid Dynamics 2000: Trends and Applications*. Elsevier Science Ltd., first edition, 2001. Cited on page(s) 2, 20

[53] P.C. Kanellakis, D. Michailidis, and A.A. Shvartsman. Controlling memory access concurrency in efficient fault-tolerant parallel algorithms. *Nordic Journal of Computing*, 2(2):146–180, 1995. DOI: 10.1007/3-540-57271-6_30 Cited on page(s) 76

[54] P.C. Kanellakis and A.A. Shvartsman. Efficient parallel algorithms can be made robust. *Distributed Computing*, 5(4):201–217, 1992. A preliminary version appears in the *Proceedings of the 8th ACM Symposium on Principles of Distributed Computing (PODC 1989)*, pages 211–222, 1989. DOI: 10.1145/72981.72996 Cited on page(s) 19, 40, 76

[55] P.C. Kanellakis and A.A. Shvartsman. *Fault-Tolerant Parallel Computation*. Kluwer Academic Publishers, 1997. Cited on page(s) 19, 40, 76

[56] Ch. Kari, A. Russell, and N. Shashidhar. Randomized work-competitive scheduling for cooperative computing on k-partite task graphs. In *Proceedings of the 7th IEEE International Symposium on Networking Computing and Applications (NCA 2008)*, pages 267–270, 2008. DOI: 10.1109/NCA.2008.46 Cited on page(s) 136

[57] Z.M. Kedem, K.V. Palem, A. Raghunathan, and P. Spirakis. Combining tentative and definite executions for dependable parallel computing. In *Proceedings of the 23rd ACM Symposium on Theory of Computing (STOC 1991)*, pages 381–390, 1991. Cited on page(s) 20, 76

[58] Z.M. Kedem, K.V. Palem, and P. Spirakis. Efficient robust parallel computations. In *Proceedings of the 22nd ACM Symposium on Theory of Computing (STOC 1990)*, pages 138–148, 1990. DOI: 10.1145/100216.100231 Cited on page(s) 19

[59] D.E. Knuth. *The Art of Computer Programming*, volume 3. Addison-Wesley Publishers, third edition, 1998. Cited on page(s) 76, 127

[60] K. M. Konwar, S. Rajasekaran, and A.A. Shvartsman. Robust network supercomputing with malicious processes. In *Proceedings of the 20th International Symposium on Distributed Computing (DISC 2006)*, pages 474–488, 2006. DOI: 10.1007/11864219_33 Cited on page(s) 131

[61] E. Korpela, D. Werthimer, D. Anderson, J. Cobb, and M. Lebofsky. SETI@home: Massively distributed computing for SETI. *Computing in Science and Engineering*, 3(1):78–83, 2001. DOI: 10.1109/5992.895191 Cited on page(s) 1, 19, 131

[62] D.R. Kowalski, M. Momenzadeh, and A.A. Shvartsman. Emulating shared-memory Do-All algorithms in asynchronous message-passing systems. *Journal of Parallel and Distributed Computing*, 70(6):699–705, 2010. DOI: 10.1016/j.jpdc.2009.12.002 Cited on page(s) 20, 126

[63] D.R. Kowalski, P. Musial, and A.A. Shvartsman. Explicit combinatorial structures for cooperative distributed algorithms. In *Proceedings of the 25th International Conference on Distributed Computing Systems (ICDCS 2005)*, pages 48–58, 2005. DOI: 10.1109/ICDCS.2005.34 Cited on page(s) 40, 127

[64] D.R. Kowalski and A.A. Shvartsman. Writing-all deterministically and optimally using a non-trivial number of asynchronous processors. In *Proceedings of the 16th ACM Symposium on Parallel Algorithms and Architectures (SPAA 2004)*, pages 311–320, 2004. DOI: 10.1145/1367064.1367073 Cited on page(s) 40

[65] D.R. Kowalski and A.A. Shvartsman. Performing work with asynchronous processors: message-delay-sensitive bounds. *Information and Computation*, 203(2):181–210, 2005. A preliminary version appeared in PODC 2003. DOI: 10.1016/j.ic.2005.08.002 Cited on page(s) 20, 40, 127

[66] D.R. Kowalski and A.A. Shvartsman. Writing-all deterministically and optimally using a nontrivial number of asynchronous processors. *ACM Transactions on Algorithms*, 4(3):Article No. 33, 2008. DOI: 10.1145/1367064.1367073 Cited on page(s) 77

[67] L. Lamport, R. Shostak, and M. Pease. The Byzantine generals problem. *ACM Transactions on Programming Languages and Systems*, 4(3):382–401, 1982. DOI: 10.1145/357172.357176 Cited on page(s) 20, 129

[68] A. López-Ortiz. Algorithm X takes work $\Omega(n \log^2 n / \log \log n)$ in a synchronous fail-stop (no restart) PRAM, 1992. manuscript. Cited on page(s) 76

[69] A. Lubotzky, R. Phillips, and P. Sarnak. Ramanujan graphs. *Combinatorica*, 8:261–277, 1988. DOI: 10.1007/BF02126799 Cited on page(s) 40, 127

[70] G. Malewicz. A work-optimal deterministic algorithm for the certified Write-All problem with a nontrivial number of asynchronous processors. *SIAM Journal on Computing*, 34(4):993–1024, 2005. A preliminary version appeared in PODC 2003. DOI: 10.1137/S0097539703428014 Cited on page(s) 77

[71] G. Malewicz, A. Russell, and A.A. Shvartsman. Distributed cooperation during the absence of communication. In *Proceedings of the* 14th *International Symposium on Distributed Computing (DISC 2000)*, pages 119–133, 2000. Cited on page(s) 19

[72] G. Malewicz, A. Russell, and A.A. Shvartsman. Distributed scheduling for disconnected cooperation. *Distributed Computing*, 18(6):409–420, 2006. DOI: 10.1007/s00446-005-0149-0 Cited on page(s) 137, 138

[73] C. Martel, A. Park, and R. Subramonian. Work-optimal asynchronous algorithms for shared memory parallel computers. *SIAM Journal on Computing*, 21(6):1070–1099, 1992. DOI: 10.1137/0221063 Cited on page(s) 19

[74] C. Martel and R. Subramonian. On the complexity of certified Write-All algorithms. *Journal of Algorithms*, 16(3):361–387, 1994. DOI: 10.1006/jagm.1994.1017 Cited on page(s) 19, 20

[75] S. Molnar, J. Eyles, and J. Poulton. PixelFlow: High-speed rendering using image composition. *Computer Graphics*, 26(2):231–240, 1992. DOI: 10.1145/142920.134067 Cited on page(s) 2, 20

[76] G. E. Moore. Cramming more components onto integrated circuits. *Electronics*, 38(8), 1965. DOI: 10.1109/JPROC.1998.658762 Cited on page(s) 1

[77] P.M. Musial. Computational requirements of the beam-space post-doppler space time adaptive processing algorithm. Master's thesis, University of Connecticut, 2001. Cited on page(s) 2, 20

[78] J. Naor and R.M. Roth. Constructions of permutation arrays for certain scheduling cost measures. *Random Structures and Algorithms*, 6:39–50, 1995. DOI: 10.1002/rsa.3240060105 Cited on page(s) 76

[79] N. Nisan and A. Ronen. Algorithmic mechanism design. *Games and Economic Behavior*, 35:166–196, 2001. DOI: 10.1006/game.1999.0790 Cited on page(s) 132

[80] C.H. Papadimitriou and M. Yannakakis. On the value of information in distributed decision-making. In *Proceedings of the* 10th *ACM Symposium on Principles of Distributed Computing (PODC 1991)*, pages 61–64, 1991. DOI: 10.1145/112600.112606 Cited on page(s) 138

[81] A. Pelc. Fault-tolerant broadcasting and gossiping in communication networks. *Networks*, 28(3):143–156, 1996. DOI: 10.1002/(SICI)1097-0037(199610)28:3%3C143::AID-NET3%3E3.0.CO;2-N Cited on page(s) 127

[82] D. Peleg and A. Wool. Crumbling walls: A class of high availability quorum systems. In *Proceedings of the 14th ACM Symposium on Principles of Distributed Computing (PODC)*, pages 120–129, 1995. Cited on page(s) 126

[83] R. De Prisco, A. Mayer, and M. Yung. Time-optimal message-efficient work performance in the presence of faults. In *Proceedings of the 13th ACM Symposium on Principles of Distributed Computing (PODC 1994)*, pages 161–172, 1994. DOI: 10.1145/197917.198082 Cited on page(s) 19, 40, 126

[84] R. Samanta, J. Zheng, T. Funkhouser, K. Li, and J.P. Singh. Load balancing for multi-projector rendering systems. In *SIGGRAPH/Eurographics Workshop on Graphics Hardware*, pages 107–116, 1999. DOI: 10.1145/311534.311584 Cited on page(s) 2, 20

[85] R.D. Schlichting and F.B. Schneider. Fail-stop processors: An approach to designing fault-tolerant computing systems. *ACM Transactions on Computing Systems*, 1(3):222–238, 1983. DOI: 10.1145/357369.357371 Cited on page(s) 20

[86] A.A. Shvartsman. Achieving optimal CRCW PRAM fault-tolerance. *Information Processing Letters*, 39(2):59–66, 1991. DOI: 10.1016/0020-0190(91)90156-C Cited on page(s) 19

[87] D. Sleator and R. Tarjan. Amortized efficiency of list update and paging rules. *Communications of the ACM*, 28(2):202–208, 1985. DOI: 10.1145/2786.2793 Cited on page(s) 135

[88] D.R. Stinson. *Cryptography: Theory and practice*. CRC PRess, 1995. Cited on page(s) 2, 20

[89] M. Tambe, J. Adibi, Y. Alonaizon, A. Erdem, G.A. Kaminka, S. Marsella, and I. Muslea. Building agent teams using an explicit teamwork model and learning. *Artificial Intelligence*, 110(2):215–239, 1999. DOI: 10.1016/S0004-3702(99)00022-3 Cited on page(s) 20

[90] E. Upfal. Tolerating a linear number of faults in networks of bounded degree. *Information and Computation*, 115:312–320, 1994. DOI: 10.1006/inco.1994.1099 Cited on page(s) 40, 127

[91] S.G. Ziavras and P. Meer. Adaptive multiresolution structures for image processing on parallel computers. *Journal of Parallel and Distributed Computing*, 23(3):475–483, 1994. DOI: 10.1006/jpdc.1994.1159 Cited on page(s) 2, 20

Authors' Biographies

CHRYSSIS GEORGIOU

Chryssis Georgiou is an Assistant Professor in the Department of Computer Science at the University of Cyprus. He holds a Ph.D. degree (December 2003) and a M.Sc. degree (May 2002) in Computer Science & Engineering from the University of Connecticut and a B.Sc. degree (June 1998) in Mathematics from the University of Cyprus. He has worked as a Teaching and Research Assistant at the University of Connecticut, USA (1998-2003) and as a Visiting Lecturer (2004) and a Lecturer (2005-2008) at the University of Cyprus. His research interests span the theory and practice of distributed computing, in particular, design, analysis, verification and implementation of algorithms; fault-tolerance and dependability; communication protocols; cooperative distributed computing; and dynamic computing environments.

ALEXANDER A. SHVARTSMAN

Alexander Allister Shvartsman is a Professor of Computer Science & Engineering and the Director of the Center for Voting Technology Research at the University of Connecticut. He holds a Ph.D. from Brown University (1992), M.S. from Cornell University (1981), and a B.S. from Stevens Institute of Technology (1979), all in Computer Science. Prior to embarking on his academic career he worked for a number of years at Bell Labs and Digital Equipment Corporation. His professional interests are in distributed computing, fault-tolerance, and integrity of electronic voting systems. He is an author of over 130 technical articles and two books.

Index

Printed in the United States
by Baker & Taylor Publisher Services